SAP Excellence

Series Editors:
Professor Dr. Dr. h.c. mult. Peter Mertens
Universität Erlangen-Nürnberg

Dr. Peter Zencke
SAP AG, Walldorf

Springer

Berlin
Heidelberg
New York
Hong Kong
London
Milan
Paris
Tokyo

Peter Buxmann · Wolfgang König
Markus Fricke · Franz Hollich
Luis Martin Diaz · Sascha Weber

Inter-organizational Cooperation with SAP Solutions

Design and Management of Supply Networks

Second Edition
with 123 Figures
and 8 Tables

 Springer

Professor Dr. Peter Buxmann · Luis Martin Diaz
Freiberg University of Technology
Chair of Information Systems
Lessingstraße 45, 09596 Freiberg, Germany

Professor Dr. Wolfgang König · Markus Fricke
University of Frankfurt
Institute of Information Systems
Mertonstraße 17, 60054 Frankfurt, Germany

Dr. Franz Hollich
SAP AG · Global Custom Development Projects

Dr. Sascha Weber
SAP AG · Development GBU Manufacturing

Neurottstraße 17, 69190 Walldorf, Germany

Springer-Verlag Berlin Heidelberg New York

ISBN 978-3-642-53457-7   ISBN 978-3-540-24763-0 (eBook)
DOI 10.1007/978-3-540-24763-0

Bibliographic information published by Die Deutsche Bibliothek
Die Deutsche Bibliothek lists this publication in the Deutsche Nationalbibliografie; detailed bibliographic data available in the internet at *http://dnb.ddb.de*

Springer-Verlag is a part of Springer Science+Business Media

springeronline.com

© Springer-Verlag Berlin Heidelberg 200x, 2004
Softcover reprint of the hardcover 2nd edition 2004

Cover design: Erich Kirchner, Heidelberg

SPIN 10959893   42/3130 – 5 4 3 2 1 0 – Printed on acid-free paper

Preface for the Second Edition

Since the appearance of the first edition of this book, the importance of inter-organizational cooperations in supply chain networks has been continuously increasing. The economic success is substantial: an empirical study recently carried out in the European automotive industry, for example, identified average cost savings of 18 percent in the stockholding area and a reduction of the transportation costs by 10 percent.

We have completely revised the text for the second edition in order to stay abreast of the current challenges on establishing cooperations both from the management and software perspective. On the one hand, the author team was extended for this purpose: SAP employees Franz Hollich and Sascha Weber, who have been dealing with SAP implementations in supply chains for years now, joined the team. Markus Fricke and Luis Martín Díaz are research assistants at the chairs for Information Systems of the Universities in Frankfurt/Main respective Freiberg and work in the environment of supply chain management and electronic marketplaces. On the other hand, we were able to extend the case study section of the first edition: The available version now contains five case studies of well-known companies from the automotive industry.

Special thanks go to many people who contributed in creating the second edition. This first of all includes Prof. Dr. Dr. h. c. mult. Peter Mertens and Dr. Peter Zencke as initiators of the SAP Excellence series.

We would like to especially emphasize the outstanding cooperation of the consulting firm Schmuecker and Partners from Frankfurt/Main (www. schmuecker.de) who allowed us to use their demonstration laboratory so that we could test APO in particular. In this context, we benefited very much from the experiences and the know-how of the employees. In addition, Schmuecker and Partners were to a large extent involved in the implementation of the SAP systems at Bosch in Eisenach (see our case study in section 7.4). Especially Wolfgang Schmuecker, Dietmar Salzer, Michael Klostereit, Robert Boensch, Michael Brunn, Wolfram Busch, Werner von den Driesch, Klaus Hamp, and Sven Schwenecke were of great help.

Special thanks also go to the employees of the case study companies for their open and friendly support. These are Bernhard Panther and Armin Zeiß from Bosch, Thomas Adler and Jürgen Herb from Goodyear, Stefan Arnold and Wolfgang Göpfert from Porsche, Bernhard Oymann and Thomas Peilert from Schenker, as well as Ute Leppert and Jörg Mieger from SupplyOn.

From SAP, Martin Edelmann, Claus Grünewald, Christian Lienert, Frank Klingl, Klaus Kreplin, Dr. Andreas Otto, Karsten Schierholt, and Dr. Stefan Theis gave us extraordinary support by sharing their know-how.

Special thanks also go to Uwe Neuner from IBM for providing his know-how in the area SAP Business Connector.

Finally, we would like to thank Matthias Kamberg, Daniel Horstkotte, and Zoe Tsesmelidakis from the Frankfurt/Main University as well as Isabel Küttner, Tina Werthmann, and Patrick Johnscher of the Freiberg University of Technology (TU Freiberg) for their continuous friendly support while this book was being written. Moreover, we would like to thank Jennifer Brundage from SAP for translating the manuscript.

The authors

Preface for the First Edition

The formation of *inter-organizational cooperation* is increasingly used to improve the partners' competitive position in a global world economy. This tendency can also be observed in logistics. Several "layers" are involved in a supply chain: vendors, manufacturers, retail companies, logistics service providers, and finally the end customers. *Supply chain management* attempts to optimize the flows of goods and information between companies.

Logistics service companies play an increasingly important role in the supply chain. Their task here is no longer restricted to just providing basic logistics services such as transport, warehousing and transshipment. Rather, logistics service providers are ever more becoming complete providers of service and information. For example, they provide basic services, such as financing for inventory, or offer after-sales services. Because of the fundamental importance of the exchange of information for the coordination of the supply chain, logistics service companies are also increasingly becoming information and communications systems specialists.

To support logistics processes, SAP provides various systems for the parties in the supply chain. These include modules for the logistics functions in the R/3 system, such as Sales and Distribution (SD module) and Materials Management (MM module), and EDI and Workflow Management to link companies using the Internet. In addition, SAP provides various components to optimize the supply chain.

This book concentrates on the business processes linking companies and investigates the opportunities and limits on the use of SAP systems. Also, it compares the known task requirements to the SAP methodology. Special attention is paid to how SAP supports the function of logistics service providers.

Although this book aims to provide a practical presentation of these concepts and solutions, it does not ignore the scientific foundation. Whereas chapters 1 and 2 concentrate on providing a compact representation of the available method knowledge, chapters 3 to 6 show solutions based on SAP systems. The practical orientation is enhanced by the inclusion of case studies: The Schenker case shows how logistics service providers are increasingly changing to become complete service providers and specialists in the provision and use of information and communications systems (chapter 6). We use the example of Goodyear to show how modern information and communications systems can support the coordination of logistics between companies (chapter 7). The use of SAP R/3 and the Supply Chain Management Initiative are discussed in both cases.

This book belongs to the SAP Excellence series, which initially contains the following works:

- Appelrath, Hans-Jürgen; Ritter, Jörg: R/3-Einführung – Methoden und Werkzeuge

- Becker, Jörg; Uhr, Wolfgang: Integrierte Informationssysteme in Handelsunternehmen

- Buxmann, Peter; König, Wolfgang: Zwischenbetriebliche Kooperationen mit SAP-Systemen – Perspektiven für die Logistik und das Service Management

- Knolmayer, Gerhard; Mertens, Peter; Zeier, Alexander: Supply Chain Management auf Basis von SAP-Systemen – Perspektiven der Auftragsabwicklung für Industriebetriebe

A feature of all these works, and thus also this book, is that employees of SAP have recently validated all statements made about the software. We have created a discussion forum under www.wiwi.uni-frankfurt.de/sap to exchange experience gained with the use of SAP systems for the cooperation between companies and, in particular, for the supply chain management. We hope that our readers actively participate in the discussion forum.

Finally, we would like to express our thanks to a number of people who supported us in many ways in the production of this book. These include Prof. Dr. Dr. h. c. Peter Mertens and Dr. Peter Zencke, the initiators of the SAP Excellence series, and Dr. Franz Hollich, our central contact partner at SAP AG. We also thank our partners for the practical examples, Dr. Joachim Klein and Bernhard Oymann at Schenker, Jürgen Herb at Goodyear, and many employees from SAP for their exemplary cooperation. Last but not least, Markus Fricke, Sven Grolik and Claus Hittmeyer, all employees at the Institute of Information Systems, earn our grateful thanks for their valuable support in preparing notes for this book. Moreover, we would like to thank Anthony Rudd for translating the manuscript.

Peter Buxmann   Wolfgang König

Table of Contents

Chapter 1 Inter-organizational Cooperation in Supply Networks

This chapter first describes basic objectives of establishing cooperation before concentrating on collaboration in supply networks in a next step. Then possible usages of information and communication systems in supply chain management are introduced.

1.1 Forms and Motives of Building Cooperation

There are many examples for inter-organizational cooperation, such as the merger of airlines to global alliances, the cooperation between original equipment manufacturers and vendors in supply chains or the joint software development within open source projects. In addition, further cooperation forms exist, for which the partners either pursue a common goal or the one party helps the respectively other to reach their goals ("You scratch my back and I'll scratch yours").

In this book, cooperation is an implicitly or contractually agreed collaboration between independent companies. Here, we assume that these agreements are made for a medium- or long-term cooperation and require investments from the participating companies (Bakos/Brynjolfsson 1993). These investments, for example, can be the time spent for negotiating outline agreements or investments in information and communication technology.

The economic effects, resulting from cooperation for the actors involved, are ultimately achieved by effectively combining resources, such as production plants, employees, or information, for example. The following advantages can be achieved:

- *Cost reductions* are regarded as a classic advantage of cooperation for the partners involved, which can be realized in particular due to economies of scale or economies of scope.

- The *time* factor is another reason for establishing cooperation agreements. The term "time to market" indicates the interval from an idea or vision all the way up to the product launch. A large amount of empirical research indicates that the life cycle of products is becoming increasingly shorter and there is a statistically significant relationship between the time of entry to the market and the market share. For this reason, cooperation agreements are attractive because the involved partners, for example, can perform tasks in parallel, which leads to reduced development times.

- The *reduction of risks* has also been frequently mentioned as being a motivation for cooperation between companies. A division of effort can also lead to a shared risk of failure. This applies for instance to projects in research and development, where a large potential risk is involved.

- *Quality advantages* through cooperation can, for example, permit alliances of airlines, car rental companies and hotels to provide additional services, such as a coordinated availability and return of rental cars and the crediting of bonus points.

- Cooperation can also result in an increased *flexibility* by permitting access to additional production capacity of the partner (flexible capacity expansion).

- In particular the linking of employees and their know-how open up new potentials of an increased *innovation activity*. Product innovations may differentiate the product offerings and thus provide additional competitive advantage.

- Cooperation can simplify the *access to new markets* as well as resolve traditional industry limits. Or, cooperation can provide a high market share, which then increases the barriers to market entry.

1.2 Inter-organizational Cooperation in Logistics: Supply Chain Management

This book focuses on inter-organizational cooperation in logistics. The actors of a supply chain consider themselves as partners that cooperate with each other in order to achieve their common purpose. The center of attention here is to better accommodate the demands of the end customers, for example, through a faster product provision. Furthermore, potentials for rationalization can be tapped. The actors of a supply chain are suppliers, manufacturers, wholesalers, freight forwarders, warehouses and merchandise distribution centers, logistics service providers, and the retail sector. Examples for cooperation in the supply chain are:

- Within partnerships, suppliers and recipients work together on the product development, starting with the initial idea, including the process development, the implementation and market launch of the product.

- Suppliers are compensated based on the commercial success of the producer. An example is the development of the Smart Car.

- In the goods flow from the intermediate product provider to the final assembly company, only one warehouse is jointly operated; thus warehouse stocks and capital tie-up costs can be reduced.

- Logistics service providers cooperate with manufacturers for the management of a supply chain. The cooperation between Schenker AG and Daimler-Chrysler AG for the overseas production of the A-Class model (refer to section 7.1) serves as an example.

The concept of supply chain management – unlike classic business approaches – emphasizes the integration and improvement of business processes beyond company limits, that is, from the provision of the material components up to the delivery of the product, possibly manufactured in several intermediate stages, and the respective services to the end customer (Oliver/Webber 1982; Cooper et al. 1997; Handfield/Nicols 1999; Helms et al. 2000; Knolmayer et al. 2002).

Cooperation in logistics, however, is also the central focus of the Collaborative Planning, Forecasting and Replenishment (CPFR) concept (refer also to Knolmayer et al., 2002). This concept aims at improving the inter-organizational partnership between vendors and customers in the supply chain through jointly managed information and cooperatively managed processes so that an excess profit challenge results for the participants. The focus here is on reducing the inventory levels while improving the delivery service. The principle part consists of the "CPFR Voluntary Guidelines" that were prepared by the CPFR Committee (refer to http://www.cpfr.org). This committee consists of representatives from approximately 70 industrial and trading companies.

The most important guidelines of the CPFR concept are:

- *The partners develop rules for the cooperation.* These include agreements on the shared use of information and arrangements on the rights and obligations of the partners, and also for the criteria and metrics to be used to measure the effectiveness and success of the cooperation. In particular, a general plan is devised, in which the participants are assigned "core process activities". The guidelines moreover recommend to develop a common business strategy, which specifies, for example, minimum purchase order quantities and ordering intervals as well as agreements on marketing and sales actions.

- *The cooperating companies set up a joint forecast on the requirements of the end-customers.* This common forecast can be prepared by aggregating the individual forecasts of the individual members in the supply chain. The forecasts can be determined, for example, using point of sales data from traders, stock issues from distribution centers, and incoming orders at the manufacturer. The shared forecast forms the basis of the plans to be reconciled.

Cooperation between the actors, on the one hand, could thus improve the entire supply chain. On the other hand, an improvement of the overall result may possibly only be achieved in this case by impairing a member of the supply chain. This leads to the following basic problems:

- How are the business risks calculated and assigned in a supply chain?

- How is the added value of a supply chain cooperation calculated?

- How are the additional contribution margins allocated in a supply chain?

This, for example, raises the question whether it is possible to replace a manufacturers distribution warehouse and a procurement warehouse for a subsequent assembly plant with a warehouse operated together, and so reduce inventory held along the supply chain. Such changes frequently also have negative effects on both upstream and downstream companies in the supply chain. Which participants must now carry the inventory risks? And assuming that this activity produces a cost reduction and the resulting sales produce an increased profit: how will the resulting added value be distributed?

Therefore, it is possible that the supply chain as such is flourishing, although individual partners could realize lower costs or higher revenues without the cooperation. The added value of the entity and the possible losses of the individuals must be adequately identifiable to allow a value distribution acceptable for the members (which does not mean that it must be a "fair" value distribution).

A further methodical, to a large extent not yet clarified problem is that many companies are members of several supply chains in parallel. 62 percent of the companies surveyed within an empiric analysis recently conducted in the automotive industry stated to be active in several supply chains (Buxmann et al. 2003). This in turn means that companies that cooperate as part of a supply chain, might also be competitors in other value chains. The literature has coined the term "coopetition" (from the words "cooperation" and "competition") for this situation (Brandenburger/Nalebuff 1996). An example for coopetition is the cooperation of the competitors Volkswagen and Ford: Here, the models VW Sharan and Ford Galaxy were developed in cooperation. Nevertheless, both companies remain competitors on the market. Coopetition, however, can also take on a different form: individual participants of a supply chain can be simultaneously engaged in several competing value-added processes. For example, in the automotive industry one can find exactly this constellation for tire manufacturers.

How can a company meet the challenge of simultaneous cooperation and competition?

Currently, no theory-based procedures exist, which have been tested in practice to answer this question. Basically, the issue revolves around the interconnection of various supply chains: What positive network effects can be ideally achieved for all participants through the connection of the processes belonging to different value chains? Nowadays, in many cases it can be observed that automobiles of a manufacturer have motors of a competitor built in. This fact permits, for example, a motor manufacturer to increase the utilization of a new factory by supplying competitors to such an extent and thereby achieve a profitability increase so that any possible growth limitations in its own end-product market are over-compensated.

Up to now, we talked about supply chains. Today we can observe, however, that classic supplier chains are increasingly replaced by network structures. This can have the effect that, for example, an actor is member of several supply chains, a manufacturer procures a certain material component from varying (previously quality checked) suppliers through reverse auctions, or network-like production structures are established (Gebauer/Buxmann 2000). The following figure shows a classic supply chain on the left and a supply network on the right.

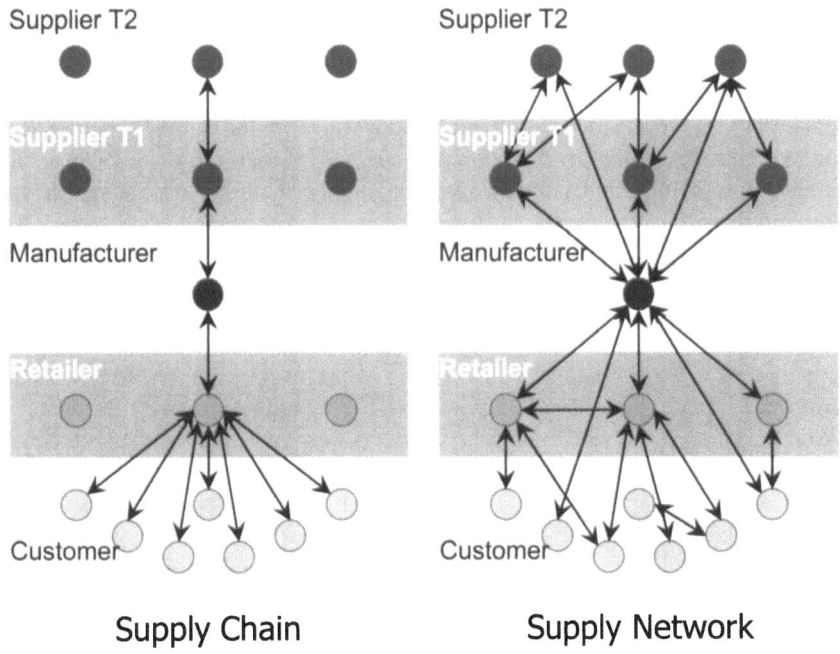

Figure 1.1: Supply chain vs. supply network

Thereby, a supply chain is a special case of a logistics network or supply network, that is, the treatment of supply networks includes the analysis of supply chains. Below we will therefore also refer to supply networks.

1.3   Using Information and Communication Systems in Supply Chain Management

An integrated data processing is a precondition for the design of inter-organizational business processes in supply chains. Ideally, all internally and externally involved parties are connected with one another in real-time, and exchange required information without delay. The automation of the data flows and the exchange of standardized formatted data, for example using EDI, makes the classic postal route increasingly superfluous. The computer-to-computer coupling from the consumer to the supplier permits not only an automated data transmission, but also a mutual immediate access to the specific scheduling files. If the supply chain is interrupted, for example, as the result of the failure of a machine at the supplier, the system forwards the appropriate information to all parties involved in the supply chain and so permits all involved companies to initiate an alternative planning, avoiding the consequences of the failure, for example, by activating an alternative supplier. After all, it is the information flow, which takes over the control of the goods movements.

In this case, it is possible that information flows in opposite direction from the goods as well as in the same direction as the goods. An example for the first-mentioned case is a delivery schedule that a manufacturer transmits to his supplier. Vice versa, information and goods flow in the same direction if a supplier transmits results of quality assurance activities to the manufacturer, for example. Information and goods flows in a supply chain are represented in the following figure.

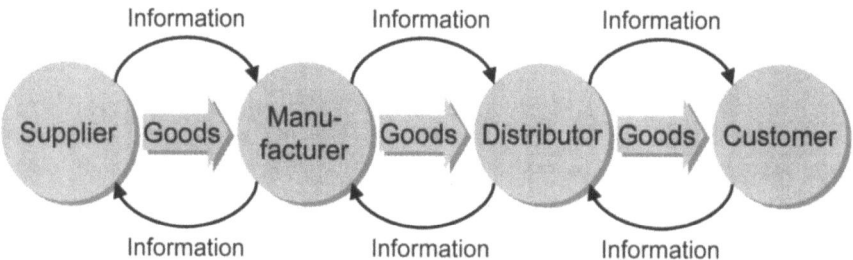

Figure 1.2: Information and goods flows in supply chains

The retail sector can serve as an example for the integrated consideration of goods and information processes: In this scenario, the sales data of various articles is collected through scanner cash desks at the "point of sale" and without delay passed on to the upstream members in the supply chain. The resulting improved sales forecasts enable – among other things – a better planning of the deliveries from warehouses and branches to the wholesalers and the manufacturers. The integrated control of the entire supply chain permits a reduction in the inventory levels and in the throughput times, which in turn reduces costs, improves the delivery service through an improved availability of the products, and increases the quality of the products, through, for example, a higher product freshness in the consumer goods industry.

Just-in-Time (JIT) production is another example. This principle is applied, for example, in the automotive industry, where suppliers provide the required goods within a short time frame after the request for delivery. In analogy to the physical level, the JIT concept can also be applied to the processing of information because the transport of information is subject to logistic considerations in the same way as the transport of real goods.

The efficient use of information and communication technology (ICT) as well as the willingness of organizational networking take on a key role when it comes to controlling the information and goods flows between the partners in a supply chain. Looking at the development stages in the ICT, it becomes evident that the trend is shifting from internal support to inter-organizational cooperation. In the 1960s, companies increasingly began to use ICT to support specific areas. Initially, these were often the accounting and manufacturing areas. In a next phase, support was also provided to cross-functional areas. This resulted in an integration of different functions, such as cost accounting with financial accounting. Since the mid-1980s, the support for inter-organizational integration has been a trend in ICT. Some ten years later, this development was intensified through the Internet which provides a worldwide available and cost-saving infrastructure for carrying out inter-organizational business processes based on open standards.

The basis of the organization and operation of inter-organizational processes in supply chains is the use of common standards at different levels. Here, Internet standards, such as HTTP, XML, Java, HTML, nowadays constitute the generally accepted state-of-the-art. Considering standard business software, these standards are more or less supported by the vendors on this market. A differentiation is made at a higher level, for instance, with the design of the data or the process models.

A common data management of the partners involved can be set up based on such open standards in order to ensure the provision of the decision-relevant information. In particular, this concerns the used communications standards as well as the type of the data maintenance and transfer. This includes, for example, the usage of EDI for the electronic exchange of business documents between the partners of a supply chain. Furthermore, information can be provided by means of a common data storage, with all participants being able to access the data pool. Modern database systems and data warehouse solutions provide various functionalities for information retrieval based on Internet standards.

Supply chain management systems enable cooperative planning of processes. These are, for example, common location, sales, production, procurement, and distribution resource planning. The vision is that an excess profit challenge results from this cooperative planning, as illustrated in section 1.2. Known suppliers for supply chain management software are i2 Technologies, J. D. Edwards, Oracle as well as SAP. Many of these suppliers provide an interface to corresponding ERP software. From an economic perspective, indirect network effects exist, which result in a competitive advantage for SAP as market leader in the ERP software area.

Finally, electronic marketplaces (EM) nowadays partially provide functionalities for the joint corporate planning in the business-to-business area, too – often under the keyword "Collaboration". These marketplaces thus combine the support of the data exchange as well as the processing of transactions with supply chain management functionalities. With partners often collaborating on a long-term basis, EM take on a cooperative character. This is achieved, for example, by the participants having to pay fixed charges over a longer period of time and thus contributing to the infrastructure costs.

This book concentrates on the support of inter-organizational cooperative business processes with the aid of SAP solutions. It will dwell on basic standards (chapter 2) and data management (chapter 3 and 4) as well as on cooperative planning within supply chain management (chapter 5) and electronic marketplaces (chapter 6). In addition, five case studies from the automotive industry will be presented (chapter 7). The structure of the book is illustrated in the following figure.

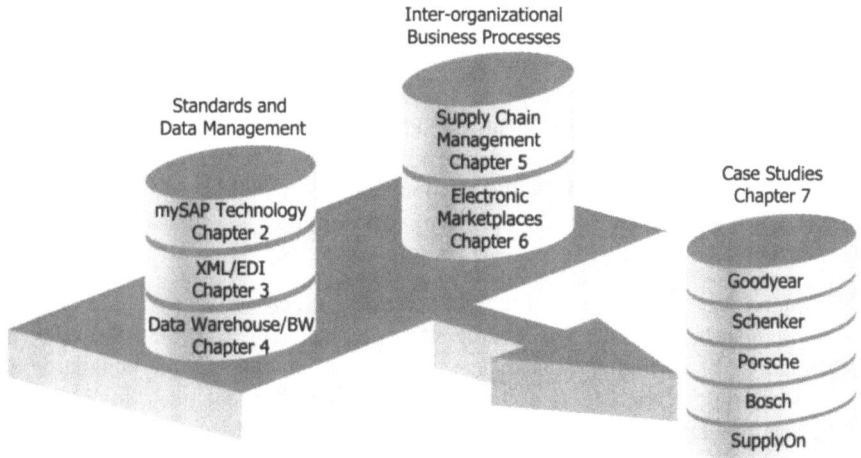

Figure 1.3: Structure of the book

Chapter 2   Basics of mySAP.com and mySAP Technology

This chapter presents mySAP Technology, the new integration architecture from SAP AG, which serves as a basis for the application of mySAP.com solutions. A fundamental objective is the support of the cooperation between companies. Like other standard software suppliers, SAP focuses on the use of open standards, such as Java, XML, or HTTP. On the one hand, this strategy aims at achieving a high flexibility in the sense of an easy extensibility of solutions. On the other hand, this openness is a prerequisite for the compatibility of systems from different suppliers. From a business point of view, this change in strategy from primarily in-house and proprietary solutions to open solutions has by all means been successful: Only one year after introducing mySAP.com, these solutions made up almost 50 percent of the income from license agreements (Jakovljevic 2000).

Section 2.1 first gives a short overview of the new product offer from SAP. Then, section 2.2 provides a description of the technological structure of the mySAP.com e-business platform. The focus here is on mySAP Technology and the employed standards, which are to ensure the openness and integration capability of all mySAP.com components used.

2.1   The mySAP.com Solutions

mySAP.com was introduced in October 1999 and is subdivided into the areas "cross-industry solutions", "industry-specific solutions" as well as "infrastructure and services".

Figure 2.1 shows which cross-industry solutions are available. These support general, that is, industry-independent functions, such as Human Resources or Financial Accounting.

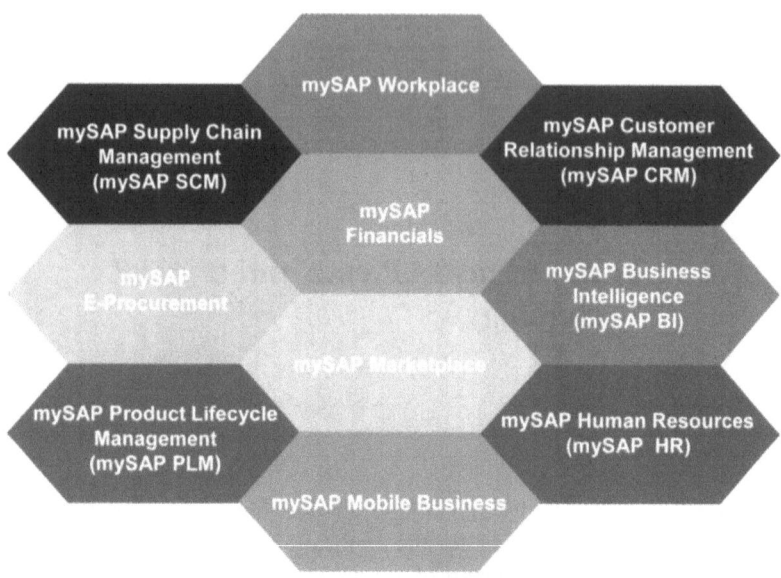

Figure 2.1: Overview of the cross-industry solutions

In addition, industry-specific characteristics are supported, where SAP distinguishes the areas discrete manufacturing industry, consumer products industry, process industries, services, financial services and public sector. Solutions for a total of 21 different industry sectors are provided (see Figure 2.2).

The specified solutions are implemented with the help of different components. A mySAP.com component is a software product of SAP, which is part of mySAP.com and fulfills certain tasks for the user or another component. The mySAP Supply Chain Management solution, for example, may consist of the application components R/3, Advanced Planner and Optimizer (chapter 5) as well as the Business Information Warehouse (chapter 4). The application components are installed independent from one another and have their own release road map. In the following, they will also be referred to as systems.

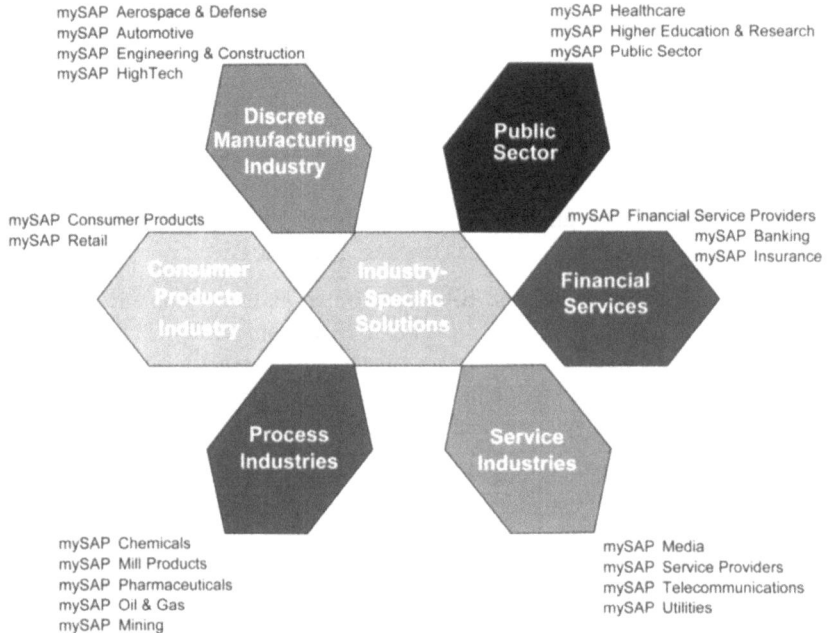

Figure 2.2: Overview of the cross-industry solutions

The technology components are software and middleware solutions used for implementing and supporting mySAP.com solutions. This category includes:

- The SAP R/3 plug-in is an interface between SAP R/3 and other mySAP.com components.

- The Workplace plug-in is an interface that allows data exchange between the SAP Workplace Server and mySAP.com components.

- The SAP Internet Transaction Server is used to make SAP solutions Internet-enabled and is the predecessor of the SAP Web Application Server.

- The SAP Web Application Server is a component of mySAP.com, which provides the technological base for other mySAP.com components (R/3, BW and so on); it was called SAP Basis in the past and was delivered as an integral part of SAP R/3.

- SAP GUI is the graphical user interface for SAP software.

- The SAP Business Connector is a middleware product for the integration of various IT architectures with mySAP.com components based on open, not proprietary Internet technologies, such as XML (refer to chapter 3).

Following this short overview of the product landscape the of mySAP.com e-business platform, the main section Infrastructure and Services is introduced with the focus on the underlying technological architecture, mySAP Technology.

2.2   The mySAP.com Infrastructure and Services

The area Infrastructure and Services consists of three parts: mySAP Hosted Solutions, mySAP Services as well as mySAP Technology.

With mySAP Hosted Solutions, SAP and other partner companies provide a service, which is to allow to implement mySAP.com solutions fast and cost-effectively without having to set up an own e-business platform. The access to applications is to be made via the Internet through a Web browser, in order to also address small and mid-sized companies as a target group.

mySAP Services include various services that SAP provides for their customers, including implementation support, training, and know-how transfer.

mySAP Technology was introduced in November 2001 and is the technological infrastructure for mySAP.com systems. It is an integration architecture based on open Internet standards, by means of which solutions from SAP as well as from third-party suppliers can be integrated. To accomplish this integration, mySAP Technology includes the four components Portal Infrastructure, Exchange Infrastructure, SAP Web Application Server, and Infrastructure Services (see Figure 2.3); they are described below in detail.

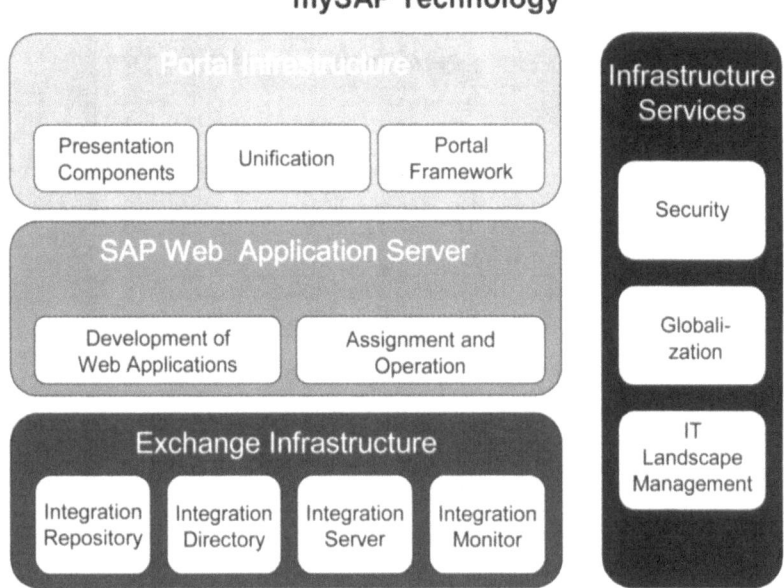

Figure 2.3: The modules of mySAP Technology

2.2.1　Portal Infrastructure

The Portal Infrastructure (see Figure 2.4; in this figure as well as in all following figures, R stands for "request") meets the precondition for a user-oriented integration and cooperation. For SAP this means that several users can share different sources of information. The (enterprise) portal in this case provides a central entry point to all information, applications and services, that employees, for example, need for fulfilling their tasks according to their role assignment. These sources of information provide vendors, customers, partners and employees with an option to easily and securely access all important contents and to be able to be part of the different business processes. Here, both platform standards .NET (Microsoft) and Java 2 Enterprise Edition (J2EE) are supported.

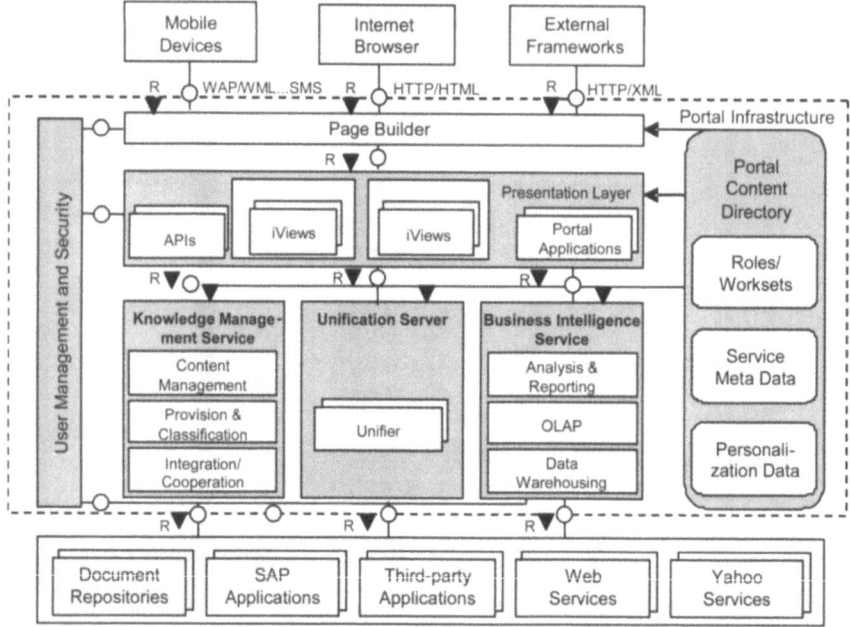

Figure 2.4: The Portal Infrastructure (based on SAP AG 2001c, p. 8)

The goal of a user-oriented integration is pursued with the help of the portal infrastructure. For that purpose, data from various sources is correlated and then combined to logical units in order to provide users with the information corresponding to their functions within the company. In this case, the information access is to be enabled through mobile devices, Internet browsers or other external infrastructures. After the one-time logon (Single Sign-On (SSO)) and authentication, users can access all areas for which they have authorization. The user does not see, however, from which source the information was originated.

The Portal Infrastructure consists of four technologies that enable to aggregate data from different sources. These technologies include iView and Unification for accessing legacy and transaction systems, Business Intelligence as analysis platform, Knowledge Management as document management solution as well as Content Management and Services Management (Yahoo!) for the provision of Web contents. The elements "User Management and Security" as well as "Portal Content Directory" (PCD) complement these technologies (see Figure 2.4), which are discussed below:

- *iView and Unification*: An iView is a congruent presentation element based on XML. iViews are set up in the presentation layer of the portal; they are to call attention to important events and allow fast development of information units from applications (SAP AG 2001c, p. 9).

In order to provide information, the iView Server uses the iView Connector to set up links to different sources, whereby these are able to access both structured and unstructured information. Object Linking and Embedding Database (OLE DB), native application programming interfaces (APIs), HyperText Transfer Protocol (HTTP), XML or Simple Object Access Protocol (SOAP), for example, can be used to access structured information. Furthermore, these links may be used to support access to applications from other manufacturers, such as PeopleSoft, Oracle, Baan, Siebel, Eroom, Clarify and Lotus.

An output in XML format is always generated, regardless of the programming language in which the iViews are written. This is the starting point for the conversion into other formats, thus allowing the information access using various devices. The Page Builder can be used, for example, for conversions into the Wireless Markup Language (WML) so that the information can be displayed on a WAP-enabled mobile phone (Wireless Access Protocol). It is additionally possible to convert to HTML 3.2 (HyperText Markup Language) and to the corresponding HTML subset for the presentation on pocket PCs.

Unification is to allow a context-oriented navigation and thus also a faster processing of events. For this purpose, monolithic applications can be subdivided into blocks, which can then be combined to complex applications (SAP AG 2001c, p. 9). Within Unification, a drag&relate function is available, which allows the user to reveal relationships between sources of information united in an iView.

The actual access to several applications is made through so-called "Application Unifiers", which are available for standard software from PeopleSoft, Siebel, Oracle, Baan and SAP. Different data sources can be connected by means of the so-called "Database Unifiers".

As already mentioned, an iView is used to display information. Hereby, Meta data on how to access the respective source of information is stored in a repository. It also includes so-called hyperrelational information, which is used to conduct data to the (user) interface of the portal based on the HyperRelational Navigation Protocol (HRNP). This protocol is tunneled through the HTTP standard. In this case, HRNP uses a browser link similar to a URL, with the HRNP link containing the meta data that is used to pass context through the HTTP protocol.

- *Business Intelligence*: Based on a data warehouse (see chapter 4), this platform allows to collect information required by decision makers. Furthermore, it provides the option to carry out simulations and supports the monitoring and optimization of business processes. Information access can be carried out through iViews or business intelligence tools, such as the SAP Business Explorer.

- *Knowledge Management*: This technology provides functions for the administration of documents, such as aggregation or classification. In the enterprise portal, the access to this system is carried out using the interface standard WebDAV (Web-based Distributed Authoring and Versioning). WebDAV specifies protocols for locking documents, meta data standards, delete and retrieval functions, characteristic value-based search functions for Web resources and namespace operations, that also allow copy and move operations. Furthermore, the interface provides the front end for different services with the knowledge management solution.

  A folder hierarchy is created and the information, at which position the document is stored in this hierarchy, is specified in the repository of the knowledge management system by a corresponding reference.

- *Content Management and Services Management (Yahoo!)*: These functions allow to access Web contents and services, i.e. company-external sources of information. The information is provided by Yahoo!, as can be assumed from the name.

Furthermore, the Portal Infrastructure provides two additional elements: "User Management and Security" and "Portal Content Directory" (PCD):

- Within "User Management and Security", user data and cross-infrastructure authorization information are stored in a directory service, which supports open standards, such as the Lightweight Directory Access Protocol (LDAP). In this area of the Portal Infrastructure, authentication and SSO are controlled. The role management is also handled here. The roles are used to set up logical units of information containing elements such as iViews and Worksets. In the SAP terminology, a Workset is a set of screens and iViews that belong to a page or a number of pages and help users to perform the tasks that correspond to their role. The information to the role is stored in the Portal Content Directory described below.

- Information on all services available through the company is stored in the "Portal Content Directory" (PCD). A large degree of personalization can be accomplished through the definition of roles: users should get access to exactly those services they need (SAP AG 2001c, p. 14).

2.2.2   Exchange Infrastructure

While the Portal Infrastructure is used for the user-oriented integration, the Exchange Infrastructure focuses on the process-oriented integration and cooperation. This process-oriented integration beyond company limits is the basic principle of establishing and practicing inter-organizational cooperations. In this case, the Exchange Infrastructure takes on the role of the "polyglot mailman" who not only distributes shipments to the correct location but also translates their contents into the correct formats.

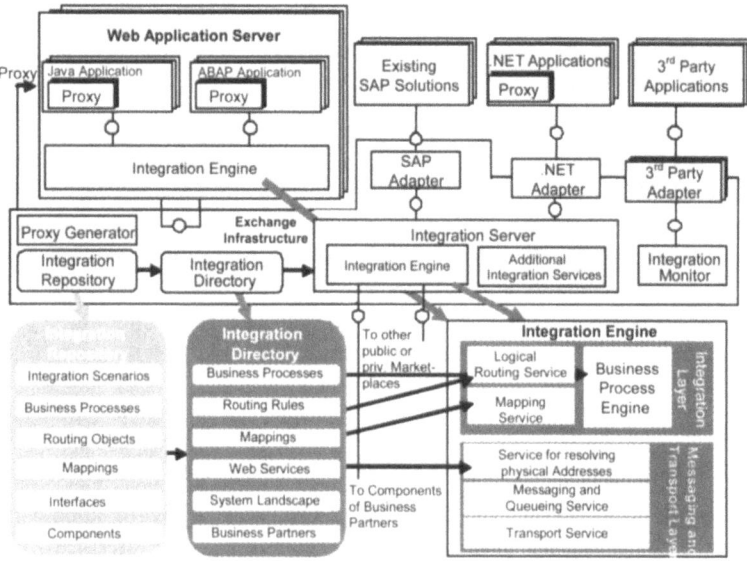

Figure 2.5: Overview of the Exchange Infrastructure architecture
(based on SAP AG 2002c, p. 24)

The idea behind this process-oriented integration is to avoid one-to-one links between all components in a heterogeneous system infrastructure. The Exchange Infrastructure marks the attempt to reduce the effort required for this integration by providing a detailed description of the cooperation knowledge required in a collective knowledge pool. This knowledge includes the functionality of cooperation-relevant elements, such as processes, business rules, Web services, interfaces, roles and so forth (SAP AG 2002c, p. 24). The thus created common knowledge base is to simplify the integration of in-house and external components since a component must be described only once in order to be accessible systemwide. Figure 2.7 provides an overview of the Exchange Infrastructure architecture with the components "Integration Repository", "Integration Directory", "Integration Server", "Integration Monitor" and "Adapter", which are described in the following.

Integration Repository

In order to share cooperation knowledge, the existing knowledge must be collected first. This is done, among other things, with the help of the "Integration Repository" programmed in Java and based on J2EE standards. There, the following elements are held ready for this purpose (see Figure 2.5):

- *Integration Scenarios*: In the future, these are to facilitate the configuration of the message-based interaction between application components or business objects. They define the message flow between interfaces and the respective components. To accelerate the configuration process of the Exchange Infrastructure, predefined integration scenarios exist that can be selected by the planner (SAP AG 2002c, p. 11).

- *Business Processes*: These are expandable composite Web services, which are executed by the Business Process Engine in the Integration Engine. This aims at organizing business processes at business level without having to consider issues regarding the technical implementation (this is realized by the interface architecture of the Web services). Various types of templates (general, industry-specific and enterprise-specific) are provided for the creation of these business processes, with every type of business process being able to identify the Web services that are needed and for which a link must be set up (SAP AG 2002c, p. 11).

- *Routing Objects*: The Integration Repository contains routing objects, through which the potential recipients of messages are determined.

- *Mappings*: Furthermore, the Integration Repository allows mappings, which describe the necessary transformations between message interfaces, message types or data types in the Integration Repository. Both, structural transformations and pure value mappings are possible. The mappings can be implemented with the help of the Extensible Stylesheet Language for Transformations (XSLT; also refer to Wüstner et al. 2002 for details on converting XML documents with XSLT) or using Java code (also see section 3.2).

- *Interfaces*: Preconfigured, SAP-proprietary interfaces are delivered with the Integration Repository, which is based on the principles of the Web Services Description Language (WSDL) (these interfaces are Business Application Programming Interfaces (BAPIs), Intermediate Documents (IDocs) and Remote Function Calls (RFCs)). In addition, other non-SAP-specific interfaces are to be supported as well (see chapter 3).

- *Components*: Finally, also installation-independent information on the individual application components and their relationships to one another are stored in the Landscape System Directory based on the Common Information Model (CIM). As a default, the repository contains information on all mySAP.com components, but it can also be extended.

After the cooperation knowledge has been entered in the repository with the help of integration scenarios, business processes, routing objects, mappings, interfaces and component information, configuration-specific information is added in the "Integration Directory".

Integration Directory

Information in the Integration Directory describes active business processes, routing rules, active mappings, executable Web services from specific system infrastructures and from active business partners (these business processes or partners are characterized as active if they are required in the current configuration). The basis of this directory is a Java platform; the contents can be represented with XML using open Internet standards. Furthermore, it is to become possible to add cooperation knowledge from third parties. The relevant description elements are explained below:

- A description, which is executed through the Business Process Engine in the Integration Server and thus enables the design of cooperative business processes, is stored in the Integration Directory for each active business process.

- Routing rules specify "content-based sender/receiver relations". They determine the recipient of a message, though this assignment is often made based on the contents of the message. Criteria, according to which the recipient is selected, are sender, message type of the sender, message for identifying the recipient and message type of the recipient. There are two possibilities to create these message rules: they can be declaratively described using XML Path Language (XPath; W3C 1999) or be programmed in Java. Exclusively logical statements are used for characterizing sender and recipient in order to separate them from the physical address delivered by the Web service described in the Integration Directory. The advantage of this separation is that the physical address can be changed any time without the business logic having to be changed. The information on routing rules is applied at runtime (SAP AG 2002c, p. 15).

- The interfaces of the Web services implemented in the current system infrastructure are available in the Web Services Area. This includes both own Web services and those from business partners involved. A Web service is a "self-contained, modularized function that can be published, discovered, and accessed across a network using open standards. (…) For the caller and sender, a Web service is a *black box*" (SAP AG 2002a, p. 2) with a predefined interface. Information contained in the Web Services Area can in the future be exchanged over UDDI-compatible directories (Universal Description Discovery and Integration). WSDL (W3C 2001) is used for the description of the Web services themselves. SOAP (W3C 2000) and ebXML (Electronic Business using Extensible Markup Language) can be used as messaging interface in connection with Web services. Furthermore, the interface description includes the physical addressing, access information or other attributes, such as URL, protocols and security information (SAP AG 2002c, p. 16). This information stored in the directory is to be used at runtime by the Integration Engine.

- Mappings are stored both in the Integration Directory and in the repository. The difference is that the directory includes only such mappings that are needed in the current system infrastructure. In addition, it is only possible to create new mappings in the directory (the same also applies to the Web services).

- The Integration Directory also contains information on the available system infrastructure, that is, information on, for example, which components are installed and available.

- It is additionally possible to store Integration Directory information on business partners, whereby every company can individually decide which information (e.g., name, URL, conditions) are to be collected.

As mentioned above, the Integration Repository and Integration Directory are used for collecting information required for the cooperation. The actual cooperation is implemented within the "Integration Server" which in this case uses the information retrieved from the directory.

Integration Server

The Integration Server includes the Integration Engine and additional Integration Services. The Integration Engine is responsible for the exchange of messages between the linked components and consists of two layers: an integration layer as well as a messaging and transport layer (see above, Figure 2.5). The integration layer consists of three parts:

- The Business Process Engine controls the interaction of the technical components within the respective business process. Web services are also executed by the Business Process Engine (SAP AG 2002c, p. 19).

- The recipient of a message is determined through a routing service. In addition, the necessary interfaces are determined through an evaluation of the respective routing rules.

- The mapping service is used to define which transformations are necessary. This depends on the message, the sender, the sender interface, the recipient and the recipient interface. In case of a synchronous communication, the direction of the message flow also matters. After the extraction of the required mappings from the integration directory, the mapping service can apply the XSLT or Java mappings to the contents of the sender message to thus ensure that the message is converted to the required format.

In addition to the integration layer, the Integration Engine also includes the messaging and transport layer, which provide messaging, queueing and transfer services for delivering the message to the recipients. After a message has been transformed to the recipient format, the physical address of the required recipient services and all other relevant attributes are read from the integration directory. Finally, the incoming and outgoing as well as incorrect and currently processed messages are persistently stored in a queueing engine. The queueing is carried out in the SAP Web Application Server (see section 2.2.3). Furthermore, SAP intends to provide interfaces for integrating queueing engines from other suppliers using the Java Message Services standard (Sun 2002) into mySAP Technology.

The transmission of a message is carried out by the transport service, through which the Integration Service is able to take on the role of a HTTP client and server. The client enables the outgoing communication, while the server can receive the incoming documents.

Figure 2.6 shows how the integration layer and the messaging and transport layer are passed through when a message is transferred.

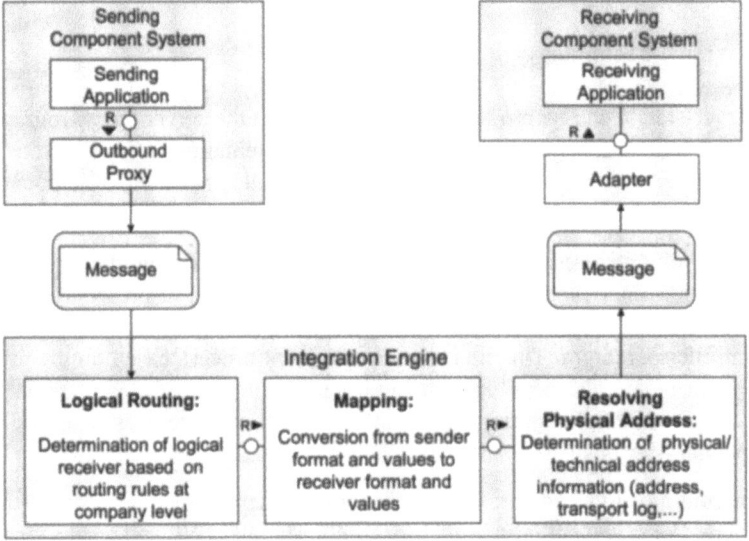

Figure 2.6: Transmitting a message using the Integration Server

Integration Monitor and Adapter

The Integration Monitor supports error handling and monitors the Integration Engine as well as the adapters (see Figure 2.5). The adapters are to ensure that the Integration Engine can accept a technical and semantic link to application components. For this purpose, XML and HTTP-based messages have to be translated into the often proprietary protocols and formats of other systems.

2.2.3   SAP Web Application Server

The SAP Web Application Server is to enable the development and provision of Web services and Web applications. Both, new Web technologies and the functionalities of the conventional SAP basis are applied here. On the server side, scripting and high-level Web Dynpro technologies belong to the Web technologies which enable the provision of Web services and Web applications. The data, system and software management capabilities of SAP are to be understood as the conventional SAP Basis. This platform supports open Internet standards, such as HTTP, HyperText Transfer Protocol, Secure (HTTPS), HTML, and XML. Both technologies – the SAP basis and the Web standards – can be used due to the integration of a J2EE and an ABAP environment (refer to SAP AG 2001e, p. 16).

First, the Web Dynpro technology is introduced, followed by a description of the architecture of SAP Web Application Server.

Web Dynpro Technology

The server-side Web Dynpro technology is based on the server page programming model JSP and consists of development and implementation tools as well as of the corresponding runtime services. Web Dynpro includes two main components for the development of applications and Web services:

- The development environment: with the creation of Web applications or Web services in the development environment, a separation of presentation design, interactive logic and business logic is made in accordance with the model view controller paradigm. This makes a development process based on the different roles feasible. The development environment provides different tools which allow, for example, setting up an interactive flow specification as well as a repository for business data types.

- The runtime environment: the runtime environment, which is based on the JSP programming model and a platform-independent BSP extension, makes a number of functionalities of the Web Dynpro available, such as input help, error handling and bandwidth optimization. The JSP programming model that uses a combination of Java and HTML allows the generation of dynamic Web pages on the server. The TagLibs are collections of reusable coding blocks in markup languages such as HTML or WML. Developers can either use the existing tags or create their own tags and use them in the page.

SAP Web Application Server

The SAP Web Application Server consists of five modules: "Internet Communication Manager" (ICM), "Presentation Layer", "Business Logic" (implemented by means of "J2EE personality" or "ABAP personality"), "Integration" as well as "Connectivity" (see Figure 2.7).

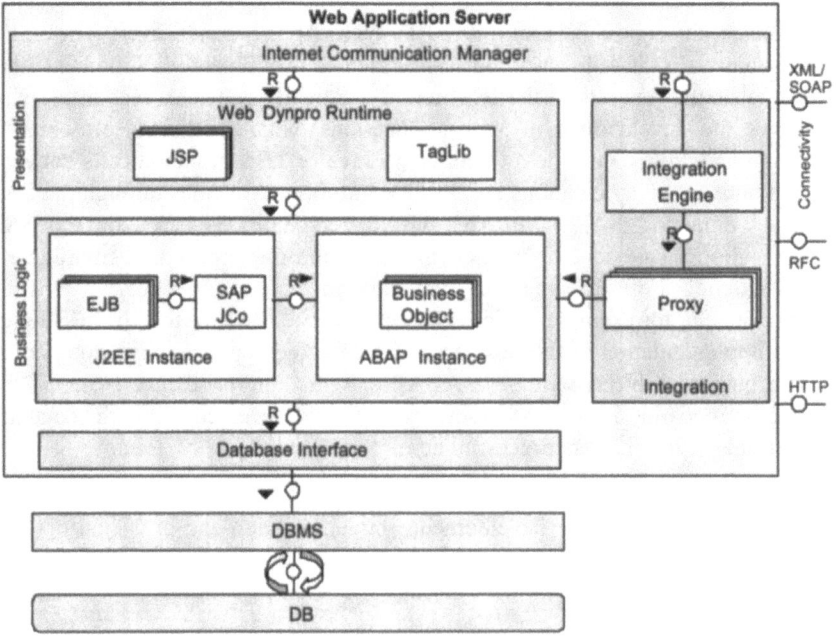

Figure 2.7: Architecture of the SAP Web Application Server (following SAP AG 2001e, p.17 and p.18)

Figure 2.7 shows the modules of the SAP Web Application Server. What these modules look like in detail is described below:

- The Internet Communication Manager (ICM) controls the communication between the SAP Web Application Server and external partners through the intranet and Internet-based standard protocols, such as HTTP, HTTPS and Simple Mail Transfer Protocol (SMTP). This communication is realized through a memory-based communication channel (the memory pipe) that, according to SAP, contributes to the improvement of the performance and the scalability of Web pages due to dynamic and active content caching technology. This communication assumes the form of requests, whereby two types are distinguished here: On the one hand, the ICM sends user interface requests (such as HTTP requests) to the Web Dynpro runtime and, on the other hand, it sends Web service requests (e.g., in SOAP) to the Integration Engine. The ICM can take on both the role of a server and of a client: It assumes the role of a server when an application or a client sets up a link to it. If the SAP Web Application Server initiates a link, the ICM becomes the client.

- In the Presentation Layer, the contents coming from the Business Logic is represented with JSP and corresponding TagLibs.

- The Business Logic includes both the J2EE and the ABAP personality (instance in Figure 2.7) of the SAP Web Application Server: The J2EE personality is based on a J2EE-certified development environment that processes the requests of the ICM and dynamically generates responses. This allows the development of Web applications, which include a presentation design as well as a business logic, using Java or J2EE. Method calls between Java and ABAP applications are feasible into both directions through the SAP Java Connector (SAP JCo). The ABAP personality is based on the SAP application server development environment and implementation environment and extends these by supporting native Web technology. Thus, all existing components, for example business objects, can be used for the business logic. The implementation of the business logic of a Web application is done either with business objects written in ABAP or with Enterprise Java Beans (EJB) programmed in Java. Databases, which are accessed through database interfaces, store the data processed here.

  Web applications can be created through the ABAP and J2EE instance of Web Application Server. The development, implementation and provision of Web services are also possible: Every independent, modularized function can be made available as a Web service through the Exchange Infrastructure based on common Internet technology.

- The Integration module contains the Integration Engine as comprehensive runtime infrastructure for Integration Services, through which links with the Exchange Infrastructure of all SAP components can be set up and messaging services between these individual components can be carried out.

- Through the Connectivity module, the integration of products, tools, Web services and applications from third-party suppliers is to be enabled based on open Web standards and formats. SOAP, XML, HTML, WML, HTTP, HTTPS, LDAP, WebDAV, WSDL, UDDI, XSLT, XPath, Common Object Request Architecture (CORBA), Common Object Model+ (COM+), File Transfer Protocol (FTP), SMTP as well as RFC are to be supported (SAP AG 2001e, p. 17 and p. 21 onwards).

2.2.4   Infrastructure Services

mySAP Technology also includes the Infrastructure Services that provide functions for the globalization as well as security procedures.

Concerning the functions for the globalization, different currencies, time zones and languages can be set with mySAP.com systems. Furthermore, translation tools and country-specific characteristics are provided.

The inter-organizational check of the system infrastructure starts with the development of extensive safety instructions. Then the functionality of all applications and processes must be checked. A distinction is to be made between an audit in closed and in open systems. In closed systems, a reporting framework that stores information on authorization, roles and other user data is sufficient (SAP AG 2001d, p. 21). The audit in open systems is more complex and requires an auditing framework, which a company uses not only to check the security of the own architecture but also the one of its business partners. This is done by applying technical audit procedures, which are part of this auditing framework.

The auditing framework allows applications to prepare themselves for the auditing from the start. For this purpose, they provide access for the analyzing tools to, for example, the process-relevant information. By using digital signatures, it can also be achieved that replaced documents are not rejected during the audit procedure (SAP AG 2001d, p. 22).

The Security Infrastructure of mySAP Technology is to provide protection against unauthorized access to applications and Web services. For this purpose, this infrastructure contains the functionalities User Administration as well as Role Management and Responsibility Management, Continuous Network and Communication Security, support of Digital Signatures for authenticity and integrity of data, Trust Relationship Management, and inter-enterprise check of the system infrastructure (SAP AG 2001d).

Chapter 3   EDI and XML/EDI: Concepts and SAP Solutions

The exchange of data between the actors of a supply chain network involves in particular sending and receiving business documents. This includes purchase orders, delivery notes, invoices, and forecast data, for example. Below, a distinction is made between classic EDI and XML/EDI. First, the basic method for exchanging such documents is introduced in each case. Then, the SAP solutions for supporting these business processes are analyzed.

3.1   Classic EDI: Concepts and SAP Solutions

3.1.1   The Basics of EDI

EDI (Electronic Data Interchange) supports the exchange of business documents between computer systems. For example, an automobile manufacturer sends its orders electronically to its component suppliers or a telecommunications company uses EDI to send invoices to its customers.

To support the electronic exchange of documents, a range of industry-specific, company-specific and national standards have been developed. Examples of industry-specific standards are VDA (German Automobile Industry Association) in the automotive industry, SWIFT in the banking sector, SEDAS in the consumer products industry, and DAKOSY in the transport sector. The British standard TRADACOMS or ANSI X12 for the USA, for example, are results from national efforts. At international level, the EDIFACT standard (ISO 9735) exists since 1987 and was developed by the United Nations, the European Community and the standardization organization ISO. Today, EDIFACT and ANSI X12 are the most widely-used. According to a survey made by the Institute of Information Systems at the University of Frankfurt/Main, 77 percent of the questioned German EDI users use EDIFACT, whereas in the USA just 32 percent use this standard compared with 64 percent who use the ANSI X12 standard.

The introduction of EDI initially results in costs that the US Chamber of Commerce estimates to average 50,000 US dollar. The main benefits are time and cost savings. The time savings result from the faster transfer of the data between the business partners and the automatic further processing in the operational software at the receiver side.

In contrast to the normal postal service, which can take several days, an EDI message takes often only a few hours or minutes to go from the sender to the recipient. The direct data transfer without media fragmentation accelerates the inter-organizational and intra-organizational processes. The wait times that result from the manual handling of a business process largely vanish. There are no storage areas, in which requests must wait for further processing, for example, and it is also not necessary to manually enter the incoming business documents. Forecasts estimate that approximate 70 to 95 percent of all data are created or entered more than once even though they are present in electronic form (Dearing 1990, p. 5). EDI makes this duplicated input unnecessary. The time savings resulting from the automatic further processing of the EDI messages also affect the costs. The prevention of manual new inputs reduces personnel costs. Other costs resulting from media fragmentation are also avoided. These are complemented by savings of postal charges for the traditional shipping of business documents and the costs for document management. Furthermore, cost savings can be achieved by reducing incorrect entries.

Despite these advantages, the use of EDI lies below the forecast. This is principally because of the high implementation costs. Another important cost factor lies in the use of so-called Value Added Networks (VANs). These form the communications infrastructure for the exchange of EDI documents between business partners. Thus, it is not surprising that the use of EDI in small and mid-sized companies currently tends to be rather limited. For the future it is to be expected that EDI will be handled increasingly using the Internet. Section 3.2 discusses the possibilities and limits of these new forms of EDI.

3.1.2 SAP Solutions for Supporting EDI

EDI based on SAP solutions is applied with the help of Intermediate Documents (IDocs). These are standardized descriptions of the structure of business documents, such as orders and invoices. This provides an interface to existing EDI standards. A conversion between the IDocs and the EDI messages is needed to use EDI. This is the reason why suppliers certified by SAP provide systems for mapping, status tracking, and conversion of IDocs into EDI standards, and vice versa. In principle, non-certified EDI subsystems can also be used.

As shown in Table 3.1, each IDoc consists of a control record, data records and status records.

Table 3.1: IDoc record types – Overview

Record type IDoc	
1. Control record	• IDoc ID • Sender ID • Receiver ID • IDoc type and message • External structure
2. Data record	• IDoc ID • Sequence number • Segment • SDATA
3. Status record	• IDoc ID • Status information

Currently IDocs support message formats comparable to those of EDIFACT or ANSI X12. The IDoc structure description in Table 3.2 makes it obvious that SAP made particular use of the EDIFACT specifications. The table lists the EDI message formats of the SD module provided by SAP R/3. A distinction is made between outbound and inbound messages.

Table 3.2: Supported EDI messages in the R/3 module SD

Description	From Release	IDoc message	EDIFACT
Invoice	2.1	INVOIC	INVOIC
Quotation	2.1	QUOTES	QUOTES
Order Response	2.1	ORDERSP	ORDRSP
Delivery Note	2.2	DESADV	DESADV
Delivery Schedule	3.0	DELINS	DELFOR
Request for Quotation	2.1	REQOTE	REQOTE
Order	2.1	ORDERS	ORDERS
JIT Delivery Schedule	3.0	DELINS	DELJIT
Invoice	2.1	INVOIC	INVOIC

The MM module, for example, supports as outbound messages exactly the same message types as the SD module for incoming messages. Similarly, because the inbound messages for the module MM are identical with the outbound messages from the SD module, we can omit their representation. To give another example, the message types available in the FI module for corporate finance are listed in Table 3.3.

Table 3.3: EDI messages in the R/3 module FI

Description	From Release	IDoc message	EDIFACT
Invoice	2.1	INVOIC	INVOIC
Remittance Advice	3.0	REMADV	REMADV

3.2   XML/EDI: Concepts and SAP Solutions

3.2.1   The XML/EDI Concept

In addition to the many advantages and "success stories" associated with traditional EDI projects, there is also – as described in section 3.1.1 – a reverse side: currently the use of EDI is primarily restricted to large companies, and in an empirical investigation pressure from bigger business partners was mentioned as being the most frequent reason for the implementation of EDI (Westarp et al. 1999). Forecasts show that only around five percent of the companies, for which its use would be beneficial, actually use EDI. In particular, small and mid-sized companies often mention the high implementation and operations costs as reasons not to introduce EDI. Also, because many of the current solutions are platform-dependent, the use of EDI would lead to additional investments for hardware and software.

The Internet with its wide availability, easy access and worldwide infrastructure could act as a catalyst for the diffusion of EDI, and provide a new impetus for EDI. The German EDI Company (DEDIG) differentiates here between WebEDI applications and Internet-EDI. WebEDI is understood to be the use of the WWW as basis for EDI applications. Existing solutions normally provide simple HTML input masks that permit an input of structured data. On the contrary, Internet-EDI designates the transport of EDI messages using Internet services. Transmission using FTP (File Transfer Protocol) or SMTP (Simple Mail Transfer Protocol) can, for example, be used here.

Commercial advantages of WebEDI and Internet-EDI compared with traditional solutions are primarily expected through the reduction of the setup effort (implementation costs and manpower) and the operating costs. The use of open standards provides a platform independence, which can be linked to a significant reduction in the investment costs. This gives rise to the hope that the entry barriers for small and mid-sized companies for the use of EDI networks can be significantly reduced.

A modern form of EDI is the representation of business documents based on the Extensible Markup Language (XML). A fundamental advantage of XML is in this case that a large number of programming interfaces as well as unrestricted accessibility to parsers exist, which makes a further processing and the integration of XML documents relatively easy. Currently, several business vocabulary collections based on XML are in the making (refer to Weitzel et al. 2001 for an overview).

For this purpose, it is self-evident to access existing know-how from the conventional EDI area. Thus, standardization initiatives such as xCBL (XML Common Business Library, http://www.xcbl.org) from Commerce One, the CEN/ISSS XML-EDI pilot project (http://www.cenorm.be/isss/workshop /ec/xmledi/isss-xml.html), the draft standard DIN 16557-4 (http://www.din.de /gremien/nas/nbue/nbue3/nbueaa3/) as well as the XML/EDI group (http://www. xmledi-group.org) draw upon EDIFACT and X12 structures.

It is specified how to define elements such as addresses, prices, discounts or currencies. These document classes are defined as a Document Type Definition (DTD), as External Data Representation (XDR) standard and more frequently also as W3C-conform XML schema.

Other examples for such approaches concentrating on the provision of documents and document classes are cXML (Commerce XML, http://www.cxml.org) from Ariba, eBIS-XML (http://www.ebis-xml.net) from BASDA (Business and Accounting Software Developers Association) and OAGIS (Open Applications Group Integration Specification) from the Open Applications Group (http://www.openapplications.org).

A study made in the fall 2000 identifies a total of 250 different e-business-vocabularies (Kotok 2000). Directories from XML.com, OASIS/Robin Cover, Schema.Net, and alphaWorks from IBM as well as vocabularies registered or maintained at XML.org (OASIS), Microsoft (BizTalk) and DISA served as source for the study.

Below we will briefly describe the xCBL initiative since many SAP solutions use this standard.

The Common Business library was originally coined by Veo Systems. Veo Systems was later absorbed by Commerce One. Now the library carries the name xCBL and is available as Version 4.0. Commerce One characterizes the xCBL as "set of XML building blocks and a document framework". This stands simply for a collection of XML specifications and modules for business documents. These documents can be product descriptions, purchase orders, and invoices, for example. The xCBL aims at a strict distinction between the contents of an xCBL document and the transport of the transaction logic. This way, the xCBL is not bound to any transport method, such as HTTP. It is thus just a question of structuring a message.

Particularly, EDI standards served as a basis for defining the contents of xCBL. The UNSMS (United Nations Standard Messages) of the EDIFACT standard and the transaction sets from ANSI X12 were the starting point for this. Due to the extent of the standards, only subsets were adopted for xCBL. Furthermore, the experience Commerce One gained as a member of several standardization bodies, such as W3C or IETF, was included in the specification of xCBL. Version 4.0, among other things, contains 44 definitions of document classes, such as purchase order, order confirmation, invoice, and product catalog.

The modular structure of the xCBL is reflected in the fact that documents can or must have the following parts:

- Header: this can be an invoice header or the header of a purchase order.

- Meta information, for example information on whether it is an original document or a copy or also which type of response is expected.

- Core modules: these can be a list of the invoice items and the invoice parties, for example.

- Optional attachments, such as an attached file.

A fundamental characteristic of xCBL is the possibility of extending existing definitions. Three methods are provided for this:

- Using existing placeholders,

- attaching any file to a document as well as

- specializing "building blocks" with the help of inheritance.

The xCBL DTDs and the schema languages XDR from Microsoft, SOX from Commerce One, and the W3C Schema Definition Language support this.

The following figure shows a sample section of an xCBL purchase order document.

```
<?xml version="1.0" ?>
<?soxtype urn:x-commerceone:document:com:commerceone:XCBL30:XCBL30.sox$1.0?>
<Order>
    <OrderHeader>
        <OrderNumber>
            <BuyerOrderNumber>PO23540586</BuyerOrderNumber>
            <SellerOrderNumber>129494575S4</SellerOrderNumber>
            <ListOfMessageID>
                <MessageID>
                    <IDNumber>Signed Purchase Order 12335</IDNumber>
                    <IDAssignedBy>
                        <IDAssignedByCoded>Other</IDAssignedByCoded>
                        <IDAssignedByCodedOther>LaMu2386</IDAssignedByCodedOther>
                    </IDAssignedBy>
                    <IDAssignedDate>20010211T15:25:00</IDAssignedDate>
                </MessageID>
            </ListOfMessageID>
        </OrderNumber>
        <OrderIssueDate>20010225T09:30:00</OrderIssueDate>
        <OrderReferences>
            <AccountCode>
            <Reference>
                <RefNum>58395776904</RefNum>
                <RefDate>20010211T15:26:00</RefDate>
            </Reference>
```

Figure 3.1: Excerpt from an xCBL purchase order document

3.2.2 The SAP Business Connector for Supporting XML/EDI

For the integration of XML documents into SAP systems, SAP provides the Business Connector (BC) which SAP customers can download from the SAP Service Marketplace free of charge. Initially, the company webMethods developed it for the Internet-based data exchange between SAP and non-SAP systems. The application of BC, however, is not limited to the XML environment. Basically, it provides integration options between different formats. Nowadays, it is mostly used for an XML integration however.

Settings concerning users, password, and R/3 system (application or database server) must be made in a way that SAP BC can communicate with the R/3 system. In addition, there is also the option to record all information that is transmitted via the Remote Function Call (RFC) channel to or from the R/3 system to BC. This can be useful during the installation and when troubleshooting.

A partner profile must be created in the R/3 system to enable business data being sent from the R/3 system to SAP BC. It is defined in this partner profile, who is to receive and who is to send which message and how it is created or integrated in the system. These settings are almost identical for EDI partners, ALE (Application Link Enabling) and for SAP BC. The only difference is the type of communication with the external system. IDocs can thus either be transmitted by means of transactional RFC directly to the external system or written to a directory as a file. SAP BC is linked to the R/3 system through transactional RFC. A further option is the direct access to BAPIs using ALE technology. SAP BC reads the recipient, the sender, and the message type from the sent IDoc in accordance with the assigned processing method, thus enabling it to process the received data. The settings are made in the SAP BC partner profile. If SAP BC now receives a message, it calls the assigned processing method and converts the inbound file. The result of the conversion can be sent to an R/3 system in the case of XML → IDoc or to a Web or mail server in the case of IDoc → XML. The settings for sending XML-messages are also set in the SAP BC partner profile. The Business Connector is able to send XML files using the logs HTTP, HTTPS, FTP or SMTP. The URL of the target server, a user and the corresponding password must be known to ensure that the parameters are maintained correctly. This parameter setting, however, requires additional administrative effort. For this case, SAP BC enables the recipient of the message to maintain the data using the POST command. Figure 3.2 shows an example of the SAP BC partner profile.

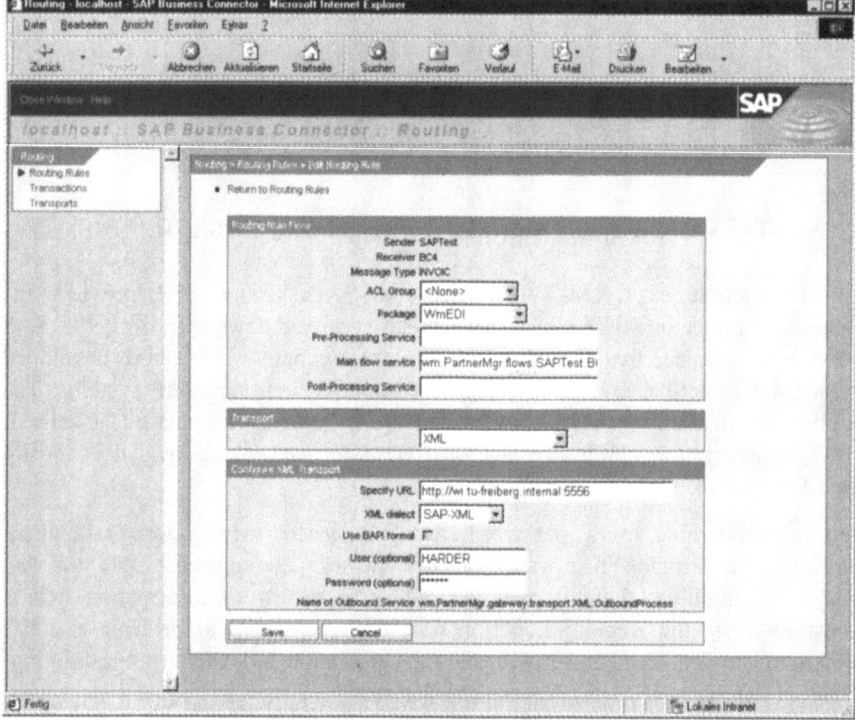

Figure 3.2: SAP BC partner profile: Sender, recipient, message type, processing

If the partner profile is now entered correctly, incoming messages can be converted in accordance with the defined processing method. The status can be controlled with a transaction monitor. Here you can also display the individual results after the conversion. Three different layout types are available:

• With XML (current prerequisite MS Internet Explorer 5 or later),

- with HTML, and

- in table format.

The following example shows the section of a purchase order after the conversion of IDoc ORDERS01 to SAP XML using SAP BC.

```
<?xml version="1.0" encoding="iso-8859-1" ?>
<ORDERS01>
    <IDOC BEGIN="1">
        <EDI_DC40 SEGMENT="1">
            <TABNAM>EDI_DC40</TABNAM>
            <MANDT>100</MANDT>
            <DOCNUM>0000000000205015</DOCNUM>
            <DOCREL>46B</DOCREL>
            <STATUS>30</STATUS>
            .....
            <SERIAL>20000624165846</SERIAL>
        </EDI_DC40>
        <E1EDK01 SEGMENT="1">
            <CURCY>DEM</CURCY>
            <WKURS>1.00000</WKURS>
            .............
            <E1EDP20 SEGMENT="1">
                <WMENG>100.000</WMENG>
                <EDATU>20000606</EDATU>
            </E1EDP20>
            <E1EDP19 SEGMENT="1">
                <QUALF>001</QUALF>
                <IDTNR>A-07</IDTNR>
                <KTEXT>Testmaterial</KTEXT>
            </E1EDP19>
        </E1EDP01>
        <E1EDS01 SEGMENT="1">
            <SUMID>002</SUMID>
            <SUMME>1000</SUMME>
            <SUNIT>DEM</SUNIT>
        </E1EDS01>
    </IDOC>
</ORDERS01>
```

Figure 3.3: Result of the conversion of a purchase order IDoc → XML

For the further usage of the IDocs as business documents in the inter-organizational exchange, a transformation to a certain XML standard is often required, such as xCBL, or to partner-specific formats. For this purpose, SAP provides the SAP BC Integrator as part of the Business Connector. It is thus possible to carry out mapping, transformation and validation tasks through a graphic user interface. For complex tasks, an embedding in a workflow is possible.

An EDI adapter, which SAP provides free of charge, is required for a simplified processing of EDI documents. This converts the EDI format specifications into a format the Business Connector can process, the so-called IData Objects. The following figure shows steps for processing EDI documents.

Architecture and Components

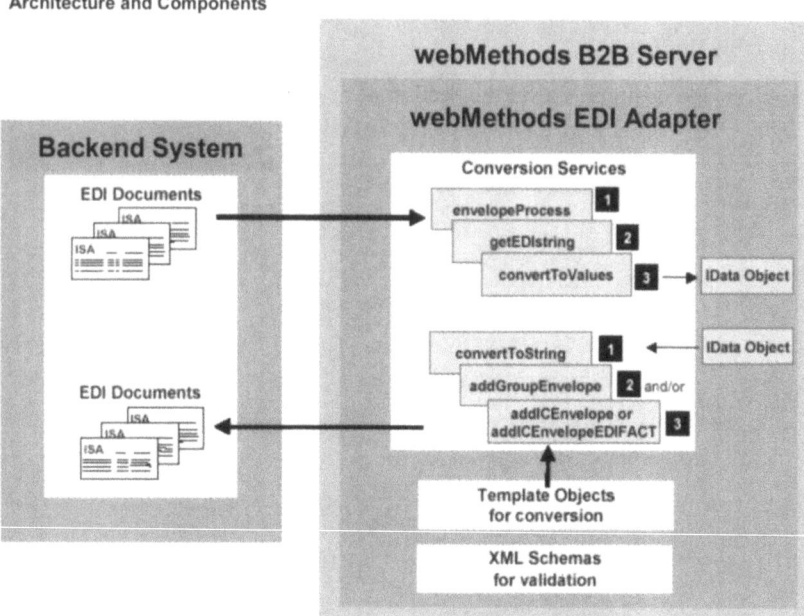

Figure 3.4 Steps for processing EDI documents

Standardized, preconfigured schemata (e.g., UN/EDIFACT) but also user-created schemata (e.g., from an IDoc) can be used for mapping and for the document validation. The following figure shows the workflow required for a mapping as well as the segment-wise mapping of an EDI message.

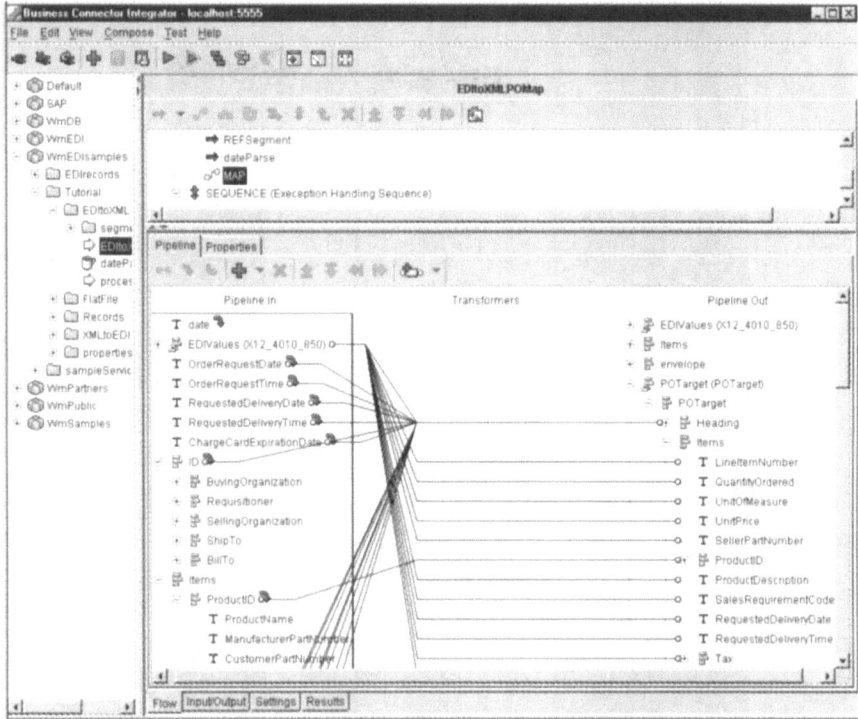

Figure 3.5: Mapping with the Business Connector

As the figure shows, the user can carry out a graphic mapping between the different formats. Generally, this method can only be used for simple assignments between the formats to be integrated. In most cases, the mapping is to be carried out based on Java programs.

With SAP BC, a system is provided that in particular enables an integration of the XML and the SAP environment. A mapping (graphic or through Java) is required here. Future developments could concentrate on defining XML business vocabularies so that the mapping can already be predefined for the partners using such a standard, thus relieving the user.

Chapter 4   Data Management: Concepts and SAP Solutions

This chapter analyzes the possibilities for data management based on data warehouse solutions. First, general concepts and methods for setting up a data warehouse are discussed. Possible applications of the SAP Business Information Warehouse are then introduced.

4.1   The Data Warehouse Concept

4.1.1   Principles of the Data Warehouse Concept

Decisions in companies require the knowledge of current and historical data. These accumulate in all areas of the company as well as in the company environment and refer to sales, products and parts, work centers, consumption activities and payment transactions as well as to the behavior of customers and vendors, for example.

Data processing usually makes a distinction between transaction systems (administration and material requirements planning systems) and planning and control systems (e.g., data warehouse systems) (Meier et al. 2003).

The central task of transaction systems is the fast processing of activities and/or transactions which generate small datasets (e.g., recording of entries). Since the underlying databases – nowadays usually relational systems – are continuously updated, for example, when new records are inserted, old records are updated, corrected or deleted, the literature also speaks of OLTP (On-Line Transaction Processing) systems.

A disadvantage regarding decision support is the fact that historical data is no longer available for analyses because data records are being overwritten. In addition, the preparation of the stored data is in many cases made difficult due to the fact that in the areas of a company, for example production and materials management, different transaction systems and thus several databases exist, which in most cases have grown over the years and cover specific company requirements. Also, OLTP systems can only inadequately meet many requirements, for example, for a quick, flexible, multidimensional analysis of data (Codd 1993). This is where the data warehouse concept applies with respect to a decision support.

By using a data warehouse (for the specific requirements regarding such solutions, refer to Inmon 1996) the goal is pursued to collect data from different OLTP systems and to make it available for analyses as factor constant over time. Modern data warehouse solutions provide tools both for the extraction of the data from the OLTP systems and for the analysis of the data contained in a data warehouse (see section 4.2).

A special feature of a data warehouse is the multidimensional data management based on the On-Line Analytical Processing (OLAP) concept (Codd 1993). Here the main idea is the representation of data in data cubes which are composed of key figures and characteristics. While key figures, such as sales or profit, quantify business correlations, characteristics are used to analyze these from different points of view, for example by period.

The representation in form of such data cubes now provides several possibilities for data analysis. This includes:

- *Drill Down:* Switch to a deeper consolidation level (detailed analysis).

- *Drill Up:* Switch to a higher consolidation level (more abstract analysis)

- *Slicing:* If data of a cube with at least three dimensions is to be displayed in a table, the data must be projected to one level.

- *Dicing:* This method only deals with certain instances of the data cube attributes, that is, smaller data cubes.

This way, certain analyses can be carried out more easily than with relational database systems, which reveal shortcomings in particular with regard to the changeability of the data view as well as the representation of different detail levels.

The multidimensional data management in data warehouse solutions can be implemented with the help of two different procedures (Bellatreche et al. 2001):

- ROLAP (Relational On-Line Analytical Processing) systems are based on a conventional relational database (storage of the data in two-dimensional tables). By successively arranging different instances of a table n times (e.g., 52 week sales of a product), a virtual data cube is created. Reading a large number of instances of a table in the case of a data analysis is time-consuming.

On the other hand, however, this method enables to process larger datasets in the data warehouse (Kurz 1999). Each query dynamically creates hypercubes, which is the reason why in literature upper limits, for instance the restriction to not more than five dimensions, are mentioned against the background of an acceptable performance.

- With MOLAP (Multidimensional On-Line Analytical Processing), the storage occurs in form of multidimensional data cubes so that a data element, such as the demand, depending on region, product and time, is "indexed". Thus, the storage effort dramatically increases with every additional dimension. This procedure allows a fast execution of data analyses (Bellatreche et al. 2001). The application of MOLAP systems is quite often limited to a data volume of up to 100 GByte.

In most cases, the ROLAP procedure based on relations is applied today. Here the data cubes or hypercubes are created from a set of relational database tables which are arranged according to the Star or Snowflake schema.

The Star schema is a combination of a fact table and several dimension tables. The term Star schema is derived from the picture of a radial arrangement of the dimension tables around the fact table (Stanford 1995). The Snowflake schema is similar to the Star schema and only distinguishes itself from it through the dimension tables being available in normalized form (Kurz 1999). The fact table remains unchanged. In comparison with the Star schema, the Snowflake schema is less intuitive from the user's point of view because of the increased number of tables. It improves the browsing functionality for queries, however.

4.1.2   Inter-organizational Data Management

So far, the setup of a data warehouse was presented from the viewpoint of an individual company. Modular organizations and inter-organizational cooperation models (e.g., supply chain management or customer relationship management), however, have new requirements regarding the quality and amount of the data (Wiegand et al. 2003, p. 55). Setting up a data warehouse in a supply chain in this case means creating a common data basis for logistics planning. This common data basis must be maintained and updated by all partners of the supply chain. Operative data from inhouse databases and systems must be imported into the data warehouse after being correspondingly formatted and checked.

A data warehouse for supply chains can be implemented centrally or also decentrally with the help of the data mart technology. Data marts are smaller implementations of a data warehouse and represent a thematically delimited collection of data. They can be completely independent or logically connected, limited by domain or task-related subsets of a higher-level data warehouse and are also called dependent data marts (Anahory/Murray 1997, Inmon 1996).

An overview of different data warehouse solutions available on the market can be found under the Internet address http://www.awi.de/leser-services/markt00/04/csc-0400-56.pdf. Below, the data warehouse solution of SAP AG will now be described.

4.2   SAP Business Information Warehouse

The SAP Business Information Warehouse (BW) exists since the end of 1997. In the meantime it is available in version 3.0B and has been delivered to more than 4000 customers (status April 2002). In the SAP environment, the BW is assigned to the mySAP.com Business Intelligence solution. The keyword business intelligence (BI) designates a concept for generating knowledge about the situations, abilities and intentions of the own company as well as of competing companies from a large amount of often unstructured information. This means specifically entering, processing and analyzing fragmented information from internal and external sources for own and inter-organizational decision processes (Liautaud/Hammond 2000). The BW supports the following functionalities (see Figure 4.1):

- The extraction of data from source systems (e.g., SAP R/3, other BW, legacy system),

- the generation of Operational Data Store (ODS) objects,

- the generation of InfoCubes (data cubes) as well as

- the access to data and information.

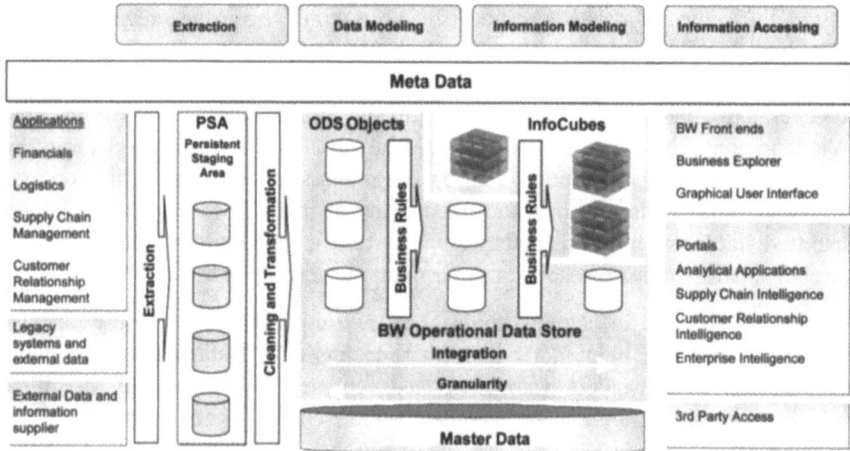

Figure 4.1: Integration architecture of the BW

In accordance with Figure 4.1, the methods for extracting data and the setup of a data basis will be discussed before the multidimensional data and information modeling as well as the possibilities of a Web-based reporting are analyzed. The section closes with a description of the Business Content and the interaction of the BW with the Advanced Planner and Optimizer.

4.2.1   Data Extraction and Structure of a Data Basis

The BW contains extractors for the creation of a data basis. These are programs that are used for transferring company-internal and external data. Extractors are particularly designed for a high throughput of a large number of parallel uploads. They filter and transform transaction and master data from the possibly different source systems. All systems providing data for the BW are referred to as data sources. Depending on type of the source,

- extractors for customer-specific, personalized R/3 tables,

- extractors for R/3 standard tables (e.g., the Logistics Information System (LIS), in which data for instance from the areas Materials Management and Sales and Distribution are stored),

- generic extractors for non-SAP data structures,

- extractors for legacy systems (e.g., flat file input) or

- extractors for mySAP.com application components, for example Enterprise Buyer Professional, MarketSet Procurement or Advanced Planner and Optimizer

are used, for example. For the extraction of transaction data from the R/3 system, a new generation of DataSources and extractors, which is not based on LIS information structures (standard tables) anymore, was developed for Release 2.0B. All InfoCubes delivered with the Business Content (see section 4.2.5) can be updated from these DataSources into the BW. SAP recommends to use these DataSources. The update for DataSources delivered earlier remains possible.

While data records are automatically extracted from the SAP DataSources, an identification and selection of relevant data records and fields must be carried out first in case of non-SAP systems.

The data extraction is controlled by the delta method. The data volume is kept as small as possible by only transferring such data records, which have changed compared to a reference point in time. The BW provides two different procedures for this:

- *Timestamp*: The data records are provided with a timestamp in the OLTP system in case of updates and the extractor, which is installed at the transaction system, transfers those data records into the BW, whose timestamps are younger than the date of the last data transfer.

- *Change Log*: The BW-relevant data of the transaction system are written to separate log tables when an OLTP transaction is processed. BW imports these change logs at extraction time.

The data (DataSource) provided by an extractor is first saved to the Persistant Staging Area (PSA) in tabular form. This is a type of incoming storage, in which the requested data is saved without being changed, this means, no summarizations or transformations are carried out. The PSA detaches the loading process from the further processing of the data within the BW and thus enables a high loading performance.

In a next step, the data temporarily stored in the PSA is saved in an InfoSource. It is always possible to aggregate several DataSources, which describe coherent facts and originate from different source systems, to a single InfoSource. This is relevant, for example, if two different systems are used for same processes within a corporate group or parts of a business process are handled by a service provider within an inter-organizational cooperation. Thus, the user can for instance aggregate orders of the regions North and South in one InfoSource.

In addition to this data, which serves as the basis for the analysis of the data cubes, an extractor can also transfer other descriptive data to the BW. This master data is entered only once in the BW and is stored in separate tables to enable the users a quick access to the information without the data having to be further processed. In the case of transaction data, it is often interesting to provide the user with the most recent dataset represented in the BW. In the BW, this is called "active data". In addition, the user frequently demands time-dependent analyses, so that attribute values have to be read and processed at various times. For this purpose, the transaction data is stored in the ODS. This concept is described below.

4.2.2   Generating ODS Objects

The ODS designates a multilayered area in which the cleaned up and transformed transaction data is stored in form of ODS objects at different levels of granularity (e.g., on document level). Before the individual ODS objects are generated, transformation programs are activated in the BW, which unify the possibly different formats (e.g., currencies, data types). An ODS object describes a consolidated dataset and consists of a key (e.g., document number, -item) as well as different data fields (e.g., order status, customer).

While with the update of data in an InfoCube only a cumulative updating of key figures is carried out, also further data fields can be overwritten in case of ODS objects. This is particularly important in the context of document-related structures, for instance if documents are changed in an OLTP system and the modifications made not only concern numeric fields, for example the order quantity, but also non-numeric fields, for example ship-to party, status and delivery date. So that these changes can also be represented in the ODS objects in the BW, the corresponding fields must also be overwritten in the ODS objects and set to the current value.

All meta data is stored in a (meta) repository. Technical and business-related features of the data are described in this case, for example, the data structure, the origin of the data, the completed transformation process, the existing summarization levels including the chronological process as well as existing evaluations and analyses (refer to the following section). Elements for the control of the BW data management can be directly imported, for example, from the R/3 system (McDonnald et al. 2002, pp. 37-38).

4.2.3   Generating InfoCubes (Multidimensional Data Cubes)

There are various options for preparing data based on the ODS objects according to individual rules in a decision-relevant way. The data is summarized according to different management viewpoints (e.g., "orders and order deliveries", whereas SAP publications refer to the later simply as "Deliveries").

By aggregating ODS objects, it is possible to reduce the accumulated data volume per time unit and to thus accelerate the analysis range. In addition, ODS objects can be aggregated for one or several InfoCubes, for example the delivery quantity, the delivery delay in days and the order status for each order item. As a basic principle it is also possible to populate InfoCubes with data of the PSA.

InfoCubes designate the central objects within the BW, on which reports and analyses are generally based. They describe (from a reporting view) a coherent dataset (e.g., sales classified by product (groups), salesperson, region and time) in a multidimensionally structured way. Although physically only two-dimensional ODS tables exist, an OLAP processor integrated into the BW generates a "virtual multidimensionality" in accordance with the ROLAP procedure introduced in section 4.1.

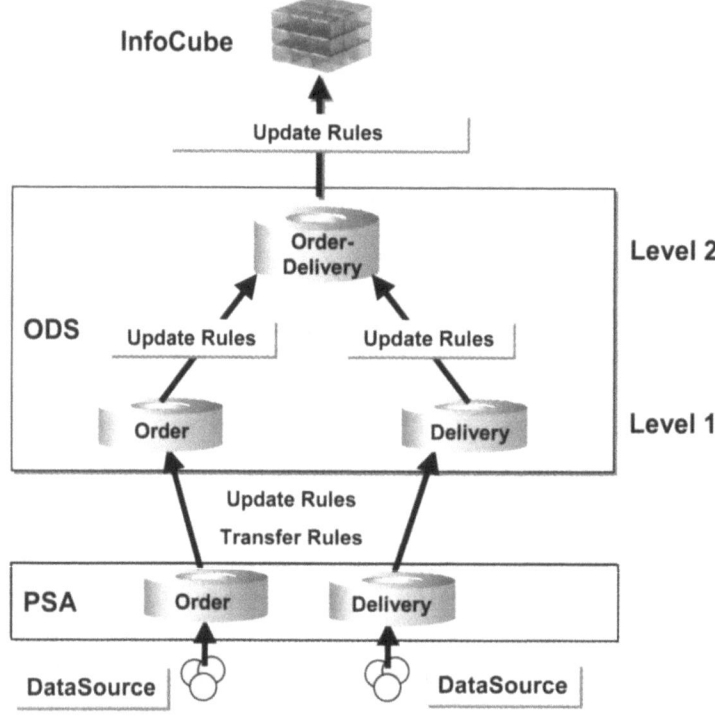

Figure 4.2: Generating InfoCubes based on ODS objects

Upload Performance

Uploading data from the ODS memory into an InfoCube can be carried out in two ways:

- Data is directly loaded from the ODS memory into the InfoCube or

- data is indirectly loaded from the ODS memory through the PSA into the InfoCube.

The upload duration and/or the processing speed within the BW is decisively influenced by the used hardware and software environment. The larger the available resources are, for example, processors and random access memory (RAM), the less time is spent for uploading data.

Below, the InfoCubes of the BW are analyzed. Three different types are distinguished:

- *BasisCubes*: Data is managed within the BW.

- *RemoteCubes*: Transaction data is managed by another system, for example another BW or an Advanced Planner and Optimizer.

- *MultiCubes*: View on data from several BasicCube or RemoteCubes.

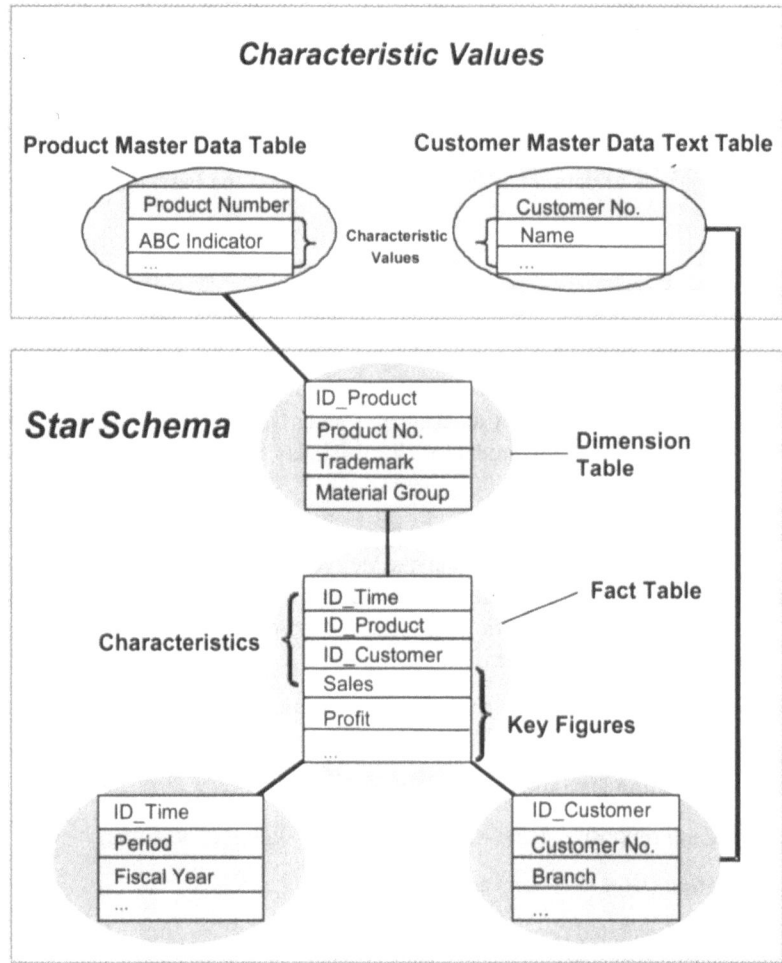

Figure 4.3: Link of master data with the Star schema

The data structure set up through the Star schema is completed by the master data within the BW (see Figure 4.3). A particular advantage is that the assignment of the (characteristic) attributes to characteristics can be changed later, without the data of the facts table having to be changed or reorganized.

In comparison to ODS objects, InfoCubes are particularly suitable for the evaluation of mass data with lower granularity, for example, the sales of products by customer and month. They deliver a navigation structure which is to enable an analysis of data across the different dimensions.

Since release 3.0A, MOLAP data cubes or aggregates can also be created in the BW with a Microsoft SQL Server database. The definition of an InfoCube allows to store individual aggregates as MOLAP aggregates. MOLAP aggregates often offer a better performance (see section 4.1.1), but no additional functionality.

Within the BW, existing InfoCubes can be converted both from ROLAP to MOLAP and vice versa.

Below, the options of data analysis and presentation on the basis of the InfoCubes are described.

4.2.4   Data Analysis and Presentation

Various applications for the analysis and presentation of the data are available on the user side. The access can be made directly, for example, from other mySAP.com components, such as from the areas supply chain management or customer relationship management or the Business Explorer (BEx), a BW-own user front end.

The Business Explorer is a Web-based front end comparable with the Microsoft Internet Explorer, that is included in the delivery of the BW and serves as an interface for the user (McDonnald et al. 2002, pp. 50-54). The connection of non-SAP OLAP tools and presentation applications, so-called *Third Party front ends* is possible through different certified interfaces.

The Business Explorer supports the following functions:

- Definitions of queries and applications with the BEx Query Designer and the Web Application Designer,

- analysis and reporting (BEx Analyzer and BEx Web Applications),

- organization (BEx Browser) and

- a specially formatted reporting called "Crystal Reports".

The BEx Query Designer is a tool that can be used to set parameters for queries. The more precise the definition of a query or the contained InfoObjects, the faster the navigation or the aggregation of the data. Threshold values (key figures) can be defined through the query definition with the help of the exception reporting so that variances of the operative data are displayed within the framework of an alarm message. Figure 4.4 explains the definition of "Exceptions" using sales data:

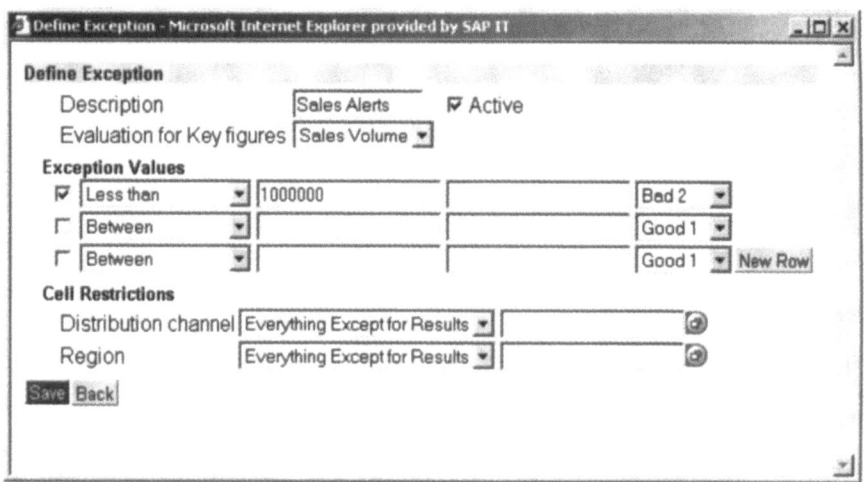

Figure 4.4: Definition of "Exceptions"

Below the line "Exception Values" displayed in Figure 4.4, company-individual threshold values can be defined, that trigger a corresponding alarm message in case the value is exceeded. The queries specified with the BEx Query Designer are suited both for the OLAP reporting and for the flat reporting on ODS objects.

The Web Application Designer (see Figure 4.5) can be used for creating Web pages that contain BW-specific contents. User can use drag&drop to transfer different "Standard Web items" (see left side of the screen), for example graphics, tables and alarm monitors, into one or several HTML pages (see center of screen). The properties of the individual Web items, such as size and title, are defined in the screen bar on the right.

The layout of the Web pages can additionally be supported by a Web Application Wizard embedded in the Web Application Designer, that step-by-step leads the programmer through the specification of his document (for instance texts, screens) as well as its positioning in the network (e.g., in an extranet). The generated Web pages are stored on the BW server in form of HTML templates (see Figure 4.5).

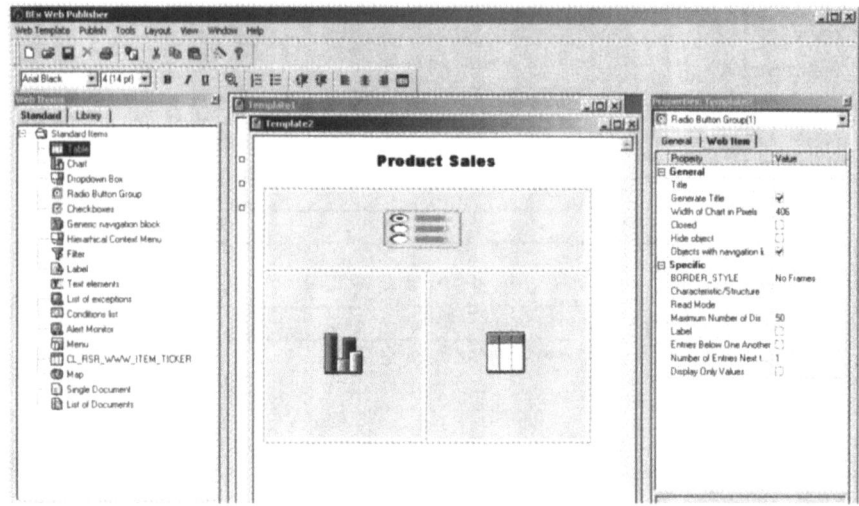

Figure 4.5: Web Application Designer

The created Web pages serve as a basis for different Web applications and can be extended to form a Business Intelligence Cockpit (BI Cockpit). This can be understood as a Web-based "control panel", which for instance gives the management of a company or the companies participating in a cooperation an overview of decisive business data.

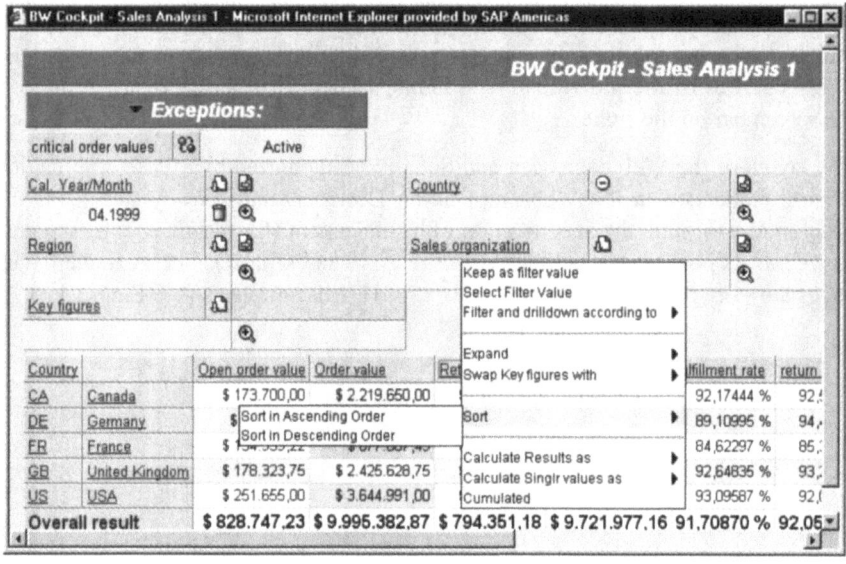

Figure 4.6: Display of alarm message in the BI Cockpit

Exceptional situations can be displayed via an alarm monitor integrated in the BI Cockpit. A reporting agent running in the background constantly compares the threshold values specified in the query with the current status. Figure 4.6 shows the example of a cockpit configured for sales analyses, in which open purchase order values are displayed by country.

BI Cockpits provide the option to retrieve data from different sources through a standard user interface. Formatted data, for example sales figures saved within the BW as well as unformatted data, such as references to Web pages, can be equally integrated in the interface. Here it is possible to support the roles and task areas of different users by the data relevant for these consumer groups being automatically loaded into the cockpit with the login.

The BEx Analyzer, from which for example the queries created with the BEx Query Designer are executed, runs based on Microsoft Excel. All queries can be stored in corresponding workbooks (these are Excel files) so that the user can suppress, for example, time-consuming data accesses in the course of planning tasks if it is clear that primary data changes only every week. Figure 4.7 shows the results of a vendor assessment in the BEx Analyzer.

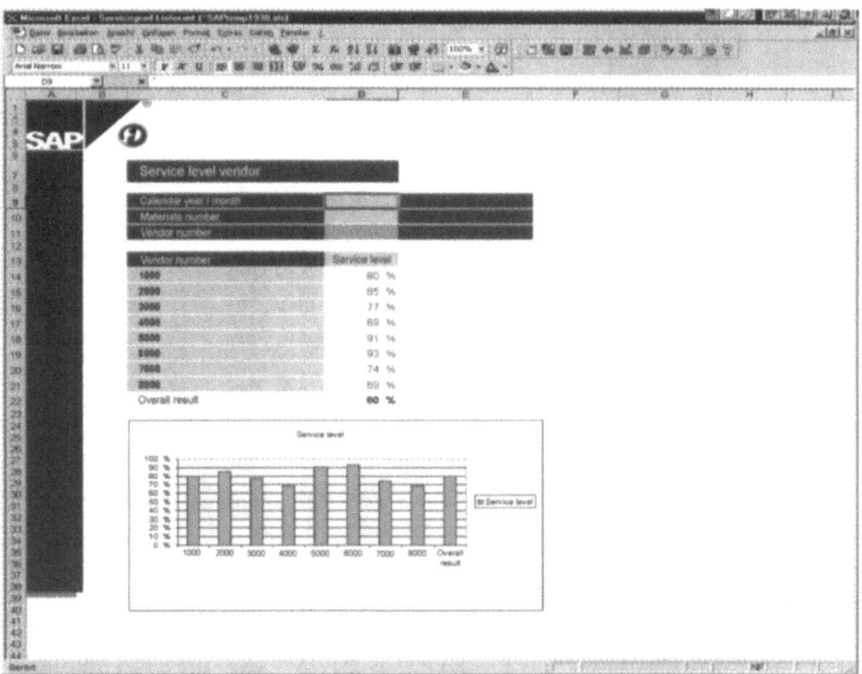

Figure 4.7: Vendor assessment in the BEx Analyzer

The BEx Browser is a graphic user interface through which queries are organized and controlled. The component provides the option of a role-specific (e.g., controller) and function-specific (e.g., logistics) adjustment and thus facilitates access to information resources. This can be workbooks, links to the file system, Internet pages of external partners (e.g., Extranet), SAP transaction calls, Web Applications or Crystal Reports. Queries can occur through direct access to the BW server or through the Internet (see Figure 4.8).

Furthermore, the BEx includes a special Geographical Information System, with which significant business objects and their attributes, for example customers, regional sales figures and countries, can be represented and analyzed in detail.

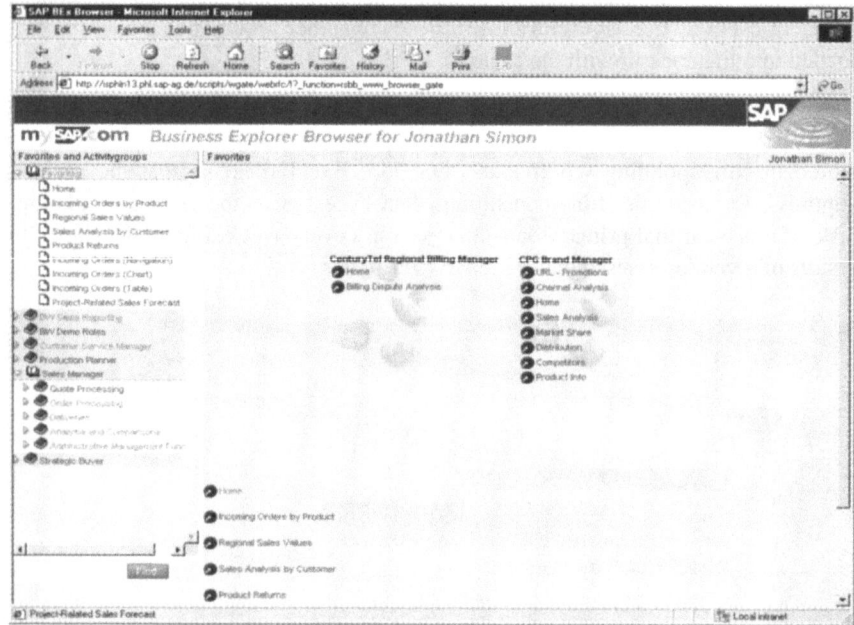

Figure 4.8: BEx Browser

Web-Reporting

Starting with BW Release 3.0, the mySAP Web Application Server (see chapter 2) serves as a central component for the Web-based access to BW-specific data contents. It thus replaces the Internet Transaction Server (ITS) (Appelrath/Ritter 2000), which was used as Web gateway for different SAP application components before. Compared to the ITS, the mySAP Web Application Server distinguishes itself by a better performance and an enhanced scalability. Web charts and figures are generated using a special Internet Graphic Server (IGS) (see Figure 4.9).

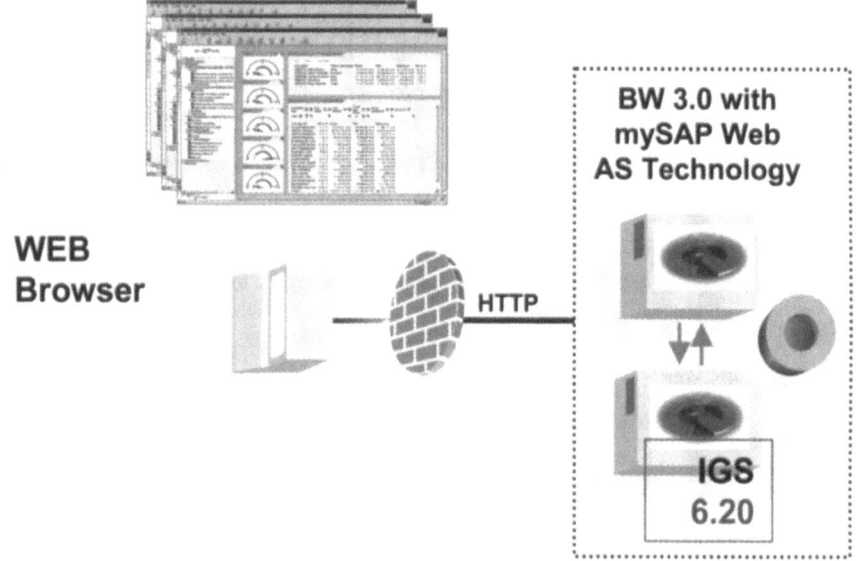

Figure 4.9: Web reporting infrastructure

The access to HTML templates as well as the contained data is supported within the BW by a Web Service that belongs to the components of the IGS, just like the Charting Engine sketched in Figure 4.10. While the Web Service retrieves data from the data basis of the BW, necessary graphics are generated through the Charting Engine.

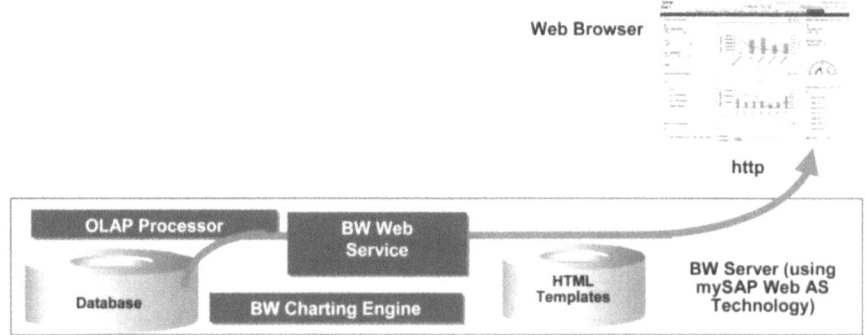

Figure 4.10: Web infrastructure (BW 3.0A)

4.2.5   Business Content

The BW has predefined information models for certain company-internal application areas. In the BW context, SAP refers to them as Business Content. This includes:

- Extraction programs,

- DataSources,

- InfoSources,

- InfoObjects (business objects to be evaluated, such as customers and sales, which are sub-classified into characteristics and key figures),

- data targets (InfoCubes, ODS objects) (SAP refers to the fact, that incoming data is to be aggregated according to predefined rules, as a data target),

- queries,

- roles/tasks, and

- workbooks.

A significant advantage in using the Business Content is that the entire process of data extraction up to information modeling and analysis does not have to be completely reprogrammed or customized for a large number of questions. Thus, data can be extracted from other SAP and non-SAP systems, transformed into BW-specific structures as well as assigned and analyzed within the data memory, for example.

By providing such a standard Business Content, the attempt is made in also meeting the requirements of different user groups, for example a buyer (in the procurement department) or a customer service representative (in service management). On the other hand, these are standard definitions, with which the problem is often associated that it is not possible to comprehensively meet specific user requirements.

An analysis of the Business Content available in the BW shows that the majority of the information models support tasks from the areas customer relationship management and supply chain management:

- Thus, pre-configured reporting and analysis functions, which automate the source of supply determination and assessment, are available. To find out which vendors are to be given a task, information on the purchase quantity as well as the results from quality inspections and inspection lots can be used.

- The vendor assessment allows an analysis of all order transactions and the associated deliveries. This includes evaluations of the quality, on-time delivery performance and delivery quantity reliability, service levels or price agreements. If data is extracted from the Quality Management of the R/3 system, results of inspection lots or reasons for return of a delivery can additionally be included in the assessment.

- Complex procedures allowing an insight into information up to the single document are available for the analysis of orders. Discrepancies between order, delivery and invoice quantity thus become visible. It also enables the retrieval of information regarding cost center or product budgets, that allow a direct comparison with actual expenses.

Since BW Release 3.0A, also parts of the Supply-Chain Operations Reference-model (SCOR) are represented in the BW Business Content. Within the model, key figures, which are also referred to as key performance indicators (KPI), are defined for different processes (and their subprocesses).

Processes can be compared if business partners orientate themselves to these definitions within a cooperation. The goal is, on the one hand, to analyze the capability of a supply chain and, on the other hand, to set up a comparability to other supply chains. Table 4.1 shows an example for the key figure "Capacity Utilization" and its composition within BW:

Table 4.1: Capacity Utilization in BW

Name	SCOR Process Elements	KPI in BW	Positioning in the BW	Technical Name
Capacity Utilization	P1, P1.3, M1, M1.1, M1.3, M1.4, M2, M2.1, M2.3, M3, M3.1, D2.3	0C_T_CAPA UTIL_% Target Capacity Load Utilization	InfoCube: Plan/Actual Comparision/Operation Work Center View 0PP_C03 Queries: 0PP_C03_Q007 0PP_C04_Q001 0PP_C13_Q001	0SCM_SCOR _008

The key figure "Capacity Utilization" is used to determine the utilization of a special resource, for example, within a production process. For this purpose, different process elements must be taken into account from the viewpoint of the SCOR model. In the case discussed here, the SCOR indexes Make-to-Order (M1), and Make-to-Stock (M2) are represented. The individual elements or their indexes are summarized within the BW under the term 0C_T_CAPAUTIL_%. All necessary information converges within the InfoCube 0PP_C03 which is created through three different queries. Examples for further SCOR metrics in the BW 3.0A are:

- *Yield*: With the help of Yield, a company can calculate the economic viability of producing a production order. Only those orders are used, for which no more confirmations are expected.

- *Material Overhead Cost per Material Expenditure*: This SCOR key figure describes the relationship between material overhead costs and material direct costs.

- *Build Cycle Time*: This key figure determines approximately how long it takes to manufacture a production unit (either several units or the standard lot size). The build cycle time is the average production time for make-to-stock products. It is calculated by dividing the average number of units in production at any given time by the average daily production rate in units.

- *Asset Turns or Asset Turnover*: This key figure determines the relationship between product revenues and the average value of the fixed and current assets. Asset turns or asset turnover (capital turnover) is viewed as a key figure for financial activities. The key figure contains information about how efficiently attachments of an enterprise were managed. The idea is to find out how many attachments can be used to generate sales. The general definition of such a relationship is the measurement of gross revenue in relation to the fixed assets.

- *Ratio of actual to theoretical Cycle Time*: This key figure compares the actual execution times with the theoretical execution times.

- *Item/Product Changeover Time*: This SCOR key figure compares the planned changeover times with the actual changeover times.

- *Machine Wait Time*: The machine wait time represents unused workplace capacity in relation to the total capacity available.

4.2.6   Interaction of BW and APO

The BW can be directly connected to the Advanced Planner and Optimizer (APO) and can thus become an elementary basis of planning processes in various areas. The APO retrieves historical data used for planning from the BW. The Data Mart Interface serves as an interface (see Figure 4.11). Its task is to update data from a data target, for example an InfoCube or an ODS object, to another data target.

Here, it is always distinguished between the update within only one BW and a cooperative update in several BW systems. Since the APO and the BW have identical data structures (the BW is included in the delivery range of the APO and fully integrated), the update between two BW systems corresponds to that between a BW and an APO system. If such a constellation is given, the supplying system is designated as BW source, the acquiring system correspondingly as BW target.

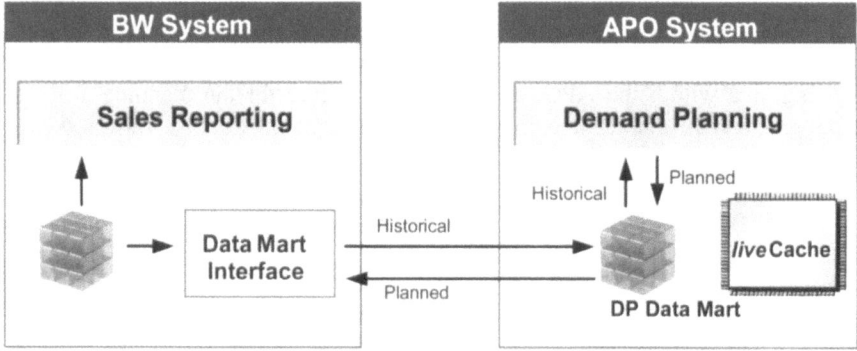

Figure 4.11 Interaction of BW and APO

The results of an APO planning run can be stored in the BW and used for benchmarking processes after the operative conversion.

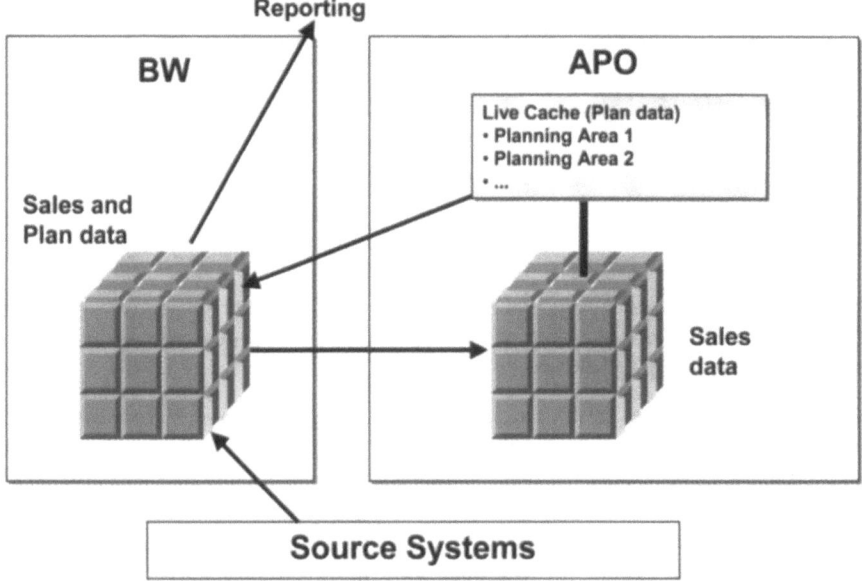

Figure 4.12: SingleCube

Concerning the data management within the BW, Figure 4.12 shows how both the historical sales data and the APO planning data are stored in a single InfoCube (SingleCube).

A further option enables sales data and planning data to be stored in separate InfoCubes which are aggregated to a MultiCube within reporting (see Figure 4.13). Principally, it is possible to retrieve BW data through the front end of the APO and APO data through the BW front end. From a BW viewpoint, aggregated actual data of the InfoCubes as well as all order and time series objects of the APO *live*Cache can be evaluated. Prerequisites for the *live*Cache reporting are a planning area within the APO, an extraction structure for the planning area, an InfoSource and a RemoteCube, in which the data of the *live*Cache is mirrored.

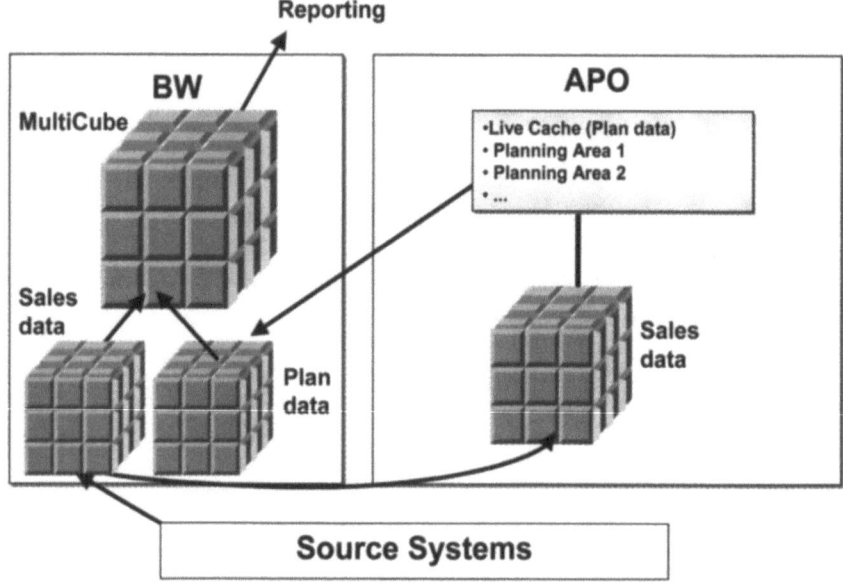

Figure 4.13: MultiCube

RemoteCubes are used during the so-called ad-hoc reporting. In this case, data of the APO liveCache are mirrored and aggregated with the data of a BW BasisCube, for example, to form a MultiCube.

The sketched concepts of the multidimensional data management are also applied in case of an exclusive use of APO, which is the focus of the following chapter. Thus, data (e.g., sales data) of various source systems is aggregated within APO to form an InfoCube that provides the basis for further planning tasks (e.g., demand planning). The results of a planning run (planning data) are stored in a further cube, which is integrated, for example, with the historical data of the first cube within reporting to form a MultiCube.

Chapter 5   Collaborative Planning in Supply
             Networks: Concepts and SAP Solutions

This chapter focuses on procedures as well as options and limits of using mySAP solutions for the support of collaborative planning processes in supply chains. Here, the use of the Advanced Planner and Optimizer (APO) is of particular interest.

First, we provide a description of the APO system, which SAP provides for planning, controlling, executing, and monitoring goods and information flows within a supply network. Then, the options of the APO in supporting planning processes in logistics-related functions are analyzed. In this context, methods for demand, procurement, production, and transportation planning are introduced, the application of the APO in these planning areas is explained and options for its usage for coordinating the planning in supply chains are made clear. The chapter closes with an example of collaborative scheduling agreement processing, showing how mySAP solutions can be applied at cross-company level in a process-oriented way.

5.1   Basics of the SAP Advanced Planner and Optimizer (APO)

For the support of supply chain management, SAP provides the cross-industry solution "mySAP Supply Chain Management" (see also chapter 2). The center of attention is APO for planning and optimizing logistics networks (Knolmayer et al. 2002).

Since its introduction in 1998, APO has been delivered to 1,724 customers up to June 2003. This corresponds to 1,922 installed SCM systems. In 2002, SAP realized a turnover of € 464 million with mySAP SCM. This sector represents 22 percent of the total licensing turnover of SAP. Companies from various industry sectors belong to the customers, such as Aventis, Bosch (see chapter 7), Bulgari, Carlsberg, Colgate-Palmolive, Elsa, Goodyear, and Lockheed Martin.

The mySAP SCM solution is complemented by the logistics modules of the R/3 system and the Logistics Execution System (LES). In addition, function modules of other mySAP solutions, for example mySAP Customer Relationship Management, mySAP Product Lifecycle Management, and mySAP Business Intelligence, can be integrated.

The next sections explain the APO application components, the *live*Cache and the integration technology as well as the optimization architecture.

5.1.1   Application Components

The APO includes different logistic planning functions, which can be used in connection with a transaction system (e.g., SAP R/3) but also independent of such a system.

The planning and optimization of a supply network from procurement over production and assembly up to distribution are supported. This is realized using various interacting planning modules that are supplied with data from OLTP or OLAP systems through interfaces. The planning components are:

- *Network Design & Modeling* (NDM): This component in particular supports long-term procurement, production and distribution decisions for optimizing and reorganizing the logistics network. NDM was available as a planning component up to APO Release 3.0. From Release 3.1 on, SAP no longer actively markets it. The functionality, however, is still available.

- *Demand Planning* (DP): This planning component allows both an aggregated and a detailed demand planning with different forecasting techniques.

- *Supply Network Planning* (SNP): This module allows a finite cross-location medium-term to long-term production and procurement planning with simultaneous material and capacity requirements planning.

- *Production Planning and Detailed Scheduling* (PP/DS): This component allows the finite detailed production planning.

- *Transport Planning and Vehicle Scheduling* (TP/VS): This module carries out a transportation planning and thus determines for instance routes and means of transport. Also, deliveries and transport requests are generated.

- *Available to Promise* (ATP): The global availability check allows statements to customers as to whether a product can be delivered in a desired quantity at a desired point in time. Stocks and receipts at different locations as well as product allocations and rules for the product substitution can be taken into account here.

These components are integrated through a common random access memory area called *live*Cache. There, information relevant for planning is available for quick access.

5.1.2   *live*Cache and Integration Technology

The *live*Cache as considerably extended main memory of the APO server is a high speed infrastructure for complex, data-intensive applications, whose information is loaded and managed there. The goal is to allow cross-system, cross-location, and inter-enterprise simulations, planning, and optimization in real-time. The system can be utilized by all APO components. The *live*Cache technology uses the multi-processor and multi-computer configuration that permits parallel and distributed processing.

With an inter-organizational application of APO, the thus required integration with the execution systems is carried out, in the case of two R/3 systems, using the R/3 plug-in technology, which is available since Release 3.1I. In this case, the data transfer between the R/3 and the APO system is controlled in real time via the Core Interface (CIF). This interface is an enhancement of the known (Application Link Enabling) R/3 interface.

While the CIF is the interface for connecting APO to existing R/3 system environments, the integration with non-SAP solutions is realized through the SAP BAPI technology, which in most cases requires an individual interface adaptation. Furthermore, the use of open standards will play a more important role with the new architecture of mySAP (see chapter 2).

The planning in APO is based on master data and transaction data. Master data consists of information on locations, customers, material (parts), task lists, BOMs (Bill of Materials) and so forth. It can be either created by the user or automatically provided by the execution system, for instance R/3. The transaction data can for example be purchase requisitions, transport requests, and so on.

APO only copies the information relevant for planning from the R/3 system managing the master data, first in form of an initial data transfer, later as changes, and only the parameters not managed elsewhere (e.g., geographic data) are maintained in APO.

The particular benefit of integrating APO with an R/3 system environment lies in the transfer of the transaction data in real-time. Data relevant for planning, such as warehouse stocks and sales orders, are transferred from R/3 to APO through the CIF interface, just like the other way round, planning results are transferred to the R/3 system and are executed there.

5.1.3   Optimization Architecture

APO makes a number of optimization algorithms and heuristic procedures available within the framework of the logistics planning of the supply chain. Thus, these procedures are used for simultaneous planning of procurement, transport, and production in the SNP planning component (see section 5.3). Also within the framework of the Detailed Scheduling (in the module PP/DS, see section 5.4) and Transportation Planning (in the module TP/VS, see section 5.5) one can use the optimization algorithms and heuristics for the arrangement of efficient logistics processes.

The APO optimization architecture is based on a 3-level concept. The master data model, the core model and the basis optimizer model support different levels of abstraction within the framework of APO-based planning. The idea behind this multi-level concept is keeping the optimization models as independent as possible from the master data without reducing their expressiveness. This allows solving a planning task using different optimization algorithms as well as also processing several planning orders using one method. For the various problems, APO provides both standard optimization algorithms and procedures adjusted to the APO modeling options, such as the Branch & Cut procedure in SNP. The methods applied for the optimizations are based on the products of the company ILOG. SNP, for example, uses the ILOG CPLEX Library and TP/VS the ILOG dispatcher.

Here, the cost values on which an optimization in APO is based are model costs that can be created by the planner in the system. They are not extracted from the OLTP system (for instance, from the controlling module of the R/3 system) and inserted into the optimization models, but instead have to be maintained in the master data model by the planner.

5.2   Demand Planning

5.2.1   Concepts and APO Application

Sales orders, the reaching of repurchase order dates or stocks, and the specifications due to a sales forecast can be the starting point of production and of logistics activities in supply chains. In the following, we will concentrate on sales forecasts as the trigger for further planning activities. The goal is to predict the market demand for products and to generate a demand plan on this basis.

In APO, SAP provides the Demand Planning module (DP) to solve these problems. The company Carlsberg Denmark, a beverage producer, is an example for a successful application of the system. It has a product range of more than 350 different beer and beverage types which are delivered to 23,000 customers in

Denmark. Furthermore, the company operates three production sites, two main warehouses and 16 distribution points. The forecast of the demand in this area heavily depends on the season and weather. Therefore, Carlsberg uses promotions to stimulate the demand. Corresponding activities are to be considered in demand planning as a further factor. By own account, Carlsberg has been able to reduce the stocks by 30 percent and accelerate the delivery precision by 20 percent since it introduced the DP.

The current methods for the sales forecast can be subdivided into univariate and multivariate (Kachigan 1986). The first include procedures of creating floating averages of past sales which can then be used if no outliers distort the time series and a constant demand is to be expected over time. The exponential smoothing stresses younger values more than older ones, so that vague trends are reflected in the forecast with only little delay. Second-order exponential smoothing allows modeling linear trends and third-order exponential smoothing allows describing exponential growth or decline. As long as seasonal effects superpose the trends, the time series are to be multiplied, for example, with seasonal indexes. Furthermore, regression models are available to calculate a trend in the simple case based on one explanatory variable, the value specifications of which are available in past periods, by using the method of the least squares. With the multiple linear regression, the sales quantity is explained using several factors.

In APO, the Demand Planning module is used for demand forecasting and, based upon this, for generating demand plans (see Figure 5.1).

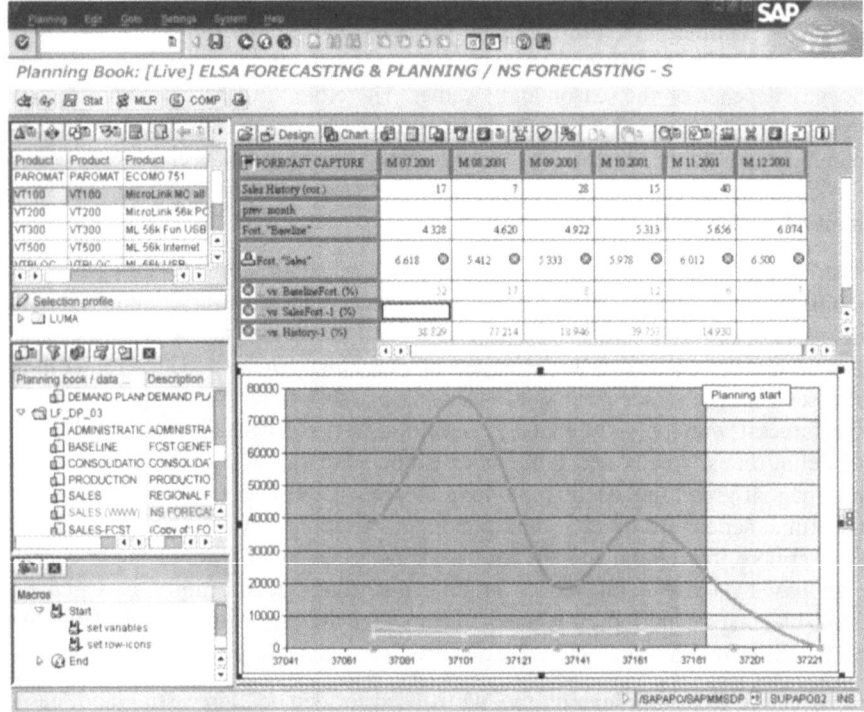

Figure 5.1: User interface of the APO Demand Planning component

The statistical techniques and macro methods available within Demand Planning allow to conduct various tests on forecasting models and results as well as to consolidate demand plans of different companies using a consensus-based approach.

Starting point of the planning process is either the extraction of past and actual sales values (e.g., point-of-sale data) from the executive OLTP system, for instance R/3, or the import of this data from BW (see chapter 4), from Excel, or from other systems. The demand history required for the forecast can be extracted from BW in form of InfoCubes and made available for planning in the APO Data Mart (see chapter 4). To increase the accuracy of the forecast, the system allows making various corrections to the imported data, such as the elimination of outliers in the sense of one-time influences, which superpose the regular time series development of the historical values. Sample events, which will probably not occur in the period to be forecasted, are one-time promotional measures and delivery problems as well as environmental catastrophes. The planner can perform the correction of the actual data; APO also provides a number of options for automatic correction:

- *Phase-in/phase-out profile*: This information on a life cycle controls the correction of the data with the introduction of new and the discontinuation of old products.

- *Workday correction*: It ensures that higher values are forecasted for periods with a large number of workdays than for periods with a small number of workdays. This way, a varying number of workdays per month can be taken into account. Prerequisite is that the historical data is standardized and an average number of workdays is taken as a basis for each forecast period.

- *Past promotions*: This data enables the isolation of effects of promotional actions from the historical values.

- *Outlier control*: This procedure allows the planner to automatically remove all actual data from the time series appearing outside of a determined tolerance range.

The thus corrected demand history is now the starting point for applying the forecasting techniques. This data is aggregated and serves as a basis for the forecast creation. Therefore, a set of statistical methods is available for this allowing the consideration of further factors, such as:

- Availability of sales personnel,

- expenses for research and development,

- expenses for advertising,

- price structures,

- use of promotional measures,

- weather, and

- seasonal fluctuations (e.g., in the tire industry; see chapter 7).

In this case, the planner has the option to define different horizons for the demand plan. It is thus feasible to create sales forecasts for a small number of days in order to provide short-term transportation capacities or to generate them for several years in case where, for example, determining factors for longer-term contracts are to be specified.

Once the demand plan has been released it is available for other application components. It is thus possible that, for example, an optimization of the production and procurement activities is based on the sales forecasts. Furthermore, orders (e.g., for production or external procurement) can be directly created from the sales data. The Production and Transportation Planning can then be used to initiate and optimize corresponding follow-up functions.

Demand Planning includes a number of statistical methods that can be used for the quantitative forecast of future demands. APO, for example, provides the moving formation average, the trend and seasonal models, exponential smoothing, the Holt-Winters procedure, and the Croston method as univariate forecasting techniques. These can be combined with one another and also with multivariate methods to achieve different types of material requirements forecasts.

The suitability of the different procedures can be evaluated with the help of an ex-post forecast or alternative simulation runs. Such an ex-post forecast starts with the forecast of past values based the former know-how, which results are then compared with the actual observed values. The error rate of the procedure, thus the deviation between planned and actual values, can then be calculated based on different measures. In APO, the following error measures are available for univariate forecasting methods: Mean absolute deviation, mean square deviation, error total, mean absolute error, mean square error, and square root of the mean square error as well as mean percent error.

For the measurement of the quality of multivariate procedures, a set of so-called measures of fit exists. These calculate different attributes of the created forecasting model which can provide indications regarding the quality of the results. The values provided with APO are: R square, adjusted R square, Durbin-h, Durbin-Watson, t-test, and mean elasticity (Kachigan 1986).

In combination with alerts, these error and adjustment measures have the purpose of adjusting the forecasting model in cases where confidence specification limits are exceeded.

The error and adjustment measures are also the basis for an automated method selection which APO provides in the Demand Planning module. The system in this case analyzes the data of the past and tries to detect unique time series developments in order to determine a suitable forecasting model. Here, the planner can select between two analysis levels differing in extension and preciseness. In both cases, the system checks the possible presence of a significant development corresponding to the trend model type with season overlap. In the time-consuming analysis mode, the model of the first, second, and third-order exponential smoothing optimally reflecting the past process is determined with the help of extensive simulations. Alternatively, simple procedures are used.

The decision maker can weight the individual forecasts by combining the forecasting techniques. The forecasts obtained through univariate, causal, or combined procedures are first of all basic forecasts that can be manually changed at the end if, for instance, additional factors influencing the forecast previously not contained in the database have become known.

5.2.2   Collaborative Forecasting

The most important key success factor of demand planning in supply chains is the creation of sales forecasts and demand plans accepted by all partners of the supply chain. Prerequisite for this is the access to this planning environment by all collaboration partners at any time, for instance via the Internet. In addition, the consistency and redundancy-free status of the plans are to be ensured and also that the exact number of commonly accepted factors influencing the expected future sales are taken into account. Collaborative administration and recording of historical sales data have proven to be a useful basis for an inter-organizational demand planning. Furthermore, special influencing factors, such as past or future promotions or personnel fluctuation, can be included in the planning.

Within Collaborative Forecasting, forecasts from different supply chain partners or business areas, which have different focuses regarding planning, are analyzed and consolidated for a common result (SAP refers to this as consensus-based forecasting; see Table 5.1).

Table 5.1: Collaborative forecasting in APO (predicted demand for a product)

Forecaster	Period 1	Period 2	Period 3	Weighting
Business partner A	35	48	37	40%
Business partner B	44	45	50	30%
Marketing department	40	30	30	30%
Consensus-based forecasting	40	42	39	100%

When different forecast values are presented, the first task is to agree on a common weighting. The system supports corresponding what-if calculations.

Collaborative Forecasting can be used to identify and eliminate possible problem areas so that all participants are able to influence the decisions of the entire supply chain. The result is thus to be accepted and supported by all participants. The following figure represents the interface of the planning book, which can be viewed and changed by the business partners via the Internet.

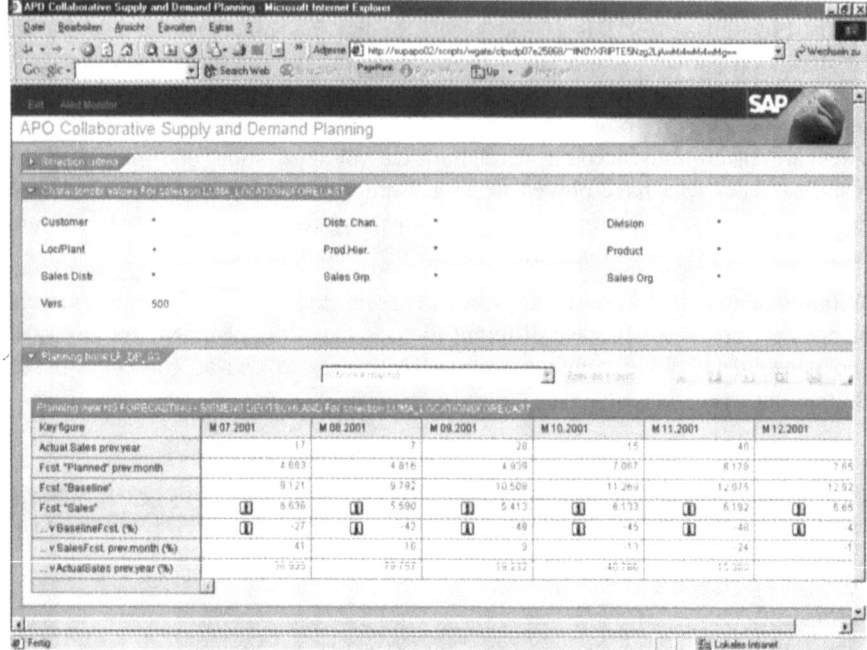

Figure 5.2: Internet-based demand planning with Collaborative Supply and Demand Planning

In addition, the planners are able to use Collaborative Demand Planning to exchange information, for example on sales promotion measures and the product life-cycle, between the partners of the supply chain and to change the planning results correspondingly. For example, a product that has reached the end of its life cycle is in the phase-out area and is not likely to obtain the sales quantities of the past. If these conclusions are exchanged between the partners of the supply chain, the planners can either reduce the planned sales quantities or adapt it to the phase-out quantities of similar products. This is referred to as a "like modeling" in APO.

5.3   Procurement Planning

5.3.1   Concepts and APO Application

The appropriate supply of the company with the required materials, parts, products, and other factors of production under adherence to business criteria is the objective of procurement planning.

SNP is the instrument of APO for simultaneous planning of procurement, production and transport in the supply chain. SNP, considering existing restrictions, creates a quantity-based supply, production, and distribution plan for a medium-term as well as long-term horizon. This plan is based on the supply chain structure and the forecasted sales quantities modeled by the planner. The procedure is based on BOMs and task lists with a maximum accuracy of one day. The thus acquired rough result can be transferred to further planning modules that create detailed plans on this base, for instance, in the area of production the PP/DS (see section 5.4) as well as the Transportation Planning module (see section 5.5).

The Mexican steel producer Hylsamex serves as an example for the successful use of SNP. The company has some 5,000 employees and an annual sales volume of approximately 1.5 billion US $. It delivers to some 300 direct customers, has two production plants and six warehouse locations. Since the implementation of APO, SNP planning in interaction with DP has increased the quota of the fulfilled orders from 70 percent to 90 percent. In this case, Hylsamex was able to increase the service level and lower the stocks at the same time. The forecast accuracy was increased from 40 to 80 percent. By their own account, these results allowed Hylsamex an amortization of the investments amounting to 850,000 US $ in six months.

Starting point of procurement planning based on SNP is the demand plan transferred from DP that first contains independent requirements as well as possibly production, transportation, and distribution restrictions.

The following supply concepts are distinguished for the procurement of the individual material groups:

- *Individual procurement*, for example in case of order-related make-to-order production and procurement of a Z part (unsteady, sporadic demand),

- *inventory procurement*, that is, the uncoupling of the production from the input market through introduction of warehouses and the triggering of a purchase order when the inventory quantity falls below a defined level, and

- *sequenced (just-in-time) procurement*, that is, minimizing the stockholding at the recipient by delivering externally procured parts so that they are consumed immediately.

Through the ABC and the XYZ analysis, objects such as parts, customers and vendors can be differentiated and allocated to the corresponding supply concepts. The ABC analysis measures the importance of the goods by share of business volume, while the XYZ analysis distinguishes the flows of goods and services with regard to their planability (Silver/Peterson 1985).

Upon determination of a procurement requirement, the vendor selection and the determination of the optimal order quantity are carried out. Valuation models based on part-specific criteria catalogs are used with the search for suitable vendors or for the check regarding the suitability of existing supplier partners. In the basic model for determining the business lot size, the trade-off between purchasing and stockholding costs and the point of minimum total costs is determined.

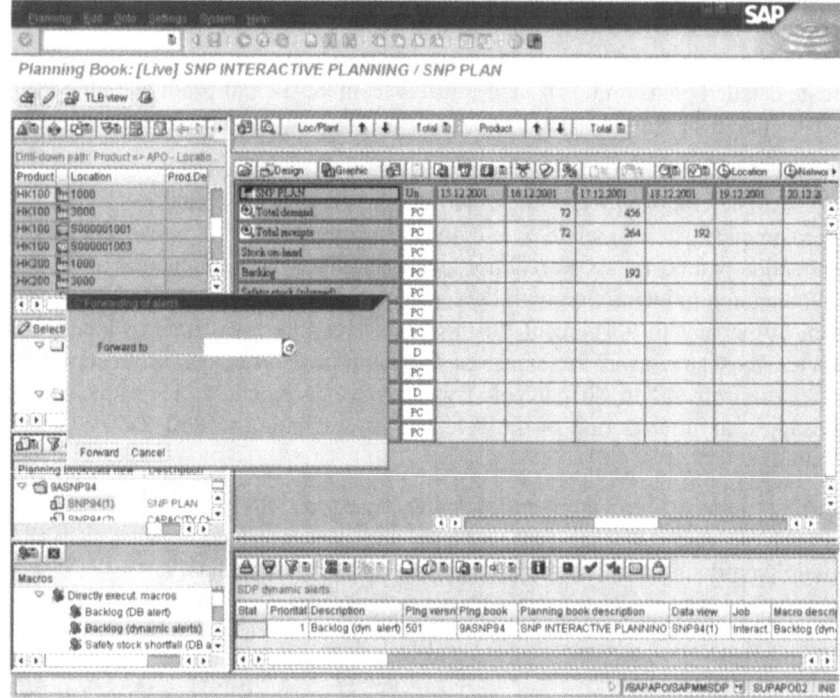

Figure 5.3: SNP Planning Book from the planner's viewpoint.

A detailed description of an SNP planning run now follows. Starting point is a scenario, in which a shortfall quantity of 192 pieces of a certain component has occurred for the production of a finished product. The Supply Chain Cockpit allows the planner to view and manage these shortfall quantities throughout the company. Figure 5.3 shows the already specified shortfall quantity (Backlog in the figure) of a total of 192 units. This planning book can now be sent to potential vendors by e-mail or be published in the Internet.

Consequently, the vendor who caused the shortfall quantity can be assigned a lower priority in the priority list for possible sources of supply. Figure 5.4 shows the screen in which the planner can assign a priority key figure to the vendor. Since APO does not set any automatic priority key figures, the planner must carry out the valuation of vendors and sources of supply manually.

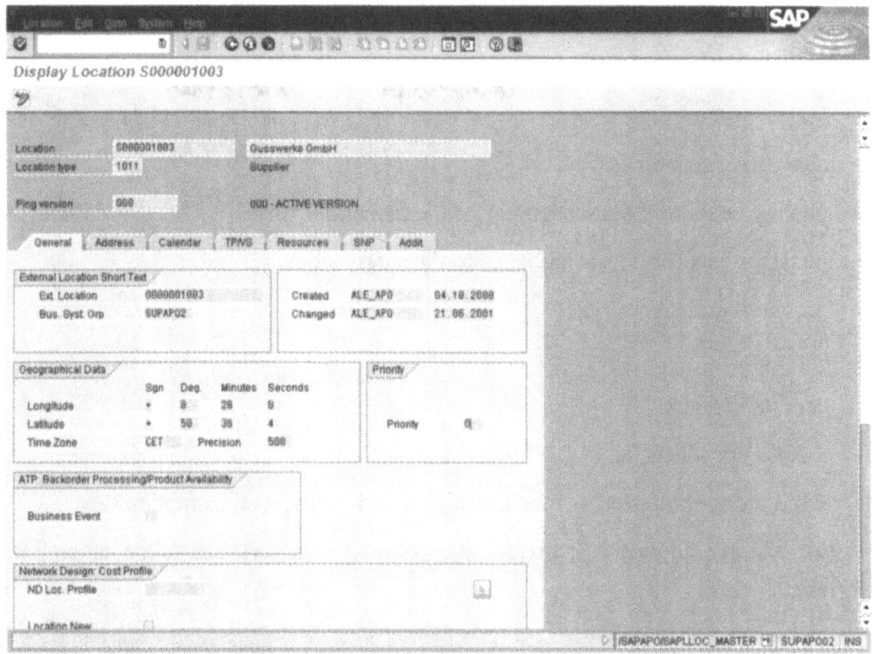

Figure 5.4: Setting priorities for sources of supply through the master data of the possible sources of supply

The priorities defined by the planner are the basis for the SNP planning. They are used during the planning run for the source selection. Further selection criteria are (see also section 5.6.2):

- Procurement quotas,

- procurement costs (procurement price as well as transportation costs),

- procurement type (external procurement or internal procurement) as well as

- penalty costs for missed deadlines.

To now find a source of supply for the shortfall quantity, the planner can start a planning run. Beforehand, the following factors have to be weighted in the system:

- Valid transport relations,

- lead times,

- transport capacity and costs,

- handling capacity and costs,

- production capacity and costs,

- storage capacity and costs,

- time stream (location master data),
- lot size (minimum and maximum lot size as well as rounding value),
- scrap,
- alternative resources,
- penalty costs for "non-coverage" of the demand,
- penalty costs for non-compliance to the safety stock,
- procurement costs,
- shelf-life,
- cost multipliers,
- location products, and
- fixed production process model resource and material consumption.

If the planner applies a heuristic, the following factors are to be taken into account:

- Valid transport relations,
- lead times,
- quota arrangements or procurement priorities,
- calendar,
- lot size rules,
- scrap,
- component availability,
- Product Process Models (PPM) (see section 5.4),
- location products,
- Supply Network Planning demand profile,
- Supply Network Planning supply profile, and
- demand profile.

Figure 5.5 shows an example as to how the planner has provided the penalty costs for a late delivery with a relative weighting of 19.81 percent. After the optimization, the planner receives the optimal SNP plan, in which the rough supply, production and distribution plans considering the 192 shortfall units were re-calculated.

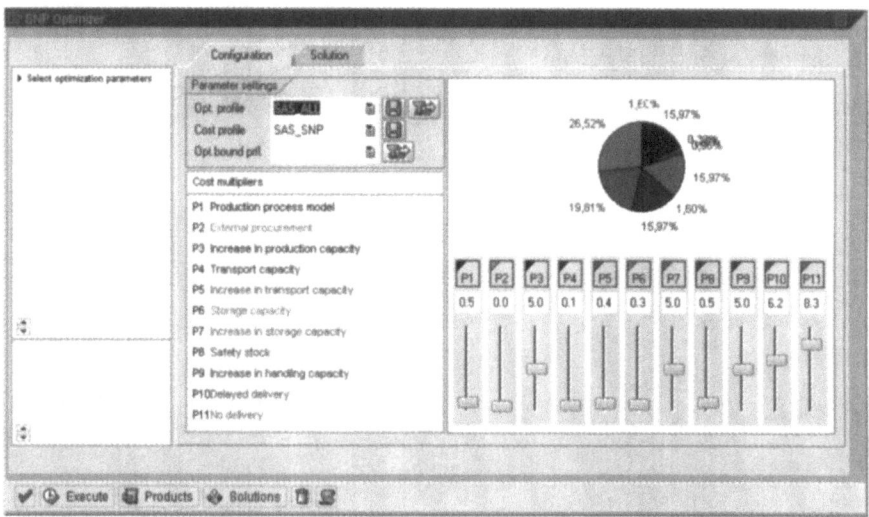

Figure 5.5: Weighting of relevant optimization factors in the SNP run

Figure 5.6 shows the result of the planning run. It has determined an SNP plan which provides transportation costs amounting to 4,179.6, storage costs amounting to 4410 and production costs amounting to 28.75 thousand monetary units (see last row of the table in Figure 5.6). The results of earlier planning runs are shown in the rows above for comparison purposes.

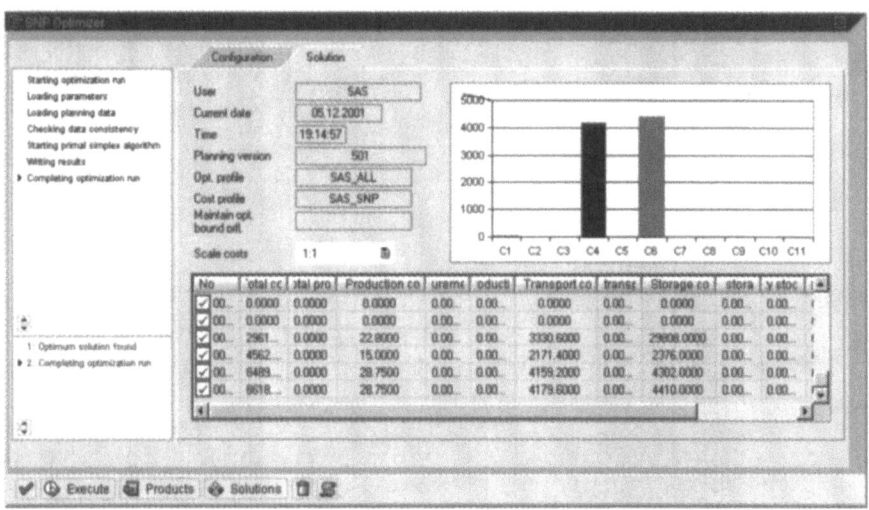

Figure 5.6: Result of the SNP optimization

The planner can release the resulting SNP plan in the system to generate corresponding detailed production, transportation, and supply plans. Figure 5.7

shows the detailed view of the planning run, which the planner can now send to
the partners of the supply chain.

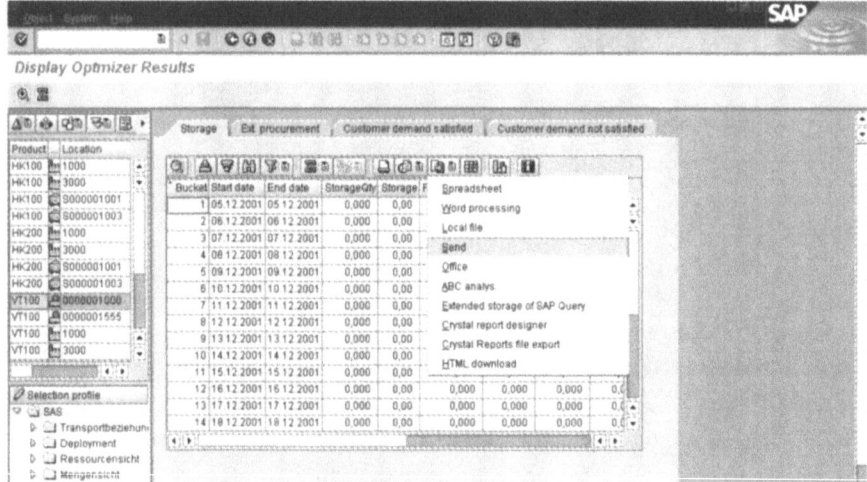

Figure 5.7: Detailed view of the collaborative SNP plan

On this basis, all partners of the supply chain can create their detailed plans; they
remain consistent within this rough-cut plan. Figure 5.8 shows the new rough-cut
plan, in which the shortfall quantity was eliminated by selecting an alternative
source of supply in the supply chain:

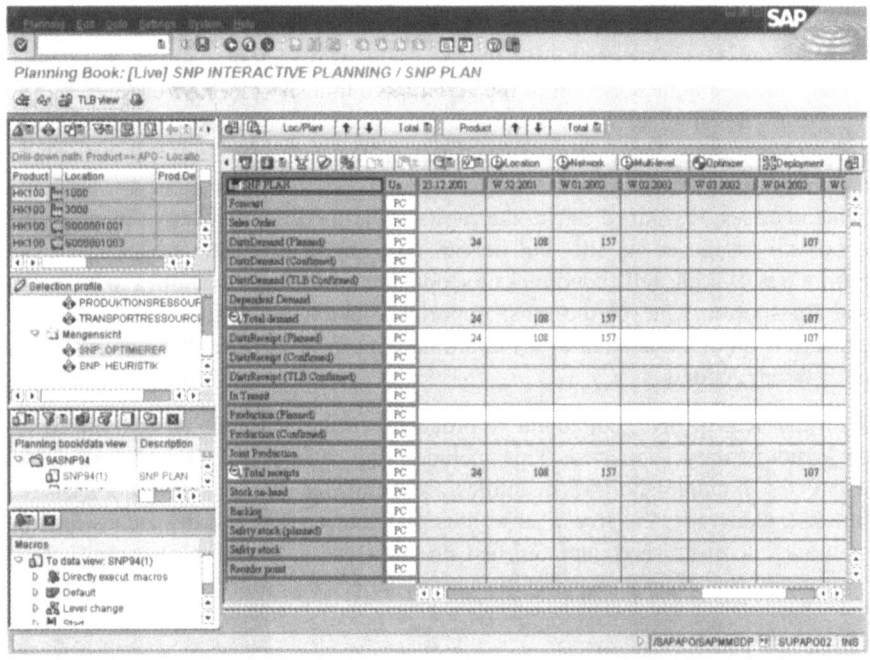

Figure 5.8: New SNP plan without shortfall quantities

The results of the planning run can now be refined with the help of further planning components of the SNP. Thus, the deployment enables short-term replenishment planning to distribute stock to distribution centers and warehouses by means of the current requirement quantities (and not from the forecasted requirement quantities, as with SNP planning). Furthermore, the TLB (Transport Load Builder) takes on the task of converting the shipment quantities determined in the SNP run into transport units, which provide the basis for loading means of transport. From these transport units, the TLB generates the necessary transport requests, which are assigned to the means of transport and external transportation service providers within the Transport Planning and Vehicle Scheduling (see section 5.5). The purchase orders in turn are executed and controlled with the help of the Enterprise Buyer Professional (EBP) (see chapter 6).

5.3.2 Collaborative Supply Planning

The so far described procedures are generally based on network structures which can be formulated internally on the one hand, but also cross-company wide, on the other hand. In the latter case, the supply chain includes for instance car manufacturers, vendors, and logistics service providers that are connected via a common network regarding the transportation of goods and information.

A collaborative supply planning in a supply chain can, for example, be carried out for the purpose of economic utilization of demand groupings as well as in the course of joint and thus less expensive transports (see also section 5.5). Furthermore, syndicate establishment and usage of warehouses can be mentioned. This concept is quite common in the automotive industry (see also chapter 7). The warehouse level of a logistics service provider, to which the various vendors deliver their products, is located not far from the recipient. The operator carries out the picking of the goods and directly delivers to the recipient as soon as a demand arises. He indeed carries the capital lockup costs for the time, in which the goods are stored at his site, but he can also obtain economic advantages from economies of scale and economies of scope due to the large quantities to be stored and transported. One of the most important objectives of this warehouse level concept is the minimization of the coordination efforts between the material flows of different vendors.

With the help of SNP, collaborative processes in the procurement area are so far only rudimentary supported. This includes the collaborative data management, where for example shortfall quantities are published in a planning book on the Internet. Generally, the stocks as well as planned receipts and dispatches for raw materials, semi-finished, and finished products are available to all supply chain partners in case of SNP planning in an interconnected network.

5.4   Production Planning

5.4.1   Concepts and APO Application

The objective of production planning is the best economical assignment possible of manufacturing orders to available production resources under consideration of the restrictions of flexible planning, for example due to technically conditioned maintenance sequences. The general goal is to minimize the lead time between starting the first and completing the last planned production step for executing the entire order program. Further factors, which can affect the assignment of series of operations to production resources, are the provision of a certain flexibility, the leveling of the utilization of the work centers, and the reduction of the tied-up capital. Three essential planning activities can be distinguished:

- *Production program planning*, which contains information regarding which product types are to be created, in which quantity, and when,

- *staging planning* that has the task of ensuring the economic availability of the required production factors (e.g., material, personnel), and

- *production process planning*, in which on the one hand the production flows are structured regarding dimension and time and, on the other hand, the actual execution of the production is planned and controlled in the sense of assigning series of operations to production resources.

The APO Production Planning occurs within the functions of SNP and PP/DS. SNP is used for medium- to long-term, rougher planning for aggregates of orders along the entire supply chain. As soon as a demand falls into the rather short-term production horizon, however, it is no longer planned through SNP but in PP/DS, where the planning can be detailed to the minute, if required.

The assignment of orders to production resources is a highly complex problem. The calculation of an optimum requires correspondingly long runtimes for the used algorithms. APO thus to a large extent does not use exact procedures and instead provides a number of strategies to solve the problems heuristically. Therefore, simple priority rules are used for selecting the next series of operations for the dispatching on a machine. The complexity of the assignment problem can be further restricted, for example by simply optimizing within a given time window and by limiting the number of resources included in the planning.

The constraint propagation procedure as well as a genetic algorithm are available in PP/DS for handling the simplified tasks. The first-mentioned procedure is typically used in cases where a planning problem is involved, in which a large number of constraints have to be adhered to, which again makes it difficult for the planner to recognize a valid solution. The procedure gradually develops a solution by changing the relevant constraints, whereby the resulting (still incomplete) solutions are checked regarding admissibility and quality in every step – for example, brevity of the overall throughput time. This way, a tree is drawn up, in which branches with impracticable solutions are deleted.

If in contrast valid solutions are relatively easily found, then it is a matter of developing a best possible option for action from these solutions with limited calculation time. Genetic algorithms simulate the processes of natural evolution in order to develop good solutions. Based on already known results, new solutions are established through crossover or mutation of partial solutions. Selection procedures are used to eliminate bad solutions from this "population". These processes keep repeating themselves until a preset number of "generations" is reached or the objective function value has not been further improved since a certain number of generations.

The production planning run is based on data stored in APO in form of a Production Process Model (PPM). In addition to the BOMs of the products to be manufactured, the PPM also contains the used task lists as well as other resources required for the production process. The information on the task list and on the BOM in this case is then combined to a master data object. The task list contains one or several activities, whereby every activity can consist of several other activities. For each activity, whose position is also managed in arrangement relationships, a specification of the required materials and resources is made, too. Costs, which are taken into account in PP/DS and SNP planning processes, can be assigned to the activities and resources of the PPMs. The data relevant for production planning is transferred, for example, from a connected R/3 system via the CIF interface to APO. To be able to carry out a production planning at all, the thus required master data, such as materials, resources, task lists, and BOMs, must first be transferred as an initial data transfer to APO. The publishing of the planning results is done by transferring data changes.

The orders generated in the course of the (medium and long-term) SNP planning processes are converted to PP/DS orders upon entry into the production horizon. Simultaneously, a display keeps on showing PP/DS orders in SNP as aggregated requests for the determined period. Frequently, a problem consists in hierarchically connecting the modules with one another so that a planning over two independent planning levels results. Ketterer (Ketterer 2002) describes an interesting solution for this problem.

If the correct data is contained in an active integration model, a typical process flow between R/3 system and APO for releasing a production plan in a simplified version looks as follows: The release is triggered by the APO by first converting the planned orders generated there into production orders. This happens by defining a conversion indicator in the planned order in APO and results in the orders being transferred to the connected R/3 system. The actual conversion into a production order is then made in R/3 within the order creation.

At this point, the task list is read again and the process is rescheduled, which means dispatching orders on production resources without consideration of capacity limits. The process scheduling in R/3 does not necessarily provide the same results as in APO, which is why a mapping is carried out by adjusting the series of operations in R/3 to the dates of the activities in APO. Afterwards, when the production orders are saved, R/3 converts the dependent requirements of the planned order into order reservations of the production order. Together with the production order number assigned in R/3, these are now returned to APO, where they replace the original planned orders.

The production order is finally released in R/3. With the release, the shop papers can be printed and the goods movements for the production can be posted. Further, the respective production order in APO is also adjusted by data changes being transferred. The subsequent withdrawal of the components for the execution of the production order and the associated goods issue are posted in R/3. Then, both R/3 and APO reduce the reservations and stocks.

The production planning run in APO passes the phases requirements explosion, finite capacity planning, and scheduling. The sequence of these planning steps, according to which the results of the previous phase are included in the following planning process as a constraint, also make the break with comprehensive optimal solutions clear.

With the requirements explosion in PP/DS, independent requirements are determined for the finished products, first. This can take place, for example, due to existing and forecasted sales orders as well as expected purchase orders for filling up the warehouses. If there is neither sufficient stock nor planned receipts to cover the independent requirements for individual parts, planned orders for the production or planned purchase orders for externally procured products are issued. In case of finished products, for which a planned order exists, an explosion of the demand is carried out along the product structures of the assembly BOM for every part according to the information in the PPM. The dependent requirements result from the multiplication of independent requirements and product structure quantity (e.g., 20 doors are needed to manufacture five railway cars for passengers if four doors are built in each railway car) as well as the negative lead-time offset, which is the planned timeframe defined under the requisite of available production capacities. The production of the doors must already start at the beginning of this timeframe so that they are ready in time for the production start of the railway cars. If the company produces components itself, tests are conducted as to whether the total of their independent and dependent requirements is covered by warehouse stocks and already planned receipts. If this is not the case, planned orders for the components are generated here as well. The process of the assembly BOM explosion continues step-by-step until all component requirements resulting from the requirements explosion are covered through external procurement. In the last mentioned case, procurement proposals are created in form of purchase requisitions or, in the case of procurement using scheduling agreements, scheduling agreement schedule lines are created if warehouse stock and planned receipts are not sufficient to cover the dependent requirements.

Lot-size calculation is used to determine for the individual procurements to which extent receipts are needed for end products and components (Harris 1913, Erlenkotter 1990). The system provides different procedures for this operating under the name "Product Heuristics" in APO. They are subdivided in static, periodic, and optimum lot-sizing procedures.

In static lot-sizing procedures, standard lots, which can be created according to the following rules, are used for planning:

- In case of a *lot-for-lot order quantity*, a receipt is generated amounting to the shortage quantity individually resulting from independent requirements or requirements explosion.

- In the case a *fixed lot size* is used, the system copies a quantity firmly defined in the product master as lot size. Where necessary, several lots are created if the shortage quantity exceeds the fixed lot size.

- *"Fill in"* designates a procedure to create the amount of the receipt in such a way that a determined maximum stock level is reached.

With period lot-sizing procedures, shortage quantities within a time segment are grouped together to a lot size. The periods can be hours, days, weeks, months, years or user-defined periods according to the planning calendar.

Static and period lot-sizing procedure can be combined. For this purpose, the time axis for planning the lot size can be split into a maximum of three areas, in which different lot-sizing procedures are used. It can be useful, for example, to work with a lot-for-lot order quantity in the short period, but to use weekly lot sizes to plan in the long-term period.

Contrary to static and period lot-sizing procedures, when using the optimum order quantity creation, the lot size is defined in such a way that the costs are minimized. Important procedures in APO regarding this are the part period balancing and the least unit cost procedure.

In case of the part period balancing, requirements following each other in regular intervals are grouped together in a lot, starting with the date of the first supply shortage, until the total storage costs exceed the setup or order costs. Also the least unit cost procedure, which is particularly used for determining the order quantity for externally procured materials, tries a step-by-step bundling of requirements for different planning periods. The system determines the unit costs for every vendor, considering storage costs, fixed order costs, quantity-based discounts and proprietary shipping times. As soon as the optimal discount scale is reached in the course of increasing the order quantity and the costs start increasing again, no lots are created anymore.

After requirements explosion and lot-size calculation, the activities, that are allowed for the creation of a production plan and that are carried out within the production or procurement, are to be dispatched to the involved production resources.

The first substep in scheduling is the lead time scheduling; it dispatches the planned orders to the production resources first without considering capacity limits. First, starting from the required availability date of each ordered quantity, a calculation in seconds of the time specifications of the planned orders and purchase requisitions or scheduling agreement schedule lines are generated in the requirements explosion through backward scheduling. In this case, goods receipt processing times are taken into account in addition to the operation times in the PPM (for instance, when test processes are executed). The dependent requirements date of the components is specified for the start date of the operation, in which they are needed. Figure 5.9 shows a scheduling result for the case that two operations (10 and 20) are needed to manufacture the end product, three operations (10, 20 and 30) are required to produce the component 1, and again two operations (10 and 20) are needed to create the component 2. The procurement lead times of the externally procured parts, which are used for the finished product or components, are taken into account in scheduling. The view for each end product is therefore on the entire production and procurement hierarchy.

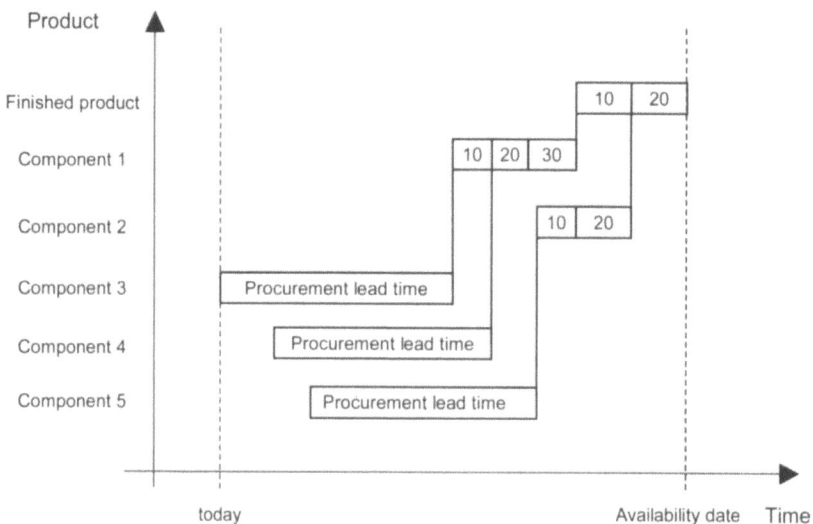

Figure 5.9: A scheduling result (without considering capacity limits)

This planning data can then be used for adding up the occupancy times of the production resources by period to determine which capacity requirements would be necessary for the execution of the production program or in which periods a surplus or a shortage exists according to current planning. Frequently overload situations can be monitored for the close future, while the capacity requirements for periods that lie further ahead decrease step-by-step. Such overviews are occasionally used for medium-term and long-term planned capacity adjustments.

In the second substep, the requests are now dispatched to the resources assigned in the PPM, considering the capacity restrictions, as they exist for example in form of limited available capacity and possibly already planned orders. If the capacities are already exhausted for the desired date, the system searches for a gap, in which the order can be dispatched to the resource. The strategy the system is to apply can be set in a strategy profile. Important settings in the strategy profile concern, for example:

- The scheduling mode (e.g., find gap and squeeze in operation if search successful, append operation if search not successful),

- the scheduling sequence (e.g., according to priority or order start date and time),

- the planning direction (forward or backward, where necessary with reversal), and

- the consideration of pegging relationships (assignment between sales orders and the purchase orders and production orders necessary for the fulfillment along all production levels, including procurement).

Figure 5.10 shows what the result looks like for a product if the scheduling mode "find gap" as well as the planning direction "backward with reversal" are set. Operation 10 of the task list is carried out on resource 1, operation 20 on resource 2. A backward scheduling starting from the desired date provides the result that operation 10 would have had to be started in the past so that with the setting "reversal", forward scheduling is required starting at the earliest start time possible. Since an interoperation time between the operations 10 and 20 is specified in the PPM, the dispatch of operation 20 is delayed until after the desired date due to the late dispatch of operation 10. In the example, it is assumed that operation 10 is to be executed prior to operation 20.

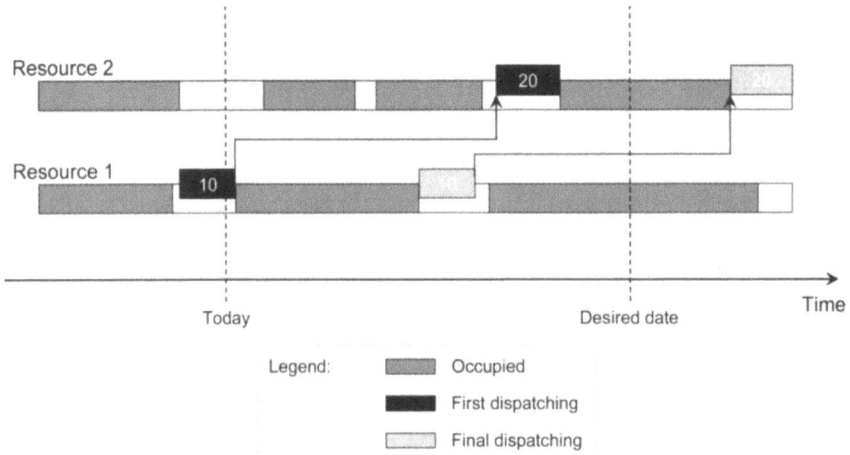

Figure 5.10: Scheduling result with scheduling mode "find gap" and planning direction "backward with reversal"

An operation can then be planned on an alternative resource instead if no remaining capacities are available for an operating facility for the required time. Respective specifications have to be maintained in the PPM.

Planned orders, purchase requisitions and scheduling agreement schedule lines are internal planning elements that can be changed, rescheduled or deleted by the processor any time. The system can be set so that changes in quantity and dates in dependent orders along the information of the production and procurement hierarchy are taken into account. These structures are represented in the *live*Cache by means of the pegging relationships.

The production plan, that is created through the described procedure or interactively by the planner, is possibly not yet allowed, for example, because new events have taken place that are not yet entered in the system or because it needs improvements regarding the production costs associated with the plan. To improve a plan, the planner can change production dates, processing orders and resource allocations of operations with regard to the currently existing order dispatching.

Operations and orders, excluded from rescheduling in advance, through their position determine to what extent non-fixed objects can be moved.

In addition to the lead time minimization, it is up to the planner to take further parameters into account when creating the production plan, for instance through weighting of target criteria taking effect from the start and in the course of interactive interventions:

- *Setup time and costs*: The total of the setup times as well as the setup costs are to be reduced with the transition of a setup status of the resources to another. The setup time and costs are taken from a matrix, in which this data is defined for every possible setup transition.

- *Entire delay costs*: The attempt is made to reduce the total of the costs associated with the delayed completion of the orders in the short-term planning horizon. A cost rate can be defined in the system depending on the order priority, which results in the delay costs of an order when multiplied with the delay duration.

- *Maximum delay costs*: The maximum delay costs of an individual request within the order quantity to be optimized are to be reduced.

- *Mode costs*: In the APO terminology, the mode designates a number of resources that are required for executing an activity. The mode costs consist of fixed and variable costs, where the latter vary with the duration of activity. If alternative modes for executing an activity are available, the mode that reduces the total costs of the production plan is selected for the optimization.

For optimization, the system additionally considers the different hard or soft constraints. While the system must adhere to the first in any case, optional restrictions can be violated.

5.4.2 Collaborative Production Planning

With the traditional form of production planning, the planning is carried out based on internal manufacturing orders that are again either based on sales orders or on sales forecasts. For activity output, mainly internal resources are used. For a collaborative production planning, on the other hand, it is possible to include the resources of the collaboration partners in the processes. These kinds of visions are discussed under various keywords, such as virtual companies.

The hope to be able to process manufacturing orders more cost-effectively and quicker is connected to this, whereby the complexity of the production process generally increases considerably with the application of such a collaborative production model. Possible advantages can result from a setup time reduction by swapping requests in the network or selecting resources with the least unit costs. The problems already mentioned in chapter 1 regarding the value distribution of the achieved value added between the collaboration participants are again encountered here if, for example, a participant renounces from executing an "own" order with the purpose of processing an order that is more profitable for the collaborative network. From an organizational view point, particularly the problem arises as to whether a central instance for the coordination of the manufacturing orders is advisable or a decentralized coordination of the players provides better results.

On an informal level, such a collaboration already exists in the automotive industry if for example production plants of a supplier break down, the production can be temporarily carried out on competitors' sites, provided that a similar production technology is used.

The application of SNP in the production planning area is so far primarily created for internal production planning and the users also use it mainly for this purpose (refer to our case studies at Bosch or Goodyear in chapter 7, for example). This is mainly due to the fact that APO in principle allows collaborative production planning but the used ERP systems get in the way of such a collaboration since these so far mainly serve intra-enterprise purposes.

5.5   Transportation Planning

5.5.1   Concepts and APO Application

The objective of Transportation Planning is the organization of the most economical transportation of materials from availability locations to demand locations, for instance from goods issue warehouses to customers. Often, the kilometers accumulated with the execution of a transport program and thus the transportation costs are to be minimized with existing vehicles or by commissioning freight forwarders. Further target values are for instance the lasting of a certain flexibility or the adherence to a supply deadline of the customers (see also section 7.3). Here, production planning takes on a particular role in cases where the interoperation time contains transportation time portions between two series of operations.

The roundtrip optimization as a standard routing planning problem, starting from a depot – for example distribution center, provides for a number of customers, whose respective required quantities and locations are known, being supplied through a vehicle. In addition, further factors quite often provide for restrictions regarding flexible planning and thus more complicated tasks to be solved, for instance if only certain vehicles are allowed to be used for the supply (e.g., no heavy-duty trucks in city centers) or if containers must be returned after a certain interoperation time.

The transportation planning process with APO 3.1 passes through several phases: once the sales forecast has been created, the quantities forecasted as demand are transferred to the SNP. There the attempt is made to meet the demand, considering the existing production capacity and the product BOMs, through the application of optimization algorithms or heuristics, whereby both internal (for instance, from the production plant to the own distribution center) and external (for instance, to customers) deployment stock transfers are generated. These recommendations contain the quantities to be transported between the nodes of the supply chain or between the partners within the period in question. The formal task is to assign transfer requirements to means of transport.

The system selects the possible means of transport, for instance during the execution of the planning process and with the help of bid invitations, or the user enters his requests before, during, and after the planning process. If external service providers are taken into account as transport carriers, the algorithm selects according to different criteria, whose weighting is defined by the planner:

- Actual freight costs,

- fulfillment of existing contracts,

- priorities determined by the planner, and

- penalty costs.

The Transportation Planning in TP/VS aims at finding a maximally cost-effective assignment of orders to vehicles. Supply sequences and transport deadlines are also determined. In this case, a large number of heuristic procedures are provided (SAP refers to these as optimizations). The following possible procedures are considered in this case:

- Differentiation between own and third-party means of transport,

- consideration of limited vehicle capacities,

- consideration of (in)compatibilities between transport groups and means of transport (containers, vehicles),

- coordination of the plans with limited loading resources in mind, also considering opening hours and loading time,

- costs minimizing of fixed and variable transportation costs (e.g., time, distance), and

- minimization of the penalty costs for earliness, delay or non-delivery.

First, an initial solution is generated through a heuristic, which carries out a first possible allocation of orders to means of transport. Then, it is modified step-by-step (e.g., by dispatching an order to another vehicle and changing the supply sequence). The attempt is made in this case to minimize the total of the costs under adherence to the secondary requirements. Upon completing a predefined number of improvements or reaching a satisfactory objective function value – for example, if further assignment changes do not provide any more advantages – the best solution found during the search run is returned.

As with Production Planning, a distinction is made between hard (e.g., capacities of a means of transport) and soft secondary requirements (such as a scheduled sales order that is supplied for late, thus accepting penalty costs):

The system determines the route, distances and costs of the shipment order and can be used for planning problems with open as well as closed routes. What-if calculations show effects on statistics and the overall result if changes are made, such as subsequent proposals from partners in the supply chain concerning the arrangement of bundling transportations.

Figure 5.11 shows the result of Transportation Planning with APO. The shipment orders assigned to the first means of transport and the corresponding route are in this case listed in the top table to the right.

Figure 5.11: Result of transportation optimization

In the case where several depots are involved, there can be open routes, unlike for the standard roundtrip, resulting in a vehicle proceeding to another distribution center at the end of the roundtrip to accept new goods, which quite often happens in the furniture and chemical industry, for example.

In addition to the objective of a maximally low number of roundtrip kilometers so far focused on, the system allows to minimize the roundtrip times and transportation costs as well as the number of the transport units. Alternatively, the planner can aim at maximizing the adherence to dates in cases where delivery locations can only be served at predefined times.

5.5.2 Collaborative Transportation Planning

While traditional transportation planning both assumes internal transport requests that are based on, for example, production planning and sales planning and uses corporate resources (own fleet as well as awarding transport requests to third parties) for activity output, the transportation planning and route planning also create collaboration potential within a supply chain. Therefore two consolidation forms are distinguished in a network:

- *Consolidation of deliveries*. The objective here is to summarize and jointly deliver shipments from different origins that are intended for a recipient. The very first effect is that the benefit for the customer can be increased since the inbound delivery costs are reduced because activities, such as the opening of the inbound delivery ramps as well as providing personnel for unloading and load turnover, occur only once. In addition, a more effective use of transportation capacity may develop from that.

- *Consolidation of routes*. This form of rationalization tries to subdivide the route areas of various sending companies so that the customers to be supplied are attended upon by the nearest carrier. This way the total distances to be covered are reduced (for details on a simulation of these advantages refer to Martín Díaz/Buxmann 2002).

From an institutional point of view, the inclusion of logistics service providers into a supply chain is interesting with regards to a collaborative transportation planning, whereby nowadays, this also adds to clear production performance for the part along with the transportation services, for example, in the automotive industry.

With the collaborative planning of the individual transports, APO provides two functions which embrace the partners of the supply chain: The consolidation of orders and shipment quantities as well as the selection of suited carriers.

With the consolidation of orders and shipment quantities, TLB takes on the task of optimally using the storage space of the means of transport. This is done under consideration of:

- Loading zone opening hours for goods receipt and goods issue,
- shift schedules and working time calendars,
- kilometer tables,

- unloading times,

- minimum and maximum weights as well as

- prices for partial and complete loads.

In a next step, VS (Vehicle Scheduling) provides the possibility to represent detailed schedules of the used means of transport, such as loading, move and break times in form of Gantt charts.

Valuation models are used for the selection of suited carriers; the criteria have to be made available to the system. Furthermore, APO enables to make an Internet-based bid invitation of the planned transports, whereby the admission of suppliers can be controlled via the system. An alternative form to transfer the planned transport requests to the partners is to publish them between the planning APO systems and the executing OLTP systems – for instance R/3 – through the CIF interface.

A further option is to use the SAP marketplaces (see chapter 6) and freight exchanges. Figure 5.12 shows an example using the freight exchange NTE.net. The following steps are to be carried out from the request for quotation:

- The transport request is created in the R/3 system.

- The transportation requirement is transferred to NTE.net with all necessary information (including upper price limits).

- NTE.net assigns a carrier to the available transportation quotation.

- The planner accepts the quotation of the service provider or rejects it.

- The transport might be processed.

- The settlement occurs through NTE.net.

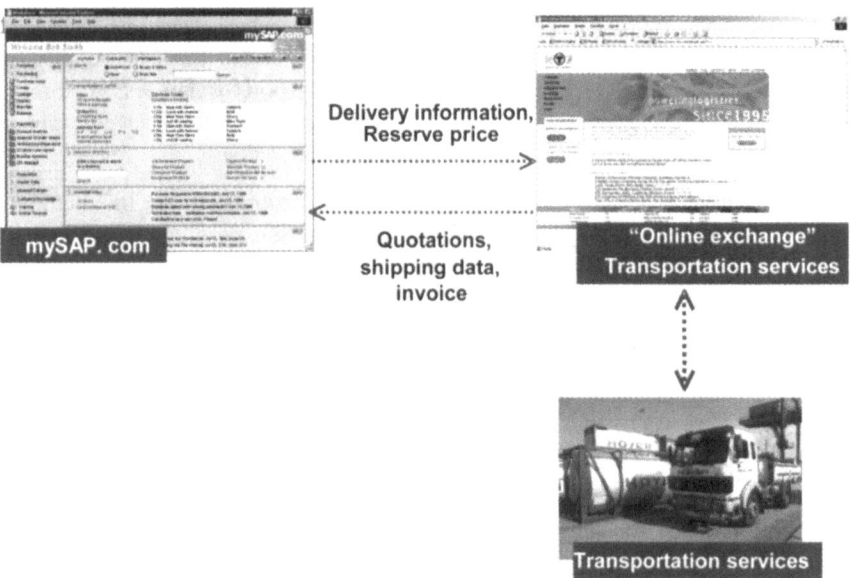

Figure 5.12: Quotation of transportation requirements through the Internet-based freight exchange NTE.net

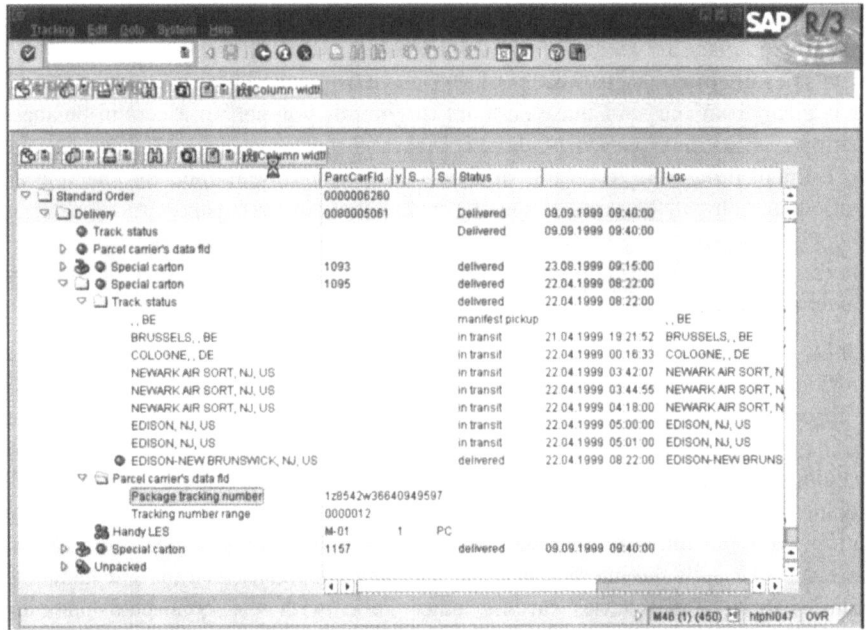

Figure 5.13: Tracking transportation loads in the R/3 system

With the processing of the transport the Logistics Execution System (LES), a part of the R/3 system that can also be implemented as independent application, provides the option to track loads. If the transport is processed through correspondingly equipped service providers, the status of the transport can be traced directly in the R/3 system or in LES (see Figure 5.13)

Here, it is possible to query the status of a delivery using EDI, the Internet and a mobile device. The truck driver, for example, has the possibility of using his personal digital assistant (PDA) to transmit a confirmation of receipt to the system after the delivery.

5.6 Process-oriented Perspective: Collaborative Management of Delivery Schedules Using APO

After the various scheduling functions and their support in APO have been described, the emphasis is now on the process-oriented perspective, in which the already introduced planning methods are applied. The presented process scenario is the Collaborative Management of Delivery Schedules that was developed within a cooperation between SAP and Robert Bosch GmbH.

The exchange of goods and services between a company and its vendors quite often takes place by means of individual (sales) orders. It is characteristic that a new sales contract on the transfer of services is concluded over and over again. If it is clear from the start that you want to commit yourself to a certain business partner for a longer period of time, it makes sense for reasons of incentive and investment protection to do this in form of a long-term contract, for example an outline agreement. The risk of specific investments in the business relationship is reduced by the long-term contractual obligation and thus both sides are incentivized to invest in an efficient exchange of goods and information between buyer and salesperson.

Unlike a simple sales order, an outline agreement does not contain any exact information on the exchanged quantity or the delivery date. Instead, the information on when which quantities are to be delivered to the customer is exchanged in regular intervals in form of releases which the customer sends to his vendor. Situations, however, in which the vendor cannot simultaneously meet all requirements of his customers are conceivable. In this case, the customer must be informed about quantity or schedule variances in form of a confirmation for his release. SAP calls the interaction of the exchange of releases on the one hand and confirmations for releases on the other hand with the connected planning processes as collaborative management of delivery schedules.

While it is the target of all participants to efficiently exchange the information the process is based on, there are different priorities regarding the definition of the collaborative management of delivery schedules: an important objective of the procuring organization is to be informed as early as possible in cases where the vendor cannot meet the demands at all, only incompletely or late. This way it becomes possible, for example, to use alternative sources of supply for the product to be procured or to adjust the production plan at an early stage. In addition, the customer can be informed early about delays in the delivery of own end products, the production of which in the case of low stockholding depends on the punctual procurement of the procured components.

On the other hand, the vendor is interested in finding out the customer requests as early as possible in order to check whether they can be met and to inform the customer about it. Since the vendor can sell several products using scheduling agreements and there can be several customers for every product, who regularly send each other varying releases, a correspondingly large data volume must be entered in the system, be taken note of and taken into account in the planning. The vendor's main target is to automate this process as far as possible. It would be ideal if the planner of the vendor had to react only in exceptional situations, for example, in cases where demands of particularly important customers cannot be fulfilled.

The activities in the Collaborative Management of Delivery Schedules for the customer and the vendor are represented in APO in the functions of the collaborative procurement and sales scheduling agreement processing. While the collaborative procurement has already been available since APO 3.0, the sales scheduling agreement processing was developed for Release 3.1.

Target groups of these functions are planners at the interfaces between production planning and procurement or production planning and sales and distribution. On the side of the vendor, for example, these are product planners who plan a certain number of sales products and keep direct contact to the corresponding customers. Through their activity, these planners in essence determine the production plan of the respective finished products as well as the confirmations for the customer.

5.6.1   Process Overview

If scheduling agreements are to be used in APO, the outline agreements must first be available in APO as master data. An outline agreement, that was concluded for the procurement of goods, can be transferred from a connected R/3 system to the APO of the customer, for example, with the help of the CIF interface. Analogously, an outline agreement regarding the sales of goods from a connected R/3 system can be represented in the APO of the vendor. A procurement scheduling agreement is created for an outline agreement through automatic planning or personally. A copy of the scheduling agreement is sent to the vendor in form of a release. At the vendor site the system automatically checks whether the quantities and delivery dates required in the release can be fulfilled. The result of this check creates a confirmation for the release, which is sent back to the customers. Here in turn the planner of the customer can react to the changed situation and adjust the production plan, for example. During the process, a continuous exchange of the relevant transaction data with the connected ERP systems takes place (for instance releases, confirmations, deliveries as well as goods receipts and issues). Figure 5.14 provides an overview of the process.

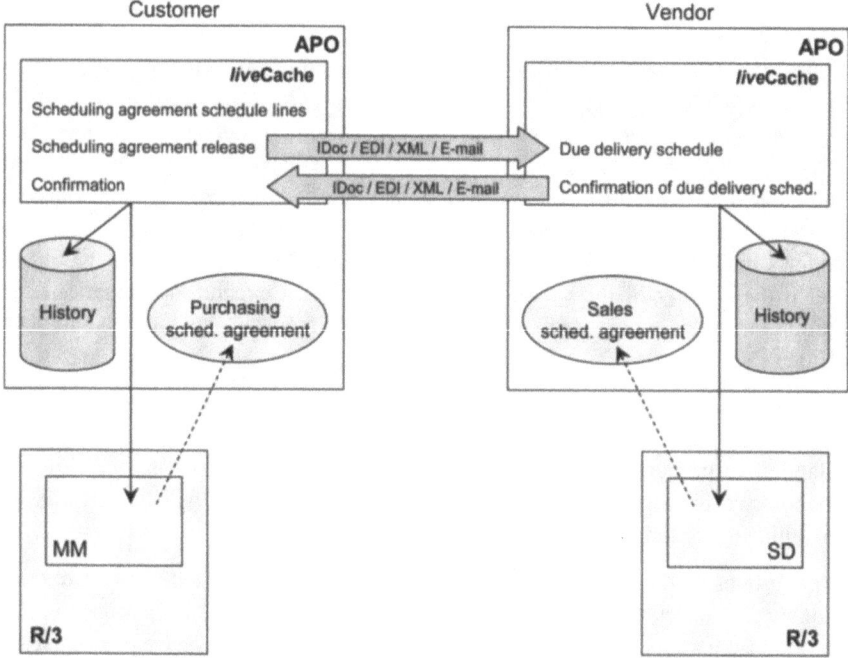

Figure 5.14: Process of collaborative management of delivery schedules between two APO systems with processing in R/3 Systems

The case of collaborative management of delivery schedules described here can be varied in detail in APO. Thus, the process on the side of the customer can be set with regard to

- release creation (frequency of the release transmission, used release types, transmitted quantities, tolerances),

- conditions, under which a confirmation is created, and

- alert processing with confirmation receipt.

On the side of the vendor, the following can be set:

- What type of releases are used,

- which parts of the releases are relevant for the requirements planning and delivery,

- which checks are to be performed upon release receipt, and

- which degree of automation the inbound processing of releases as well as the confirmation creation are to have.

Below, the process is described in more detail first from the customer's point of view, then from the vendor's viewpoint. Then, the focus is set on the underlying interfaces for the data transfer between the business partners as well as for the integration of the executive ERP systems.

5.6.2   The Customer: Collaborative Procurement

Demand, which for example can originate from the Collaborative Demand Planning in form of forecasted planned independent requirements or from sales orders, is the starting point for the planning. If a planning run is now triggered and if demand for components, which are externally procured, is determined during this process, a source determination starts. There can be more than one source of supply for the procurement of a component. In this case, various criteria are evaluated with the source determination to determine which of the external procurement relationships are to be used to procure the components in question. In this case, the sort criteria are as follows:

1. Quota arrangement: In the quota arrangement it is defined which portion of the demand is to be purchased by which source, whereby in addition to vendors also (own) producing plants can be sources.

2. Priority: The priority is stored in the transportation lane for an external procurement relationship. This way, it can also be assigned in a period-dependent way.

3. Costs: The costs of an external procurement relationship can be assigned to period-dependent cost functions by using the transportation lane. In these cost functions, fixed and variable costs records are defined for different quantity intervals. If no procurement costs function was maintained, the personally created costs are used for the transportation lane.

4. Procurement type: if a component is created internally as well as procured externally, then in-house production has priority over external procurement.

5. Time limit adherence.

If the component as a result of the source determination is produced internally, the system generates a planned order; if the component is procured externally, the system generates purchase requisitions depending on the used source or, provided that a procurement scheduling agreement is being used, scheduling agreement schedule lines. A necessary requirement for the selection of a procurement scheduling agreement is that an outline agreement with the vendor exists.

In addition to the automatic generation of schedule lines for procurement scheduling agreements, the planner can also interactively create such schedule lines. With the interactive generation of schedule lines, the planner enters demands in a planning transaction. If more than one source of supply exists for the product to be procured, source determination is called up, that then provides a selection list, in which also available scheduling agreements are displayed. If a scheduling agreement is selected, schedule lines are created for the requested quantities.

The schedule lines for a scheduling agreement or changes to schedule lines already transmitted earlier are at first not yet known to the vendor as planning elements. The planning results are transmitted to the involved vendor in a second step, the release creation.

With the release creation, a time window of the planned time series is copied to a release. The width of the used time window varies depending on the used release type. In APO, the two release types "forecast delivery schedule" and "operative delivery schedule" can be used. While the delivery schedule contains a material requirement forecast for a longer period of time and is not legally binding, the information, at which point within a short period which quantities are required, is transmitted with the operative delivery schedule, whereby the width of the time window is defined through the release horizon. In order to control the quantity of the transmitted data, it is possible to define for different period sequences how large the tolerances are to be towards delivery schedule updates before in each case a new release may be generated. It can thus be determined, for example, that a new release may be generated from every delivery schedule update or only when a certain tolerance limit is exceeded.

Figure 5.15 shows the view of the planner of the planning results for a product. In the example, demands were generated for the product ABS_MM01 through the forecast, which were converted to schedule lines for a procurement scheduling agreement in an automatic planning run. The released quantities are displayed in the row "SAgREL" as they were determined from the schedule lines.

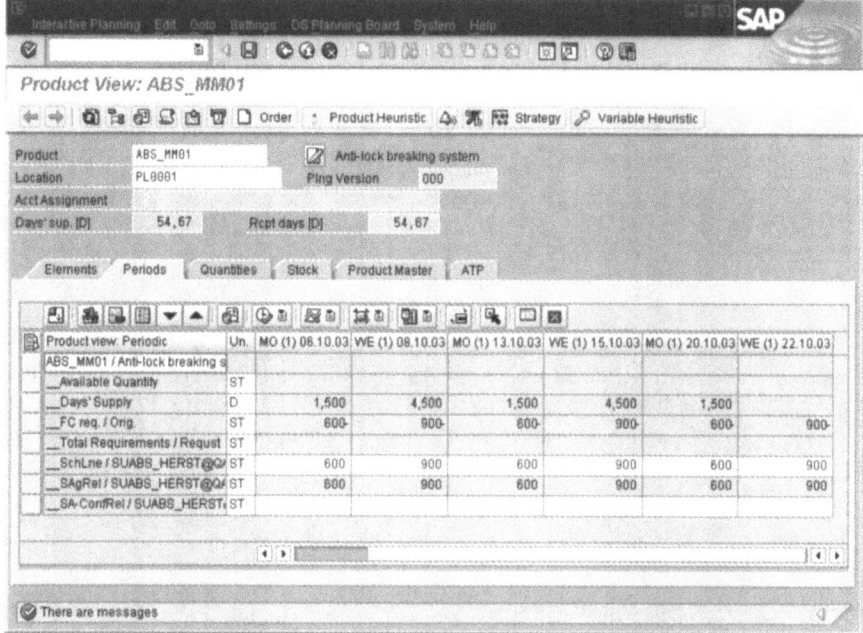

Figure 5.15: Processing interface (excerpt) of the planner in Collaborative Procurement after automatic planning and release creation

In a last step, the release is sent to the vendor. Just like the release creation, this can also occur interactively or automatically in asynchronous mode at predefined times for several releases in parallel.

Depending on made setting, either

- a confirmation from the vendor is always expected,

- a confirmation is only expected in case of variances from the release, or

- a confirmation is never expected.

The last process variant makes sense when the vendor is not able to send DP-supported confirmations for the scheduling agreement, which can be the case particularly with small and medium-sized companies. In such a scenario, it is instead possible to have the vendor confirm that he acknowledges schedule lines for a procurement scheduling agreement by using an Internet interface.

Figure 5.16 shows the planning situation after receipt of order acknowledgement. The release schedule lines from 10/06/2003 and 10/08/2003 were confirmed with alternative quantity, the schedule line from 10/13/2003 with alternative date (in each case last row in Figure 5.16).

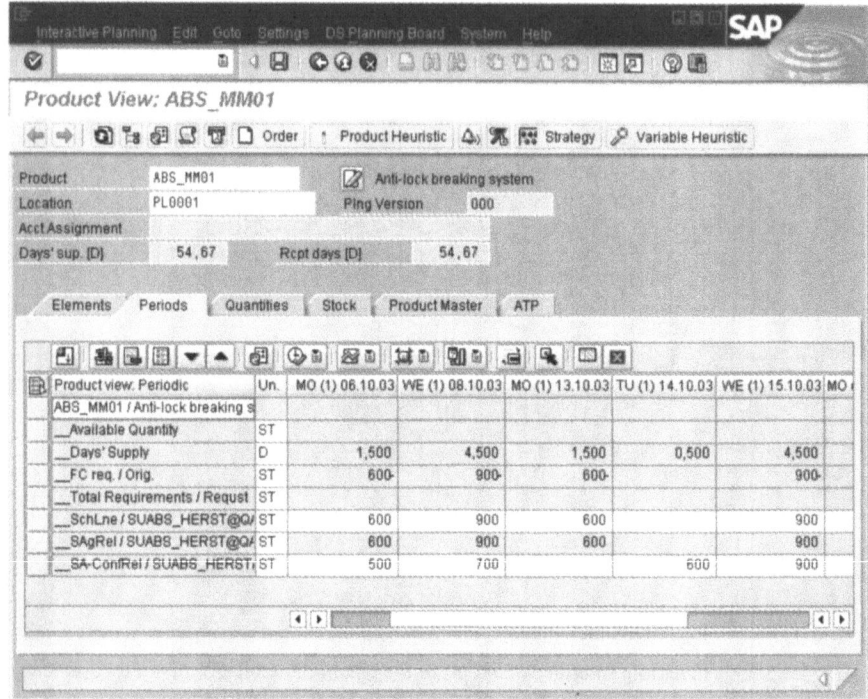

Figure 5.16: Processing interface (excerpt) of the planner in Collaborative Procurement after receipt of order acknowledgement

If a confirmation for a release arrives in the customer system, a check, that compares the current confirmation with the last received confirmation or with the respective release, can be automatically started in the inbound processing. A previously defined tolerance profile is used to determine in the check whether the planner is to be made aware of deviating confirmations by means of an alert message. The planner can react to this message and initiate changes to the production plan.

5.6.3   The Vendor: Sales Scheduling Agreement Processing

The process of the collaborative scheduling agreement processing starts for the vendor with the arrival of a release from the customer. The due delivery schedule is the planning element. This is a time series of required quantities and dates that is made up of parts of the last delivery schedule the customer sent and the operative delivery schedule. In this case, the schedule lines of the delivery schedule are replaced by schedule lines of the operative delivery schedule until the release horizon is reached.

Following the release receipt, every due delivery schedule first passes through an admissibility check and then a feasibility check (see Figure 5.17).

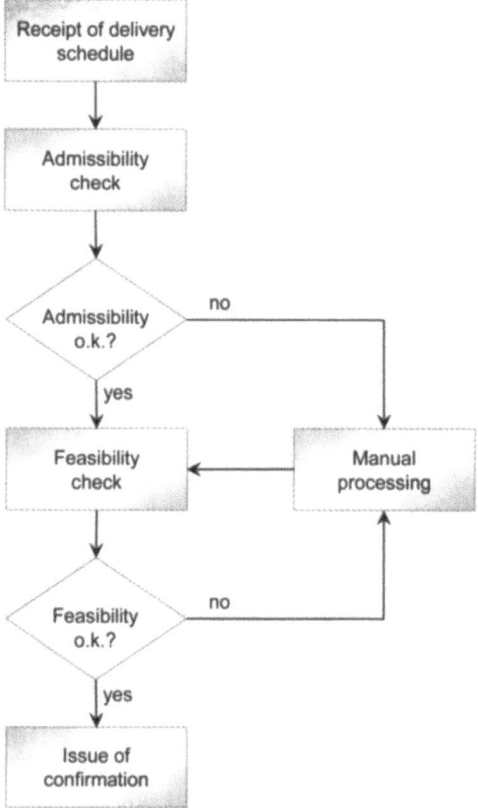

Figure 5.17: Checks in sales scheduling agreement processing

The objective of the admissibility check is to identify quantity variances which could be attributed to a transmission error. For this purpose, the quantities and dates of the last confirmed due delivery schedule are compared with the current due delivery schedule. It is determined in the tolerance check whether individual quantities or dates deviate to a larger extent than is allowed according to a previously defined tolerance profile. In this case, percentage threshold values (tolerance limits) can be defined in the tolerance profile for a maximum of three check horizons. Low tolerance limits are more appropriate for the near future, and high tolerance limits for the remote future. In the tolerance check, each individual quantity/date pair or the cumulative quantity of a planning calendar period can be taken into account here. According to the results of the admissibility check, the status of the underlying sales scheduling agreement is changed from "New" to "Admissibility o.k." or "Admissibility not o.k.".

Following a successful admissibility check, the feasibility check is carried out, in which it is stated whether the customer requested quantities and dates transmitted in the due delivery schedule can in fact be fulfilled. Unlike the admissibility check, which occurs independently for every due delivery schedule, it is necessary in the feasibility check to simultaneously consider all customer requirements for a product. The standard algorithm for the feasibility check delivered by SAP contains a simple days' supply check.

In the days' supply check it is determined for a product for how many days the available stock lasts under consideration of the planned receipts if the delivery is made according to the already confirmed customer requests and the currently received due delivery schedule. The current days' supply is compared with a minimum days' supply which is defined product-specifically in the days' supply profile. A sensible value for the minimum days' is, for example, the replenishment lead time for a product. In case of a shortfall of the minimum days' supply, the statuses of all sales scheduling agreements taken into account in the check are set to "Feasibility not o.k.".

For every sales scheduling agreement, admissibility and feasibility checks are adjustable:

- The checks can be activated and deactivated independently.

- Instead of the standard algorithms delivered by SAP, the customer can implement and include own algorithms.

- The checks can occur synchronously for release receipt or can be started in a delayed collective run.

- In case of a successful check, it is possible to automatically create and send confirmations for due delivery schedules synchronously or delayed in a collective run.

- In addition to the automatic execution, the checks as well as the confirmation generation can be started manually.

The planner must intervene if one of the checks fails, for example, because customer requests cannot be met due to missing warehouse stocks or insufficient receipts. Here he has the two basic options for action, either to influence the production in the short-term horizon in order to receive further receipts or to confirm the customer requests with differences. The latter option can occur either at the planner's discretion and possibly after consulting the customer or it can be automated by using the backorder processing in APO.

The following figure shows the planning scenario from the view of the MRP controller in sales scheduling agreement processing. In the bottom right part of screen, the planner gets an overview of the stocks and receipts of the product. In addition, he sees the time series with the demands of the customer from the due delivery schedule. The confirmation for the due delivery schedule can be manually processed here. The customer request is confirmed with differences both concerning the quantity and the date.

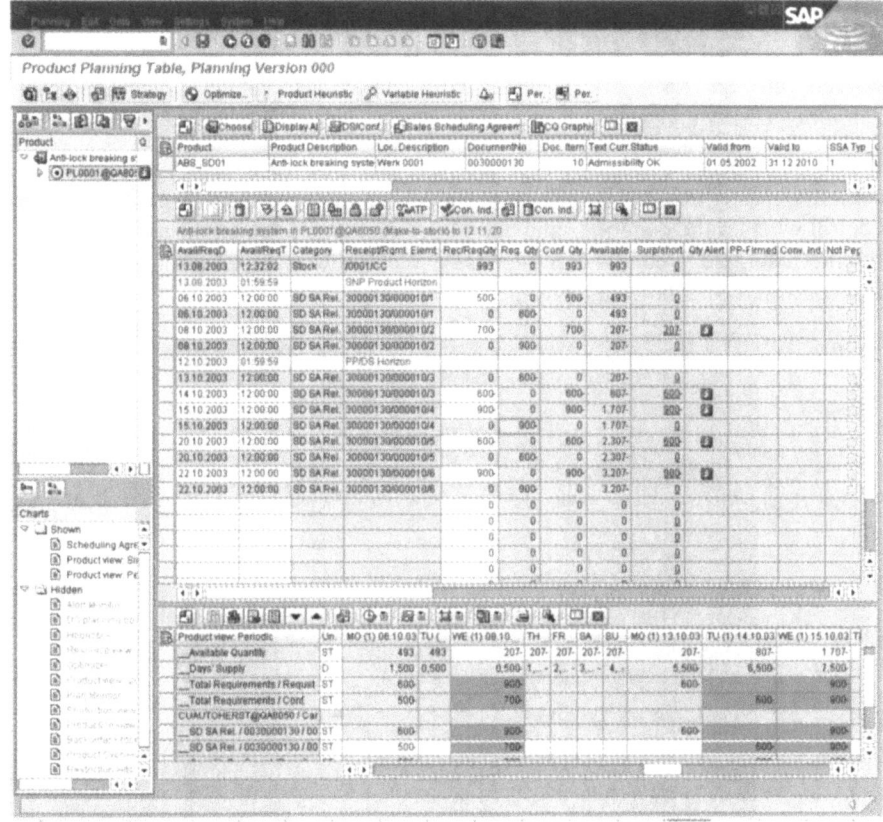

Figure 5.18: Processing interface (excerpt) of the planner in sales scheduling agreement processing

5.6.4   Data Transfer between the Business Partners

APO provides an IDoc interface for the transmission of releases for scheduling agreements and confirmations of releases. Concerning the data structure used for the IDocs, releases and confirmations belong to the same basic type DELFOR. They differ however regarding the message type. While releases are of the message type DELINS, confirmations belong to the message type DELCONF. The synchronization between customer and vendor plays a special role for the interpretation of the transmitted data.

At a technical level, the functionalities provided in the standard system by SAP are available, as they are described in chapter 2, for sending the IDocs. By selecting the suitable port, for example, the setting can be made as to whether releases and confirmations for scheduling agreements are to be transferred with the help of EDI, XML or email. In the case of an email transmission, the IDoc is sent as an attachment in MIME format (*Multipurpose Internet Mail Extensions*). If XML is selected, the decision can be made as to whether the IDocs are to be written into an XML file together with the corresponding *Document Type Definition* (DTD).

Procurement provides a special feature with the "Internet release", which can be set in the master data for the procurement scheduling agreement. It can be used to control whether the quantities and dates of releases are to be published through an Internet interface. Vendors can then use a Web browser to view the release data and confirm the acknowledgement.

Product/Locns./SchedAgreement/Item/L	Status	Quantity	Open Qty	CmlSchQty	Un.of Meas	Date	Time	
▽ ☐ PL0001@QA8050/(no planner)								
▽ ☐ ABS_MM01/SUABS_HERST@Q								
▽ ☐ 1(Operative Del. Schedule)								
▽ 🗎 0000000004	●●●	4.500	4.500	4.500	ST	13.08.2003	12:01:23	0
🗐		600	600	600	ST	06.10.2003	12:00:01	
🗐		900	900	1.500	ST	08.10.2003	12:00:00	
🗐		600	600	2.100	ST	13.10.2003	12:00:00	
🗐		900	900	3.000	ST	15.10.2003	12:00:00	
🗐		600	600	3.600	ST	20.10.2003	12:00:00	
🗐		900	900	4.500	ST	22.10.2003	12:00:00	
▷ 🗎 0000000003	●●●	4.507	4.507	4.507	ST	13.08.2003	12:00:43	0
▷ 🗎 0000000002	●●●	4.500	4.500	4.500	ST	12.08.2003	19:39:46	0
▷ 🗎 0000000001	●●●	4.500	4.500	4.500	ST	12.08.2003	18:44:37	0
▽ ☐ 1(Confirmation)								
▽ 🗎 0000000007		4.200	0	0	ST	13.08.2003	14:00:00	
🗐		500	0	0	ST	06.10.2003	12:00:00	
🗐		700	0	0	ST	08.10.2003	12:00:00	
🗐		600	0	0	ST	14.10.2003	12:00:00	
🗐		900	0	0	ST	15.10.2003	12:00:00	
🗐		600	0	0	ST	20.10.2003	12:00:00	
🗐		900	0	0	ST	22.10.2003	12:00:00	
▷ 🗎 0000000006		4.193	0	0	ST	13.08.2003	14:00:00	
▷ 🗎 0000000005		4.207	0	0	ST	13.08.2003	14:00:00	

Figure 5.19: Releases and confirmations for the procurement scheduling agreement with send status

In addition to the mentioned IDoc data structure, APO also supports processing logics for the releases transmitted in the IDocs to VDA and ODETTE, as they are commonly used particularly in the automotive industry.

While with inbound processing of releases for scheduling agreements in accordance with VDA process, the complete previous release is replaced by the new release, the older release is only partially replaced with the ODETTE process. In the ODETTE process, a distinction between a basic logic and a cumulative quantity logic can be made in this case (Figure 5.20).

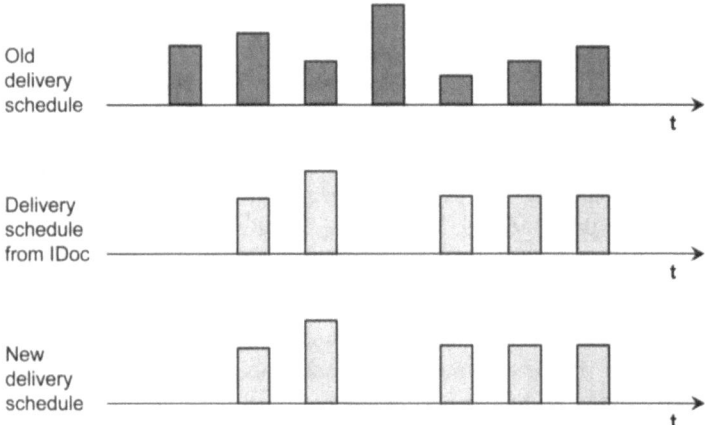

Figure 5.20: Release substitution in accordance with VDA logic

In the basic logic, a validity period is also sent in the release. Those schedule lines are copied from the existing release,

- whose date lies between the release date from the IDoc and the start date/time of the validity period as well as

- whose date lies after the end date/time of the validity period.

The schedule lines from the IDoc are now added to the transferred schedule lines (see Figure 5.21).

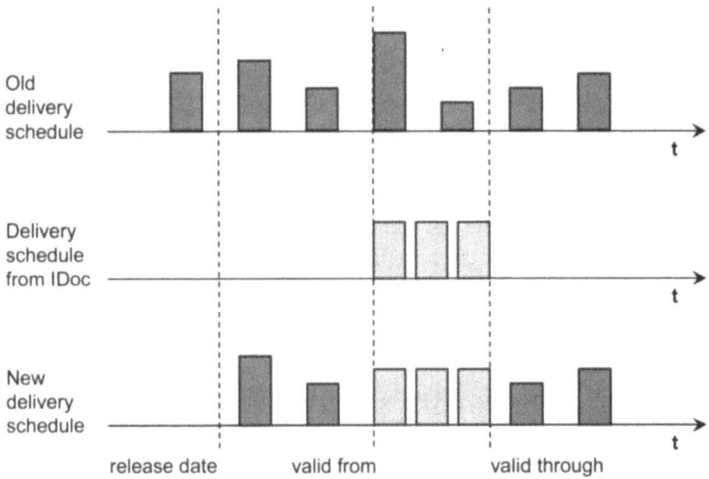

Figure 5.21: Offsetting scheduling agreement releases according to ODETTE basic logic.

A logic according to planned cumulative quantities exists in addition to the basic logic. In this case, a planned cumulative quantity with a planned date is additionally specified for the IDoc. The planned cumulative quantity includes the cumulative released quantity for the key date of the planned date. This way, the releases are to be kept synchronous on customer and vendor side.

The planned cumulative quantity can be negative, zero or positive. The planned date can be in the past, today or in the future. If the planned date is not sent but the planned cumulative quantity is not zero, then the planned date is populated from the start date/time of the validity period of the IDoc.

To determine the new release after IDoc inbound, the planned cumulative quantity is now compared with the cumulative released quantity of the older release. The latter is first converted to the planned date. If a difference results, the schedule lines of the older release are first adjusted correspondingly:

- If the planned cumulative quantity is larger than the cumulative released quantity (underdelivery), schedule lines are generated, that is, the corresponding number of schedule lines are copied from the previous releases or they are generated so that, as a result, the cumulative released quantity was adjusted to the planned cumulative quantity.·

- If the planned cumulative quantity is smaller than the cumulative released quantity (overdelivery), schedule lines are deleted or reduced until the cumulative released quantity corresponds to the planned cumulative quantity.

Then, the new release is generated in accordance with the basic logic.

With the confirmation for a release, the entire time series of the currently valid confirmation is always replaced by the time series of the confirmation transmitted in the IDoc on customer side. In this case, quantities that no longer appear in the confirmation, since deliveries have already been created for them, which however have not yet arrived at the customer, are to be appropriately taken into account as "Quantities in transit". Here, a synchronization occurs through the cumulative received quantity of the customer and the cumulative delivered quantity of the vendor. The latter is transmitted in the confirmation IDoc. The quantity in transit, that is taken into account for the schedule lines upon confirmation receipt, can be concluded from the difference between cumulative received quantity and cumulative delivered quantity.

5.6.5   Integration with the ERP Execution Systems

APO as a planning system ensures that receipts are created according to a production plan and that from this purchase orders are sent to the vendors in the collaborative procurement and also that in sales scheduling agreement processing, confirmations for them are created and sent. The actual delivery of the demands is made in a connected ERP system. For this purpose, the functions of the APO collaborative procurement and sales scheduling agreement processing can be connected to an R/3 system by means of the CIF interface.

If an R/3 system is used for the processing, an indicator must be set in the procurement scheduling agreement "external planning" on procurement side, and the scheduling agreement must be transferred to APO by means of initial data transfer. Depending on selected process variant (confirmation always, only in case of variance or never), the quantities and dates are then transmitted during operation from the release or the confirmation to the connected R/3 system by change date transmission. Conversely, inbound shipping notifications in R/3 (or goods receipts, provided that shipping notifications are not being used) cause a reduction of the scheduling agreement schedule lines, of the releases as well as the confirmations in APO.

Analogous to procurement, the sales scheduling agreement must first also be created for sales and distribution by means of an initial data transfer if an R/3 system is used for the processing. As soon as a confirmation is generated, a change transfer occurs with the time series of the confirmation. This time series is created as a release in R/3; all deliveries are posted to it. Deliveries posted in R/3 reduce the schedule lines of the respective due delivery schedule and the confirmation in APO.

Chapter 6 Electronic Marketplaces: Concepts and SAP Solutions

6.1 Electronic Marketplaces: An Overview

Electronic marketplaces (EM) are a comparably young approach of inter-organizational cooperation. EM are virtual locations that are realized with the help of modern information and communication technologies, that serve as a platform for the concurrence of supply and demand, and that support the exchange of goods, services, and information in a market as agreed on by contract (Bakos 1991, pp. 32-33; Bichler 2001, p. 2). Here, they also provide information, agreement, settlement and after-sales functions, and services in addition to the general information (e.g., news from certain lines of industry) and to a description of products and services as well as of their respective suppliers. Below, the focus will be set on B2B (bussines-to-business) marketplaces that are characterized by the fact that vendors and customers are companies. Two cooperation types are to be distinguished in this environment:

- Cooperation of companies when setting up and operating the marketplace (operator cooperation) and

- cooperation of companies through the marketplace (e.g., within logistics processes).

The cooperative setup and operation of EM result in different cost saving and revenue potentials, which include economies of scale and economies of scope:

- *Economies of scale*: Start-up and operating costs for the individual company of an operator consortium can be lowered through cooperation (Baldi/Borgman 2001).

- *Economies of scope*: The opening of new sales potentials is enabled through cooperation of the operator consortium.

Positive effects for the companies cooperating in a marketplace (this can also include operators) are for instance:

- Reduction of transaction costs (business transactions can be carried out at less costs and in less time by means of offered marketplace services),

- reduction of the purchase prices (increase in bargaining power due to demand bundling; improved market transparency due to aggregated comparisons), and

- extension of the sales and procurement market.

Below, first common classifications as well as the services and phases of transactions provided in electronic markets are explained, before dealing with SAP-specific marketplace technologies and applications in section 0.

6.1.1   Classification and Service Offers of Electronic Marketplaces

Frequently EM are classified in horizontal and vertical marketplaces: *Horizontal marketplaces* support cross-industry functions and processes, for example by offering indirectly value-added goods and services (e.g., office equipment and PC accessories), which are often summarized under the term MRO (maintenance, repair, and organization). Examples are the marketplace emaro.com (office, IT and industry supplies) operated as a joint venture by Deutsche Bank AG and SAP AG or mondus.com (books, office supplies, hardware, software, among other things).

On the other hand, v*ertical marketplaces* support business processes along the value chain for a certain line of industry and are thus targeted to specific subject areas (e.g., chemical industry). Since the traded products and services address the core business of the companies, vertical marketplaces are more important within inter-organizational cooperation. The detail and range of the provided services are in general broader than on horizontal marketplaces. Examples for vertical marketplaces are covisint.com and SupplyOn.com in the automotive industry or CPGmarket.com in the consumer goods industry.

Furthermore, *open* and *closed* systems are distinguished. As the name suggests, open marketplaces are available for all users while closed marketplaces are exclusively accessible only for selected participants, e.g. following a quality certification. Individual companies, for example, Volkswagen or BMW, neutral organizations or a group of companies can act as operators (Fricke/Hoppen 2002). An example for an operator cooperation is the marketplace Covisint (DaimlerChrysler, Ford, General Motors, among others. Baldi/Borgman 2001 describe more details of operator forms.

The services offered in marketplaces, which are frequently used for further classification, include:

- Bulletin boards,

- catalog-based services,

- exchanges, and

- auctions.

Bulletin boards designate the simplest functional marketplace type. By means of systematization, for example of products, they merely support the initiation of a transaction and can be compared to classified advertisements of a newspaper.

The focus of *catalog-based services* is aggregated product and supplier catalogs that provide the customer with an overview of the entire product range of a marketplace. Products and services are concentrated and displayed together with similar, related, or complementary articles. Provided that an integration with the enterprise resource planning systems of the suppliers exists, the availability and prices can be queried in real time.

Supply and demand for a specified product meet at the *exchange*. On this basis, the price is determined, for which the largest quantity can be traded and finally the transactions enabled for this price are processed.

In the case of *auctions*, an offer faces many demands (here, the highest demand price is usually selected) or a demand faces many offers (the lowest quotation price is searched for).

While early electronic markets mainly supported one or several of the sketched services (we refer to them as basic services for purchasing and selling goods and services), the service range today is increasingly extended by value-added services. Services in form of an application hosting or application service providing are offered, for example, which in addition to the information phase and agreement phase particularly support the settlement phase important for inter-organizational cooperation. Supply chain management and the collaborative product development are included here, for example. Software providers and marketplace operators often summarize the two under the term e-collaboration:

- Supply chain management offers various services that enable the planning, monitoring, and controlling of entire supply chains. Sales and demand information of different companies on the marketplace, for example, can be collected, consolidated (aggregated and disaggregated), and used for planning processes (e.g., a collaborative demand planning). In addition, processing-relevant business documents, for example scheduling agreements, shipping notifications, or JIT delivery schedules for the supply chain control, can be exchanged through the marketplace or monitoring and status information can be accessed. The term "e-hub" is often used in this context. A necessary prerequisite is a technical infrastructure that supports for instance the conversion of different EDI and XML formats and thus the data flow between business partners.

- With the collaborative product development (e-development), the data of a process, for example the design of a product, is documented and managed within the marketplace. The collaboration between a company and its suppliers within innovation processes is the focus. The key factors here are speed as well as the protection of intellectual property.

6.1.2 Phases of Marketplace Transactions

A marketplace transaction can be subdivided in four subsequent phases, the information, negotiation, settlement, and after-sales phase (Lincke 1998, p. 9 onward.; Scharl et al. 2001) (see Figure 6.1).

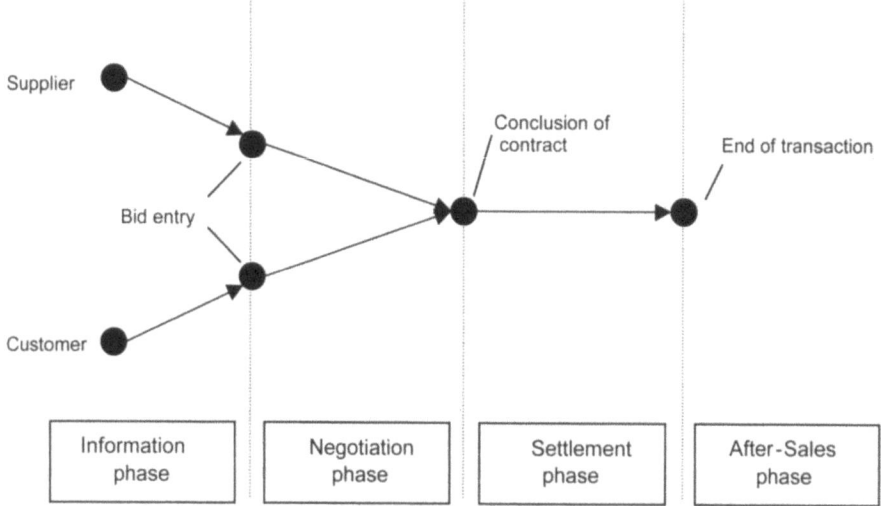

Figure 6.1: Phases of a marketplace transaction

During the *information phase*, information on potential suppliers and customers is searched for. Depending on the marketplace type, the range of information can in addition to general information also include various product or service specifications and features of the suppliers and buyers (e.g., on-time delivery performance, liquidity). These are processed within a comparison and then used for the purchase or sales decision. Information asymmetries between marketplace partners are reduced since offers and demands are transparent for both sides. The research is usually supported by search services and catalogs, for example a *business directory* (see section 6.2.1). In the case of vertical cooperation, which can be seen as a mid-term to long-term oriented collaboration regulated by contract of legally independent companies on adjacent levels within the value creation, the information phase plays a subordinate role since collaboration partners are known.

In the following *negotiation phase* suppliers and customers establish contact in the marketplace. An agreement on quantity, price, quality, terms of delivery, terms of payment as well as warranty and other services are targeted. The complexity of the phase depends on the selected pricing mechanism. Fixed prices or prenegotiated contracts for instance allow a very simple procedure while auctions and reverse auctions can include many interactive steps. A legally valid contract is concluded upon approval by the buyer and the salesperson that completes the end of the negotiation phase. The negotiation of contracts becomes more and more important in vertical marketplaces. Thus, special *cockpits* or *cRooms* (collaborative project rooms) can be used for negotiating conditions with one or more vendors.

In the subsequent *settlement phase* the services are exchanged. In the area of material goods this includes the shipping of the goods, the provision of relevant information (e.g., *online tracking* on the datasets of service companies involved), the payment processing, and possibly various value-added services. Services in connection with information products can, on the other hand, be completely exchanged online. Due to the wide variety of offered value-added services, the settlement phase is the central element of inter-organizational cooperation.

The *after-sales phase* starts when the customers receive the products. In case customers require additional services or information, for example for processing repairs and warranty services within service management, historical transaction data that is mostly saved in electronic marketplaces is used. Supplier and customer behavior can also be included in a participant evaluation, which is available to other marketplace participants, to simplify the selection in the information and negotiation phase.

6.2   mySAP Exchanges

In the SAP environment, setting up and operating open EM is supported by MarketSet, a joint solution by SAP and Commerce One. From an SAP view, MarketSet is a part of the higher-level solution mySAP Exchanges that includes both closed (company solutions) and open marketplace solutions. MarketSet has been available since the 3rd quarter 2000, and until April 2002, it has been delivered to approximately 20 customers (operators) (section 0 provides an implementation overview). According to SAP, there is no standardized price model. The solution that is currently provided with version 2.0 includes two core areas, the MarketSet Infrastructure (see section 6.2.1) and the MarketSet Applications (see section 6.2.2).

6.2.1 MarketSet Infrastructure

The MarketSet Infrastructure is made up of three areas: The MarketSet Builder, the MarketSet Services Framework, and the MarketSet Platform (see Figure 6.2). It forms the basis for all transactions in the marketplace.

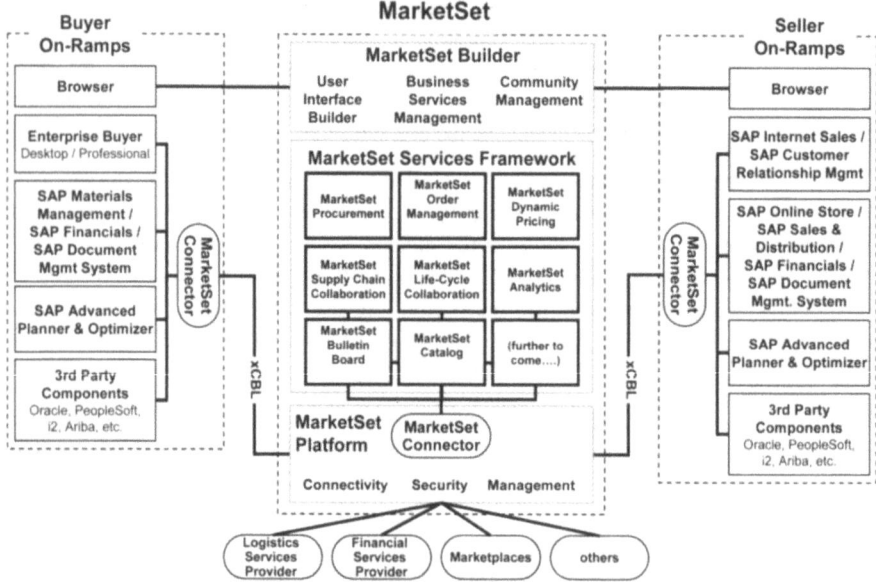

Figure 6.2: Marketset 2.0 architecture

The *MarketSet Builder* is used for the configuration of the marketplace and can be adjusted according to operator-specific interest, for instance with regard to the orientation of the marketplace (horizontal or vertical), supported processes (e.g., procurement and sales and distribution), and the respectively necessary services (e.g., product catalogs) as well as the layout of the Web pages. The configuration of horizontal EM differs from the vertical EM particularly in the provided services. Thus, services for the development of products or supply chain management solutions are not required, for example. Fewer requirements regarding the data exchange are the result and, therefore, complex processes for the routing of data must not be defined.

The core functions include the User Interface Builder, the Business Services Management, and the Marketplace Community Management. Communication takes place through an HTML-based user interface (browser) (see Figure 6.2).

The *User Interface Builder* contains a number of tools that allow both the operator and the user individualizations. Operators, for instance, can predefine access authorizations, layout, or user roles. Figure 6.3 shows the administration of business partners and users within the MS Internet Explorer. Personalizations are stored in XML-based configuration files that are automatically loaded upon login.

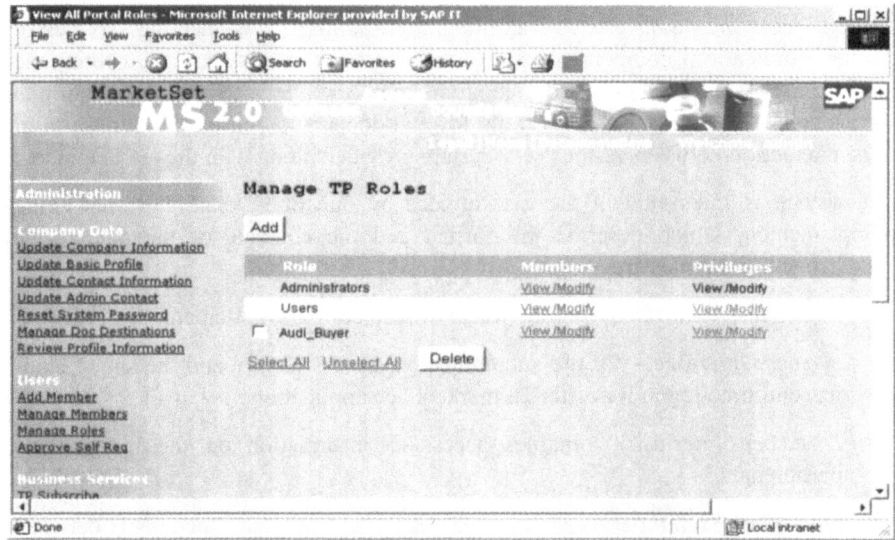

Figure 6.3: Administration of the business partner roles

The *Business Services Management* provides various tools for the operator, for example, in order to offer new services (this is then referred to as "Register"). As Figure 6.2 shows, this can involve services for procurement, for order processing, or supply chain collaboration (see section 6.2.2).

Community Management includes various tools for the creation and maintenance of multi-vendor and multi-product catalogs (SAP refers to these as Trading Partner Directories (TPDs)), that are a central element of modern marketplaces. TPDs, often also referred to as yellow pages, are used within the information phase for finding suited business partners. They contain all relevant data on the buyers and salespersons registered in a marketplace, such as:

- Product number,
- validity date (date up to which a participant can do business in the marketplace),
- contact address,
- shipment and invoice address,
- bank details,
- time zone,
- security logs,

- encryption methods as well as

- authorized users and administrators.

Interfaces (which SAP refers to as integration points) for connecting services of other application components and other systems are described within the *MarketSet Framework*. In addition, guidelines (e.g., for the registration or the document exchange) as well as tools for and documentation on the definition of the interaction between various services are provided along with the marketplace.

A service is integrated in the marketplace by one or several interfaces being implemented, which describe the format and the contents of the data to be exchanged. Examples are:

- *Registration Interface* – for the usage of services by a participant,

- *Security Interface* – for the authentication, access control and the single sign-on (one-time logon for different marketplace applications),

- *Directory Interface* – enables access to information on the marketplace participants,

- *Document Exchange Interface* – enables the exchange of documents between marketplace participants as well as

- *Tracking and Billing Interface* – enables billing of services made use of.

By means of the *MarketSet Platform*, external application systems for procurement (e.g., SAP Materials Management, SAP Enterprise Buyer Professional or an Oracle solution) as well as for sales (e.g., SAP Sales and Distribution and SAP Customer Relationship Management) and for planning (e.g., the SAP Advanced Planner & Optimizer or comparable solutions of i2) are integrated with the marketplace (see also Figure 6.2).

The platform fulfills the function of a router of business documents between marketplace-external and -internal systems. The component includes the areas Connectivity, Security and Management.

The *MarketSet Connector*, a middleware component that supports the secure exchange of business documents, is the central element of Connectivity. The connector enables the exchange of documents between the different services within the marketplace but also between the back-office systems of the marketplace participants and the marketplace. The documents available at first in proprietary (in-house) formats, such as purchase orders in the IDoc format (see chapter 3), are converted to the xCBL standard before they are transmitted to the marketplace (see also Figure 6.2). The MarketSet Connector extends the functions of the Business Connector described in chapter 3, which enables the communication of mySAP.com components with the marketplace, by adding an "XML Portal Connector" (XPC), by means of which also non-SAP systems can be connected to the marketplace.

For the communication not based on HTML, there is a special EDI interface as well as a corresponding translation service available.

Parts of the MarketSet Connector are:

- A framework for generating and transmitting XML documents,

- a Java-based mapping environment for converting from IDoc-XML to xCBL,

- the asynchronous and synchronous exchange of business documents between mySAP.com application components and the marketplace,

- security standards, for example, Secure Socket Layer (SSL),

- an administration console for the management and monitoring of the platform processes as well as

- options for extending document descriptions.

The *MarketSet Platform* supports two transfer types, HTTPS and SonicMQ, which both use the SSL procedure for securing the data exchange. The type of communication is defined within the connector. Provided that messages are to be routed to several drains, also different shipment types can be defined for a message.

A *portal router* controls the message flow between the end points of a connector, for example business partner or registered services, and the marketplace. All routing entries (sources and drains) are stored in an LDAP (Lightweight Directory Access Protocol) directory so that the router can forward the respective messages to exactly one connector. This is referred to as point-to-point routing. Upon arrival of a message, a corresponding service is triggered in accordance with the rules implemented within the connector.

A compatibility problem with the integration of market participants often results from the fact that their application systems use different coding numbers (IDs), for example material master data and vendor master data. For this reason, central master data records that do support a mapping of "non-standardized" IDs are maintained within the marketplace. The marketplace thus takes on the role of a conversion portal.

The mapping process includes two sub areas (see Figure 6.4):

- On the sender side, the data to be transferred is first subjected to mapping. This can involve the transformation of an IDoc document to an xCBL document, for example.

- Proprietary data fields are then, in connection with a special transformation service within the EM, transferred into a neutral format and passed on to the recipient of the message. The data fields to be "mapped" are defined within the MarketSet Connector.

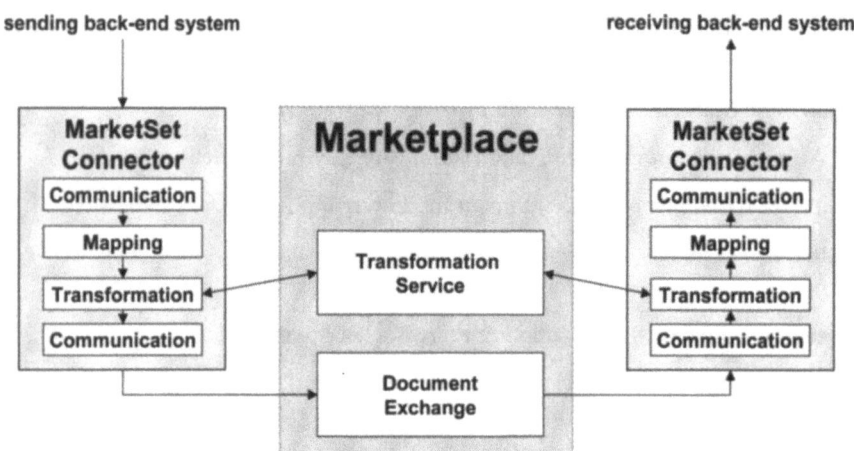

Figure 6.4: Transformation flow during the data exchange

MarketSet 2.0 supports two mapping methods:

- *Field value to Field value Mapping* – By means of the user interface, proprietary IDs are assigned to central marketplace IDs. Then, corresponding mapping entries are generated. The method is used to map customer IDs and products that cannot be assigned by rule.

- *Rule-based mapping* – Proprietary IDs are transmitted to the marketplace together with a number of key attributes, for example EADN numbers. Following a comparison with the central master data table of the EM, mapping entries are generated automatically. The method is applied particularly with the conversion of product identification numbers, since a large number of them exist and they quite often change over time (e.g., in cases where a product is replaced by its successor).

Example: Mapping-process between a purchasing and a selling company.

As the following figure shows, IDs are transformed when data is exchanged between a purchasing and a selling organization. Primary keys, which are kept in the marketplace in separate tables, are used in this case.

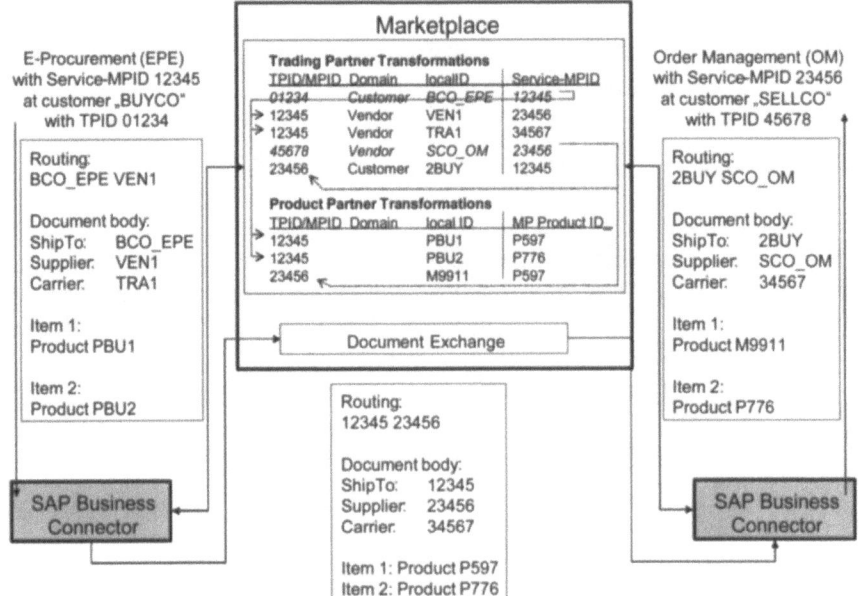

Figure 6.5: Data transformation and exchange

If a purchase order is generated within the purchasing application (the example uses the SAP application component Enterprise Buyer Professional, which will be discussed in more detail in section 6.2.2.1), the proprietary IDs of the involved business partners (Ven1⇒23456; Tra1⇒34567) must first be transformed into a neutral or marketplace-specific format. The purchase order data is correspondingly exchanged with these primary keys being used. On the recipient side (tpid 45678), these are set back to specific formats (of the recipient) (e.g., 12345⇒2BUY, 23456⇒SCO_OM) and can be viewed with the used order application (see section 6.2.2.2 for further details).

The support of certificates and encryption methods (such as *Triple DES*), for example, allow for security issues to be considered.

The MarketSet Platform Management includes

- an LDAP directory for the storage and retrieval of data,

- an archive database for archiving documents that are used for tracking within the settlement phase or for processes within service management during the after-sales phase,

- administration services, for example for controlling servers,

- an event management for monitoring databases, networks, application servers, Web servers, and other components, as well as

- the Tracking Event Collection Service, a value-added service that localizes and stores data of the documents needed for billing, for example, and transferred by means of the marketplace.

6.2.2   MarketSet Applications

The second component of the MarketSet – in addition to the MarketSet Infrastructure – are the MarketSet Applications. These are business application components that are hosted in the marketplace and support the marketplace participants in the various transaction phases. A selection of MarketSet application components are described below. These are (see Figure 6.2):

- MarketSet Procurement,

- MarketSet Order Management (order processing and sales and distribution),

- MarketSet Dynamic Pricing and Bidding (collaborative price negotiations, such as auctions, exchanges and reverse auctions),

- MarketSet Supply Chain Collaboration (collaborative planning of logistics processes),

- MarketSet Life-Cycle Collaboration (collaborative development of products),

- MarketSet Analytics (evaluation of business facts based on collaborative data management).

6.2.2.1   *MarketSet Procurement*

MarketSet Procurement (MSP) is an application that supports the procurement of goods and services in electronic marketplaces. The application component provides almost the entire functionality of the Enterprise Buyer Professional Edition (EBP), an independent SAP buy-side solution, and is positioned by SAP as an alternative for companies that do not have the required resources for the implementation of an own proprietary procurement solution (for instance, small and mid-sized companies) or refuse to do it due to a lacking procurement volume, for example.

MSP is based on EBP but was modified to enable the operation by one or several "hosted buying companies". Both applications have almost identical user interfaces. Figure 6.6 shows the view of the application in a Web browser.

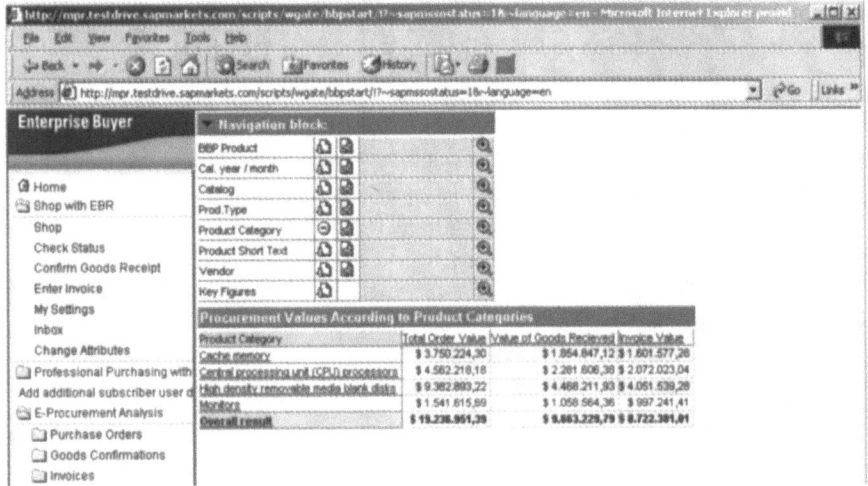

Figure 6.6: Enterprise Buyer Professional / MarketSet Procurement

Functional differences compared to EBP are basically due to the fact that the application within the marketplace communicates with the outside world (with external application systems) only in asynchronous mode. While for example in a classic setup (using an R/3 system and an EBP solution) a G/L account can be validated directly and online by calling a back-end system (e.g., SAP R/3 or Baan), such a check is usually implemented locally in the purchasing application in the case of operation on an EM and transferred to the back-end system only at a later point in time.

An essential prerequisite for the participation in marketplaces is the guarantee of data security. Generally, every company is therefore represented by an own client, that is, in terms of commercial law, an organizational and informational self-contained unit within the marketplace. This way, every company is assigned a self-contained area for its own master data and database tables.

On the one hand, the client concept still enables inter-company services, such as reporting across the datasets of the applications used by a company in the marketplace but, on the other hand, ensures a high data security for all involved companies in spite of a common database since the database system automatically assigns a client key to all business objects (e.g., purchase orders). This key ensures that only authorized users can access the data.

In addition, the marketplace software enables the consolidation of several companies within one client, which can result in reductions of the data processing costs for the participants regarding the procurement, for example, by sharing the master data (for instance, product data).

For both scenarios (exclusive usage of a client or client sharing), the procurement process can take place in two different ways: completely through EM or for parts.

In both cases, a download of account assignment data to the master data table of the procurement application in the marketplace is required.

In the case of a complete processing, the entire procurement process (see Figure 6.7) from the selection of the product(s) up to the financial reporting takes place in the "hosted" application in the marketplace. From a technical viewpoint, a financial accounting system, for example mySAP Financials, is necessary as back end, into which the invoice is transferred in xCBL format.

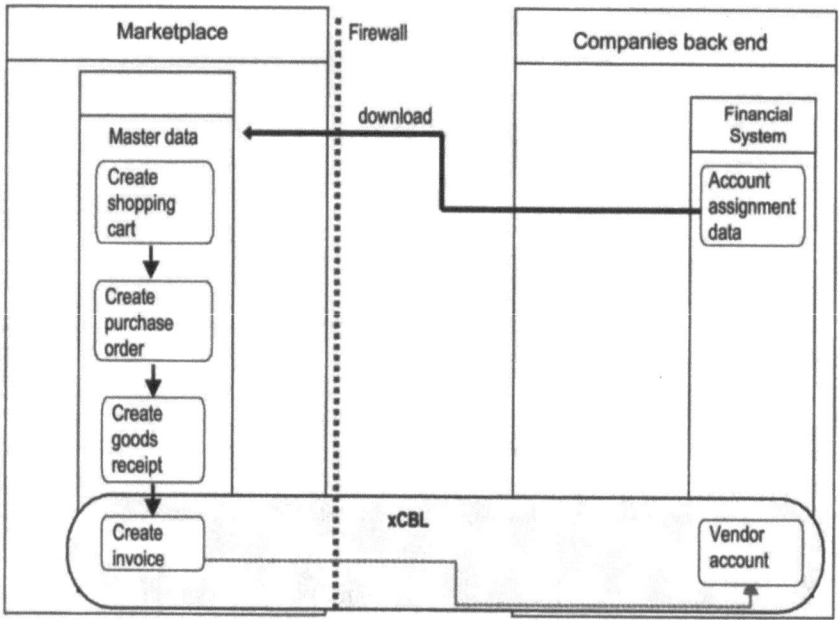

Figure 6.7: Entire procurement process takes place in the marketplace

The entire procurement process in MarketSet Procurement can be particularized by means of document flow outlined in Figure 6.7 and can include a total of seven sub steps from the point of view of the user, which are passed through one by one:

1. *Create shopping cart:* Products can be selected by means of a catalog or by directly entering the corresponding identification number, for example the product number. MarketSet Procurement provides different catalog functions which can be called from a current application using a special Java interface. The user can call complementary information on products or vendors at any time. A list of all items in the "shopping cart" is forwarded to trigger a purchase order or correspondingly flagged so that it can be processed again at later point in time. The system simultaneously checks whether the individual items or their purchase order require an approval and if so, which persons can grant them.

2. *Approve or reject shopping cart:* If no approval is necessary or it has been granted already, a follow-on document (e.g., a purchase order) is generated. Provided that no approval is granted, the sold-to party is informed through a predefined *workflow.*

3. *Check processing status:* The buyer can check the status of his purchase order (also with another processor).

4. *Transmit purchase order:* The purchase order is converted to xCBL format (see section 6.2.1) and sent to the vendors.

5. *Confirm goods receipt or performance of service:* The confirmation occurs upon receipt of the ordered goods and services. This can alternatively be done through a goods receiving department or – in the case of an externally operated warehouse – by means of a document of the business partner. After the update the sold-to party is informed automatically.

6. *Enter invoice:* Upon receipt and entry of the vendor invoice the system starts a workflow again, which places the document in the buyer's inbox for him to check.

7. *Approve invoice or service entry sheet*: The transmitted documents are checked by the buyer, who in the case of defects, for example, can block the payment from being made. In this case, the vendor is notified.

In case of "procurement in parts" the above described processes without goods receipt and invoice verification are carried out within the marketplace solution since these take place in the respective back-end system. This there assumes a materials management system in addition to a financial accounting component, for example, SAP R/3 Materials Management (MM), in which the goods receipts are updated. Figure 6.8 shows the document or data flow for the procurement without goods receipt and invoice verification.

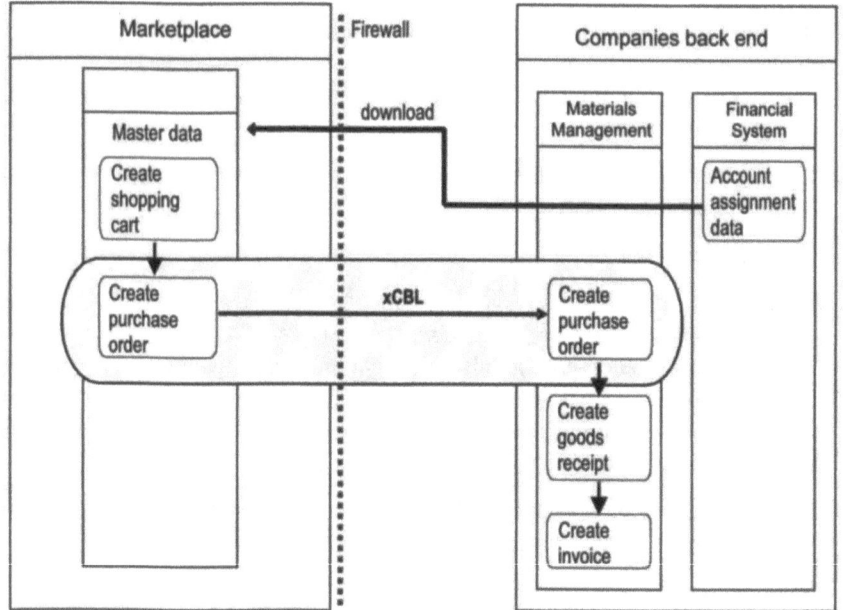

Figure 6.8: Procurement without goods receipt and invoice verification

MarketSet Procurement is currently used for example in the marketplaces Emaro and HUBWOO (see section 0).

6.2.2.2   *MarketSet Order Management*

MarketSet Order Management (MOM) stands for a Web-based application within the marketplace, which supports the sales of goods and services, the administration of material stocks, products and customers, the calculation of prices, the creation and processing of orders, the exchange of business documents with customers (e.g., order confirmations and shipping notifications) as well as financial reporting. It is thus the counterpart for the MarketSet Procurement application described in the previous section.

Prerequisite for using MOM in an EM is the registration of the supplier in a TPD (see section 6.2.1) as well as the *upload* of product and price master data into a Auto Catalog Publisher (ACP). Then, data can be transferred to the ACP by means of xCBL, Excel, Access or Notepad (CSV format), afterwards converted and transferred to the marketplace. To a large extent, MOM is based on structures of the SAP Customer Relationship Management solution. An own sales organization is assigned to every salesperson in the marketplace.

The focus of the application is the *user interface* (see section 6.2.1) which enables the access to all relevant functions of MOM through a browser. This includes:

- Order Management

- Inventory Management,

- Price Management,

- Customer Management,

- Shipping Notification Management and

- Invoice Management.

The *Order Management* includes functions for creating, selecting and changing orders, for supporting the exchange of order confirmations, for providing information on the order status as well as administrating documents. Orders are generated when a customer has created a purchase order in the purchasing application of the marketplace (see previous section) or of an external procurement system. The system generates an xCBL message that arrives in the MOM of the supplier through the marketplace. Since the order receipt is at first not known in the ERP system of the supplier, comparison processes must be specified:

- E-mail: The supplier defines an email address to which a message is sent upon receipt of new orders.

- Automatic notification: The notification can be sent directly (automatically) after order receipt or at defined times (periodically), for example every hour.

- Type of the automatic notification: A notification is sent either only in case of new orders or new and changed orders (a customer corrects delivery items, for example) as long as the user has not set the waiver of information.

- Automatic order acceptance: The system checks whether customer and supplier price match and the requested quantity can be covered by the warehouse stock. If both characteristics apply, the order is automatically accepted and a confirmation is transferred to the customer.

- Order confirmations can also be created manually.

The following figure shows an example for an accepted vendor order in the MOM application component of a supplier. The purchase order includes order number, date, customer name, customer ID and PO number. Status information, for example order status, delivery status (in this case, a delivery is planned) and the status of the invoicing, is additionally displayed (see top part of the screen). In addition to the purchase order data in a narrower sense (article number, name, quantity, and so forth) additional information, for example details of the business partner, can be viewed (see bottom part of the screen).

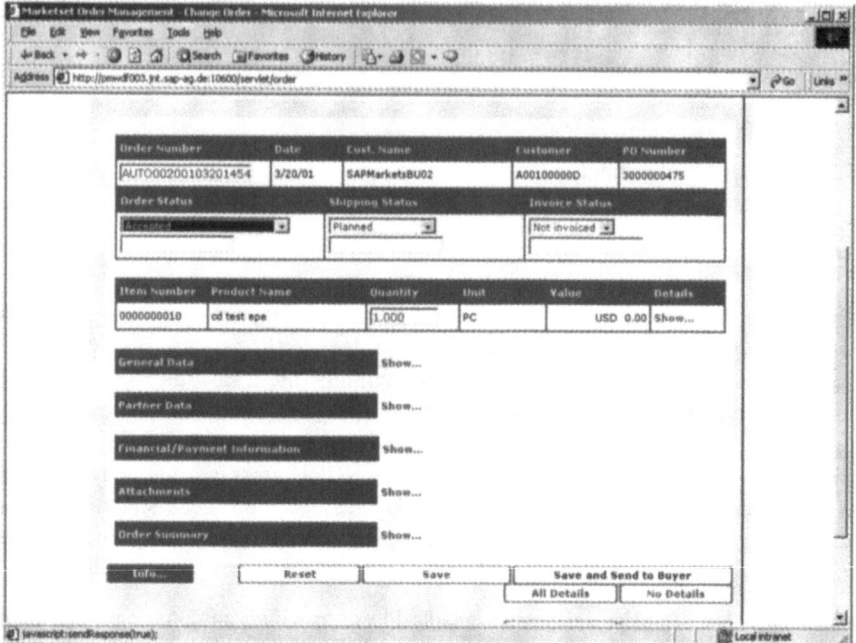

Figure 6.9: Sales order data

As soon as an order is accepted and the user saves the corresponding document, an automatic forwarding (order confirmation) to the respective customer occurs. The customer can then trigger queries regarding the order status using a special Web form.

Order changes on the part of the customer are logged thus enabling a monitoring of the order history at any time.

Within *Inventory Management* it is possible to query stocks also using operators such as "greater than" and "less than". Upon receipt of an order, three different forms of the warehouse stock check can be used:

- *No stock check*: Customers always receive an order confirmation, that is, any order quantity is automatically confirmed.

- *Stock check without quantity specification*: It is checked whether the requested quantity can be delivered but no notification regarding the warehouse stock occurs.

- *Availability check with quantity specification*: The customer receives a confirmation of the available quantity.

Within *Price Management*, list prices and customer-specific prices as well as surcharges and discounts can be determined, displayed and changed. These conditions are defined in the product master data. Prices can also be assigned to lists (such as standard prices and action lists, e.g. temporary special offers) or individually to business partners.

The system manages two price lists for every customer: list prices and cost prices. If prices are stored in both lists, the system automatically uses the list price. If no entries are found here, however, the system uses the cost price (standard price). Provided that individual lists are assigned to a customer, the prices specified there are preferred. Figure 6.10 shows an example for the definition of list prices for a "temporary" period (March 2001 through December 9999).

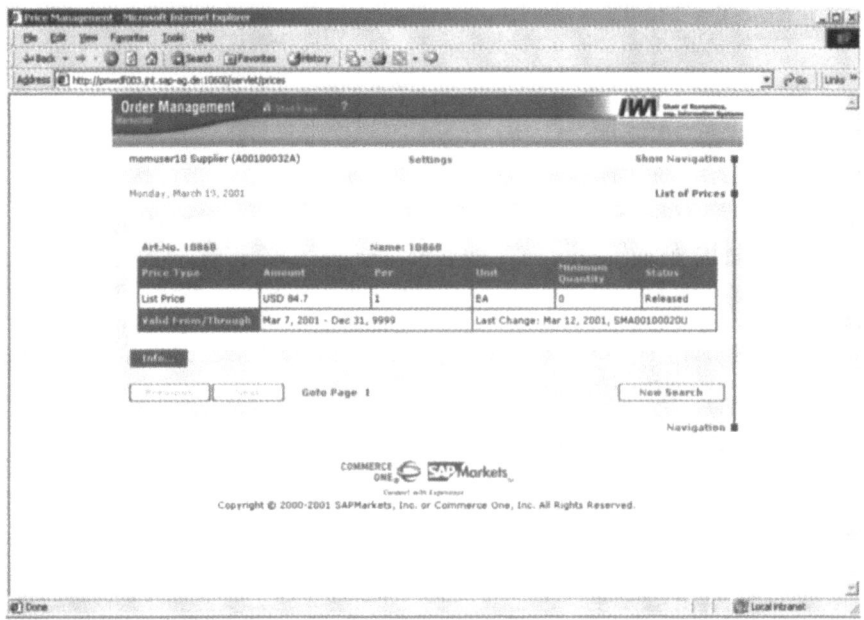

Figure 6.10: List prices

Customer Management is used for the administration of the marketplace customers. The available functions support the viewing of customer data, the updating (e.g., addresses or prices), and the creation of new as well as the deactivation of obsolete customers. The data of a customer includes customer number and name, information whether orders of a customer supposed to be accepted or rejected, possibly individual price lists as well as additional notes.

Invoice management is used for the creation and administration of invoices. Here invoices can either be generated directly from an order or manually. The invoice inquiry is supported by different functions, for example search according to document, status and date.

Shipping Notification Management includes functions for creating, selecting, changing and sending shipping notifications. Statistics on the number of the created shipping notifications are maintained within the system. A shipping notification is not transmitted automatically but upon special entry.

6.2.2.3   MarketSet Dynamic Pricing Engine

MarketSet Dynamic Pricing Engine (DPE) is another application component that through various services supports dynamic price negotiations between business partners within procurement processes. It is thus in opposition to the catalog-based services that are characterized by fixed prices. DPE includes the following areas:

- *Auctions Service*,

- *Request for Proposal and Request for Quotation*,

- *Exchange Service*, and

- *Classified Advertisement Service.*

Auctions are a mechanism frequently applied in practice for determining prices and thus for allocating resources. This is based on a rule set, in which for instance lowest bid and period are determined. In the Auction Service area, SAP supports two different auction procedures: the English-Forward (ascending-bid-auction) and the English-Reverse auction (referred to as Dutch auction in literature (descending-bid-auction)).

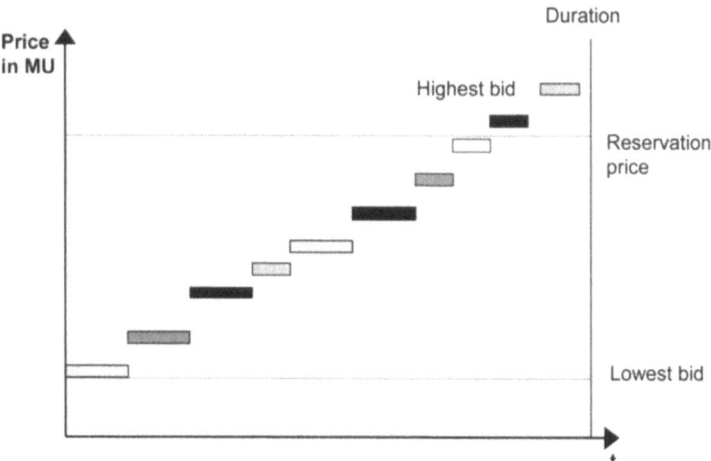

Figure 6.11: English-Forward auction

In case of an English-Forward auction, the supplier of a product must first determine a lowest bid price. With an increasing number of bids (the respectively last bid is transparent), the price is increased step-by-step (according to previously determined minimum intervals), in case of which an also predefined reservation price is to be exceeded. Above this limit, the bid of the customer with the highest bid is accepted upon expiry of the auction runtime (see Figure 6.11).

Figure 6.12: English-Reverse auction

In case of a Dutch auction, the supplier of a product specifies a maximally high initial price (start price) that is reduced according to determined criteria of the auctioneer until a customer accepts it (through his bid) (see Figure 6.12). The auction also terminates if the price drops below the minimum price required by the supplier.

Using the services *Request for Proposal (RFP)* and *Request for Quotation (RFQ)*, a customer can simultaneously invite bids for the demand for different goods or services respectively. This involves contracts that can contain one or several goods in a specific package. At first a RFQ, thus a call for the submission of bids, must be generated and be published with the necessary technical specifications of the procurement articles for all external suppliers of the contract. All incoming bids converge in a central point in the marketplace and can therefore be easily compared with one another. Figure 6.13 shows the corresponding data flow using an example:

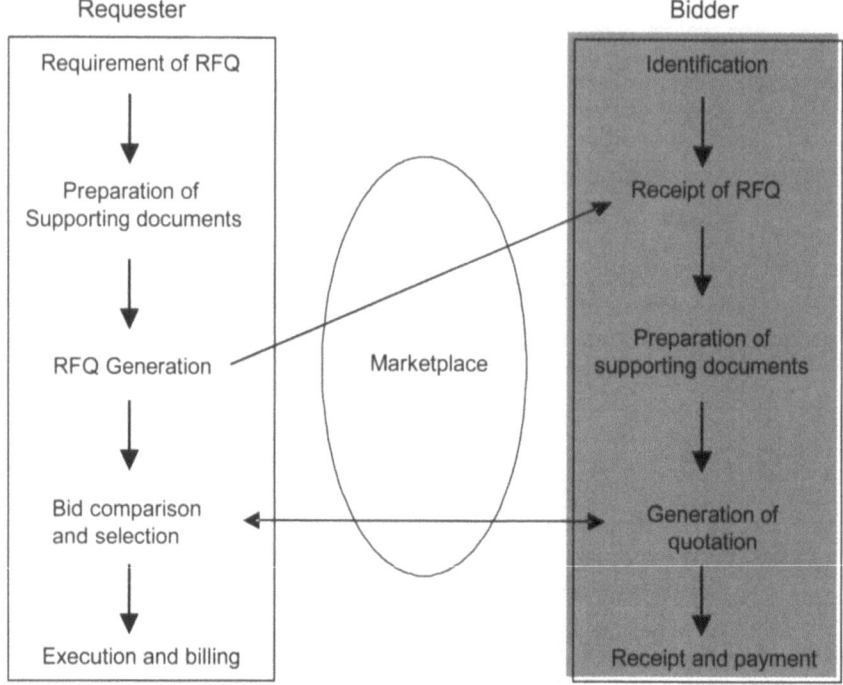

Figure 6.13: RFQ process

1. The RFQ can be generated in the back-end system of the customer or directly in the marketplace, that is, by using the corresponding service available there. It is additionally possible to generate the RFQ directly from an APO application, for example, when it identifies a raw material shortfall quantity.

2. RFQs are published in the marketplace, for example, for a limited number of possible vendors. These are informed about the publication of the RFQ.

3. The bidders generate offers (either by using corresponding marketplace services or from an own back-end system), and send them to the marketplace that, depending on the rule set, either displays the currently best offer or collects all bids until the opening and prevents unauthorized person from viewing the data.

4. The customer views the bids and, if necessary, requests additional information, before he accepts the best offer.

5. The execution and billing as well as the update of the incoming payment are carried out in the back-end systems of the RFQ requester and the bidder.

SAP refers to the scenarios realized by means of Auction Service and RFQ as Collaborative Procurement. Examples can be found in our SupplyOn case study in Section 7.5.

The term *Exchange Service* stands for a market exchange functionality that supports trading activities between several customers and suppliers. They must first communicate their willingness to sell und buy to the EM. The meeting of supply and demand is controlled via a central service that also considers subsets. The order resulting from the *matching* can be stored within the marketplace or transferred directly to involved back-end systems.

Table 6.1 classifies the described services according to customer/vendor relationship:

Table 6.1: Services and supported business relationships

Type of DPE service	Type of business relationship
Auction Service	One supplier – several customers (1: n)
RFQ/RFP Reverse Auction	One supplier – several customers (1: n)
Exchange Service	Several suppliers – several customers (n : n)

The *Classified Advertisement Service (Classifieds)* designates a further DPE service that can be compared with classified advertisements or bulletin board. Classifieds are used only for establishing contacts and are summarized in various categories within the EM. They are suitable for standardized products in particular. No legal obligation is involved in listing goods and services.

The outlined services can be individually configured by the respective initiator, for example for a certain product. SAP refers to this as Business Opportunities. A Business Opportunity is made up of four characteristics:

- *Rules* aim at a *Multi Parameter Matching*. This is applied, for example, in cases where during an auction or bid invitation the determination of the "winner" also depends on other factors than just the best price bid (e.g., the dependability of a business partner). Rules are defined in a special administration console.

- *Attributes* describe offered goods and services.

- Through a *classification, opportunities* are categorized, for example, by industry, country and price.

- The currency system is specified through the parameter *Currency*.

A BizTracker is the central entry point of all DPE services (see Figure 6.14). It is used, on the one hand, for the initiation of a service (e.g., an auction) and, on the other hand, for viewing information (e.g., individual bids and the bidding process types). Information is in this case grouped together to different categories (listings, opportunities, participations, invitations und messages). The BizTracker logs all transactions between business partners and, if necessary, sends messages to them.

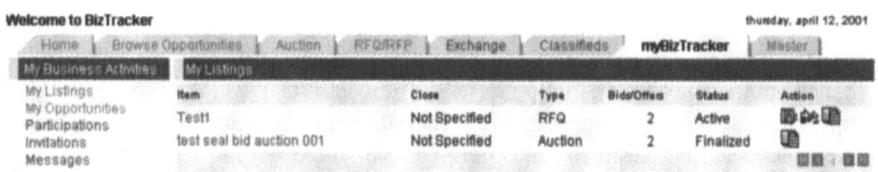

Figure 6.14: BizTracker

DPE is completely implemented in Java. The data exchange through the Internet is realized by means of XML documents that use the HTTP log and Secure Socket Layer.

6.2.2.4   *MarketSet Supply Chain Collaboration*

Supply Chain Collaboration (SCC) designates special functions that support collaborative planning and the exchange of data required for this. It is target of the application to integrate data relevant for planning, for instance, in form of a common demand planning of manufacturer and customer or a common planning of manufacturer and vendor.

The components of MarketSet Supply Chain Collaboration include:

- *Internet-based Planning Books* that are viewed by business partners and used for exchanging data, such as sales forecasts, shipping planning or marketing activities. These planning books can display data on different planning areas (e.g., products, plants (locations)) or business partners in an aggregated and disaggregated way. The method of the multidimensional data management described in chapter 4 serves as the basis for this.

- An *alert monitor* informing the collaboration partner about exceptional situations.

- A *workflow* controlling the exchange of data or plan books by means of especially defined processes and process structures. The specification of the processes is made by means of a Collaborative Planning Workflow Template.

- *Macros*, with the help of which planning tasks can be carried out automatically. It is thus possible to carry out analyses, for example, directly upon receiving new data records, the results of which are then updated in the corresponding planning books without delay.

MarketSet Supply Chain Collaboration within inter-organizational collaborations supports a number of scenarios provided through functions of APO that are hosted within the marketplace. This includes:

- *Supplier Collaboration,*

- *Internet-Enabled Consensus-Based Forecasting,*

- *Vendor-Managed Inventory* as well as

- *CPFR Compliant Collaborative Forecasting.*

The function Supplier Collaboration supports the earliest possible exchange of planning data, for example demand information and production quantities (based on xCBL). The planning horizon is medium to long-term.

The scenario Internet-Enabled Consensus-Based Forecasting supports the planning of collaborative business targets, for example, the common demand planning of products over several levels of a supply chain (see chapter 5). The individual forecasts of the companies are in this case aggregated in central planning books within the marketplace. These can be viewed and modified by authorized persons any time. In addition, a further processing of the data is possible in Microsoft Excel.

Internet-Enabled Vendor-Managed Inventory (VMI) designates a scenario, in which vendors manage the demands of their customers, for example, of one production location. The inventory quantities can be continuously monitored by viewing the planning books so that stockpiling can be limited in view of an improved estimate of the actual consumption.

Example: Vendor-Managed Inventory

1)   The inventory data maintained in ERP systems for the customer is often the basis of the VMI. Within the R/3 system, it can be found in the Inventory Management (IM) and the Logistics Execution System (LES), for example. In case of the Internet-Enabled Vendor-Managed Inventory, the stock situation is passed on to the Business Connector in form of series of consumption values (Time Series) and from there is transferred to the marketplace (see Figure 6.15). It is additionaly possible to import EDI data by means of a special EDI interface of the MarketSet Connector. In this case it is an EDI enabled VMI.

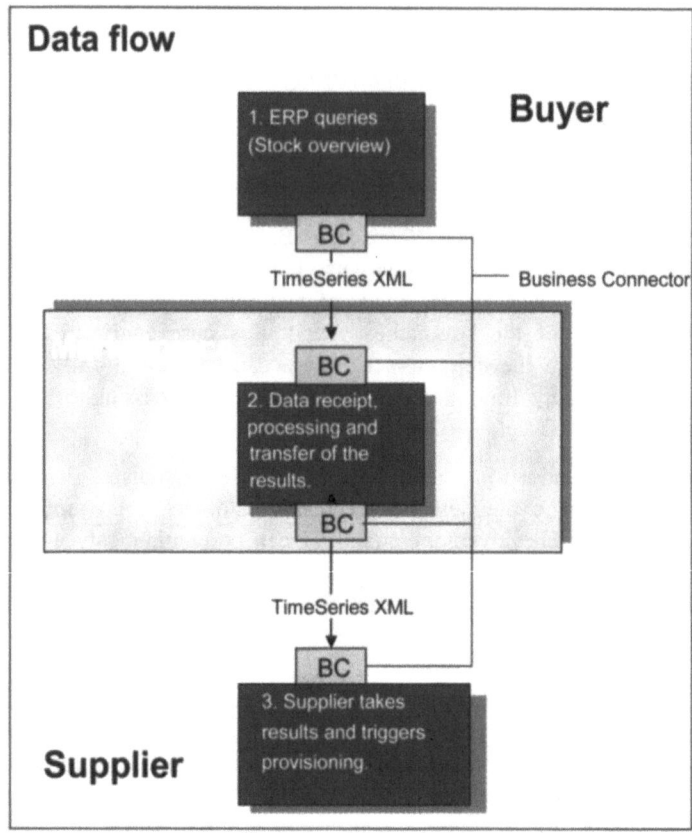

Figure 6.15: Data flow between buyers and supplier in the VMI

2) Figure 6.16In addition to the stock data, requirement information following
    from the order volume of the customer is transferred. On this basis, min/max
    price calculations (see Figure 6.16) are carried out for different consumption
    periods, the results are displayed (for individual articles) in an accessible way
    for the suppliers.

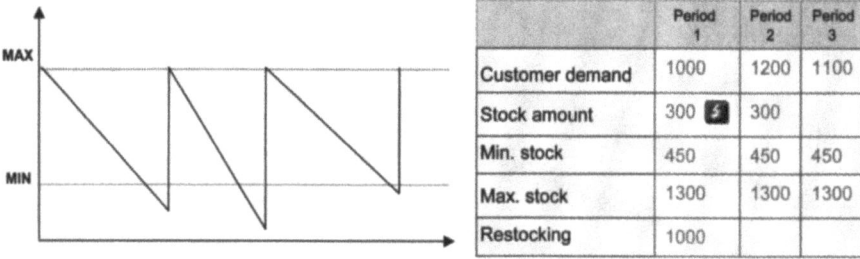

	Period 1	Period 2	Period 3
Customer demand	1000	1200	1100
Stock amount	300 ⚡	300	
Min. stock	450	450	450
Max. stock	1300	1300	1300
Restocking	1000		

Figure 6.16: Calculation of the replenishment quantity

3) The supplier takes the data from the planning book and triggers the stockpiling.

Collaborative Planning, Forecasting and Replenishment (CPFR) is a cross-industry business scenario for optimizing collaborative planning processes based on transparent information between the participants of a supply chain (prior vendors, manufacturers and customer (e.g., retail companies)). Additional uplifts are expected when creating common business plans, improving the event and promotion planning and the associated corrected goods availability. Cost reductions can be achieved by an improved forecast accuracy, resulting in the stocks being optimized at all levels of the supply chain and production, warehouses and transport capacities being better exploited. The MarketSet CPFR scenario consists of two areas (see Figure 6.17),

- *Collaborative Demand Planning* and

- *Collaborative Supply Planning.*

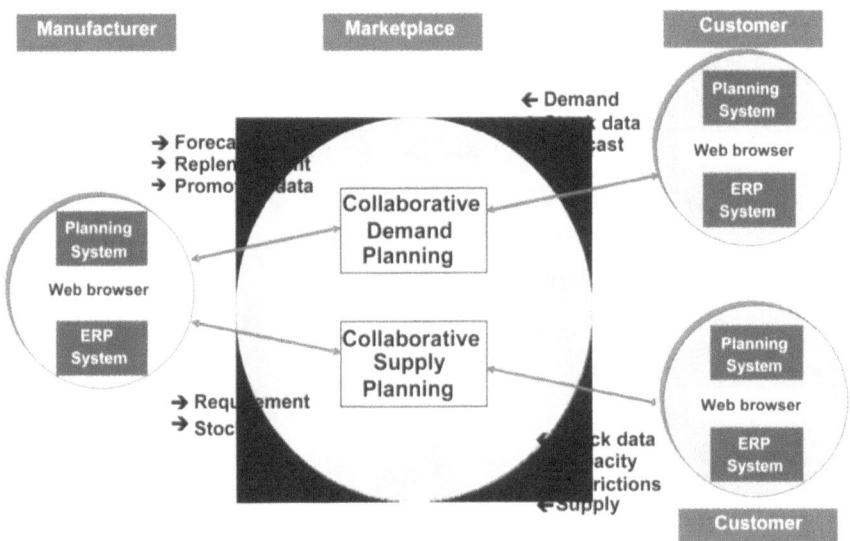

Figure 6.17: CPFR scenario

In the first case, customer and manufacturer generate collaborative forecasting that can be configured and updated via the Internet. The basis for this is, as Figure 6.17 shows, the comparison of actual and expected demand, promotion and stock data. The exchange, controlled by means of a corresponding workflow, takes place automatically (see Figure 6.18).

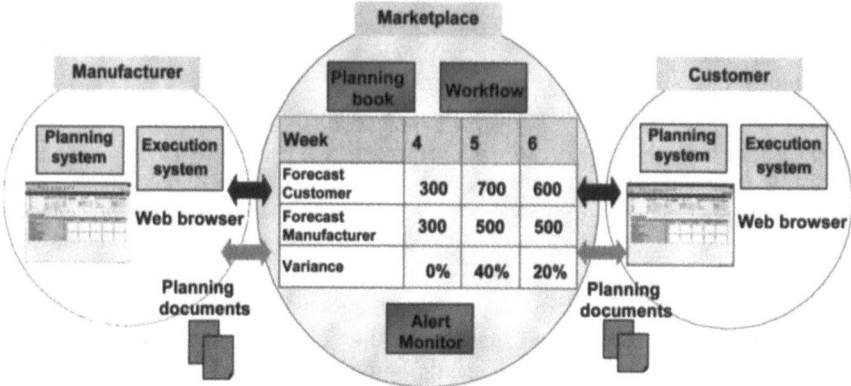

Figure 6.18: Collaborative Demand Planning

To ensure the ability to deliver of the manufacturer, his requirements are brought in line with the possibilities of his supplier in a second step. In this case as well a comparison of necessary consumption data is made. Figure 6.19 illustrates these facts showing an example of three periods. Percentage variances, that are correspondingly reflected in a new plan, are displayed.

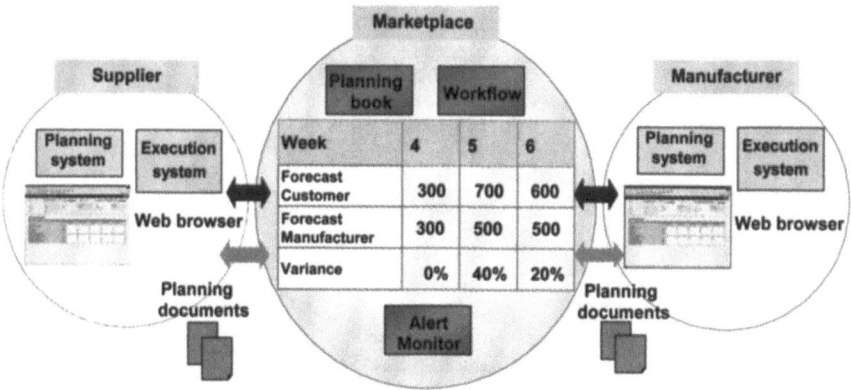

Figure 6.19: Collaborative Supply Planning

As the examples show, the CPFR concept can be understood as a link between continuous replenishment programs and vendor-managed inventory relationships. Retrieving promotion, point-of-sales, and stock data are necessary prerequisites.

In practice, these scenarios often fail because many actors of the network are not willing to provide the required data or to locally implement solutions that are favorable from the viewpoint of a central optimization since they fear an impairment of their individual competitive environment.

To increase the willingness to supply the business partners with data, access authorizations can be granted only for certain data so that sensitive information does not have to be revealed.

SAP supports the update of planning books and/or the exchange of planning documents by providing two methods, the manual and the automatic data transfer:

- Automatic data transfer: Data is converted to xCBL documents and sent to the marketplace or the contained planning book.

- Manual data transfer: Data changes are triggered by the respective user via the user interface. This method lends itself particularly to such companies or collaboration partners that do not have the facilities for an automated exchange of documents.

Unlike the SAP Supply Chain Management solution, the Supply Chain Collaboration application component integrated into MarketSet does not have functions for production planning and controlling or functions that support the logistics execution (*execution* und *fulfillment*). By using the xCBL standard, in principle both mySAP.com applications and non-SAP back-end systems can communicate with the marketplace.

6.2.2.5 *MarketSet Life-Cycle Collaboration*

While so far logistics processes, for example procurement and order processing, were the focus of our discussions, we now describe an application component for the support of collaborative development projects. The center of product development is the computer-aided design (CAD). The objective here is, for example, to accelerate the market launch of products and to limit the costs associated with it.

The exchange and the provision of data within collaborative projects, for example product specifications, technical drawings and CAD data are often hampered due to decentralized structures. By means of a centralization of information in an EM, MarketSet Life-Cycle Collaboration tries to counter this problem. For this purpose, the application provides various function modules allowing project partners to jointly manage and exchange information through Web-based front ends. This includes:

- *Secure Document Management System (SDMS),*

- *Offline Processing of Collaboration Documents* as well as

- *WebFlow: The Workflow Engine.*

The Secure Document Management System is a special document management system (DMS) within the marketplace for the central storage and administration of documents. In general, DMS are used to find stored documents, documents entered by means of a scanner and in particular also drawings by using descriptors. Documents belonging to the same context are grouped together to an electronic workflow folder, the document folder. Development partners can jointly create and use a document folder (*Data Vault*).

The individual documents are often processed offline in the CAD systems of the individual companies. Drawings or geometric data saved on the computer or the product bill of material are the result of the CAD procedure. Figure 6.20 shows a sample CAD drawing in the Microsoft Internet Explorer.

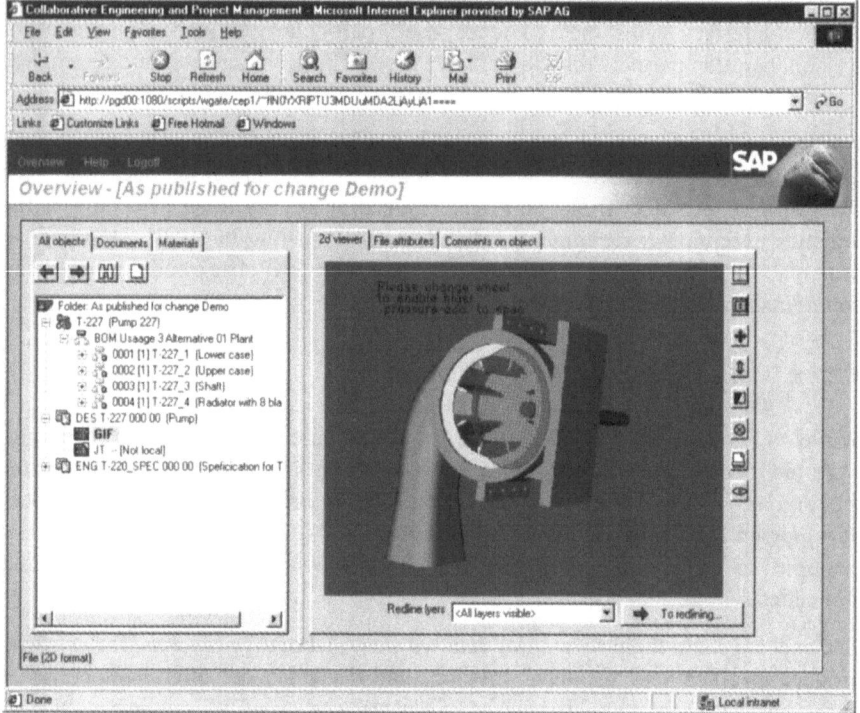

Figure 6.20: Representation of a CAD drawing

MarketSet contains a special tool for displaying two- and three-dimensional CAD drawings, which supports 24 different formats, for example AutoCAD, IGES and BMP.

With the exchange of documents between an internal application system and the marketplace, the documents to be transferred are replicated. The system saves the original file "sealed" within the central database to be able to understand modifications made by a development partner and thus the process of the product development at any time. A version control logs all changes made to a document. The locating of documents is supported by the maintenance of meta data and the associated option for drill-down reporting, for example the entry of key terms, names and document classes. A full-text retrieval is additionally possible.

Figure 6.21 illustrates the search for documents using a simple example:

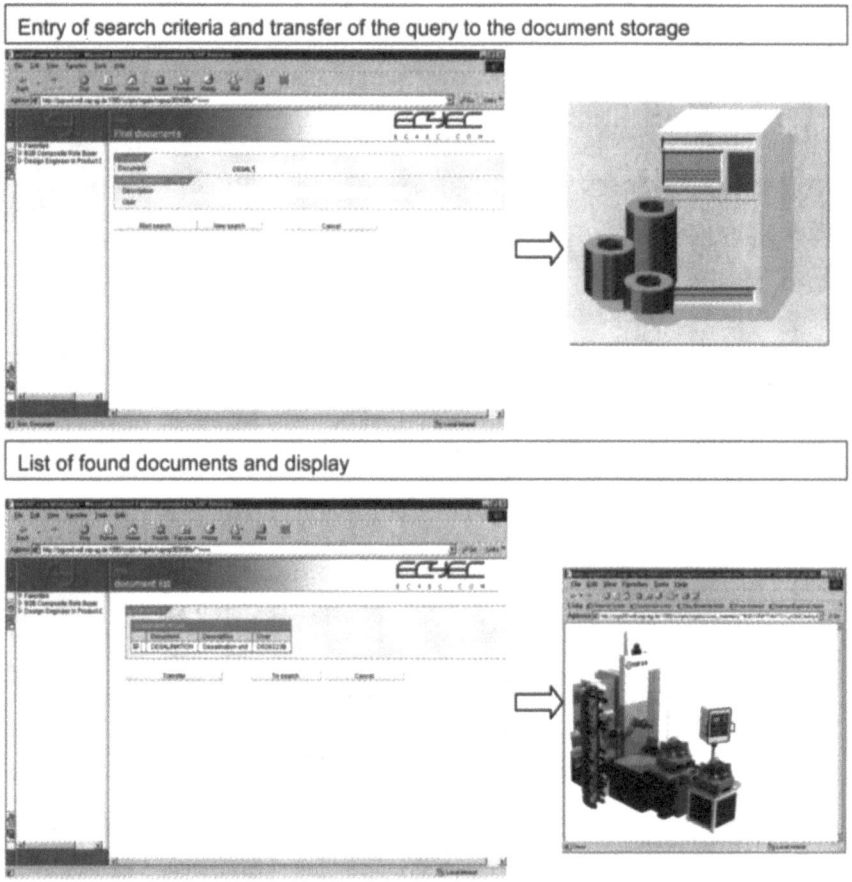

Figure 6.21: Document search and display

Once the search terms have been entered in a special search template (see top left part of screen), relevant documents are searched for in the central data store of the marketplace. The results are displayed in lists (see bottom left part of screen), from which the required documents, for example CAD drawings, are called directly.

The SAP WebFlow is a further element used for controlling the document flow. Necessary process structures are specified using a *Workflow Engine*. Furthermore, several interfaces to other MarketSet applications, for example EBP and DPE, are available. This allows the triggering of engineering-related RFQs and/or the participation in such. This method is being used since November 2000 on the EM ec4ec (e-commerce for engineered components).

Example ec4ec:

ec4ec is an open EM for the mechanical and plant engineering and construction that supports the engineering and procurement process of engineers, buyers and suppliers. The focus here is procurement management of non-standardized, coordination-intense components and services. The EM supports a special bid invitation process referred to as RFI (*Request for Information*) by SAP.

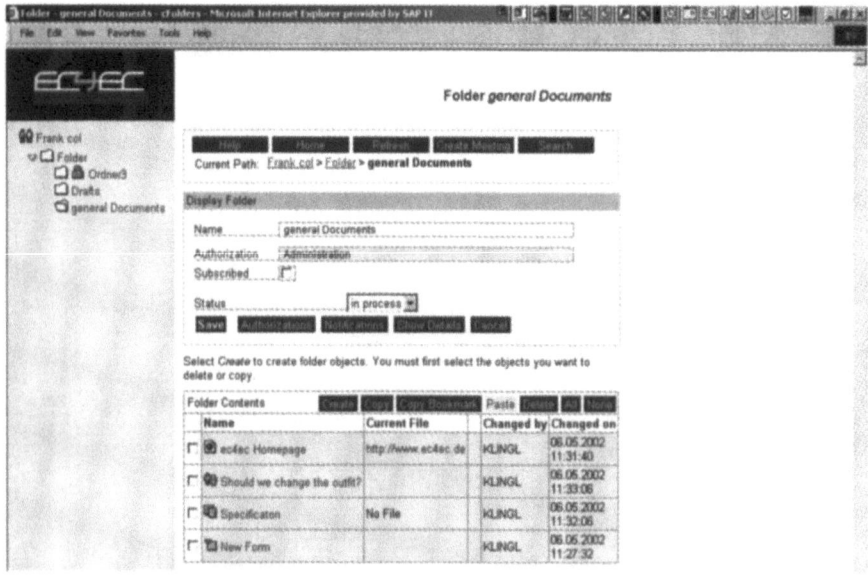

Figure 6.22: Document management on ec4ec

Consumer documents, for example product specifications, are stored within the EM in special folders (see Figure 6.22). These include standardized structures for documents and data that suppliers are to take into account with bids, provided access authorizations are granted. The initiator of a RFI first enters necessary specifications in the DMS of the EM. Then component suppliers enter quotations in the DMS that can be associated with design drawings and specification changes. According to ec4ec, in practice several iterative steps, in which specifications and design are modified, are performed prior to the end of a bid invitation. Then the component suppliers, whose quotations are accepted, are contacted.

Furthermore, the ec4ec enables central project documentation, which is particularly important for large projects with distributed actors.

6.2.2.6   MarketSet Analytics

MarketSet Analytics is a special business intelligence solution (see chapter 4), whose basis is a Business Information Warehouse operated within the marketplace.

Operators of an EM can use MarketSet Analytics to analyze the behavior of the participants, for example *click streams* and document flows. This is particularly important with transaction-oriented revenue models, for which the costs of the participation depends directly on the number of executed function. Various standard queries, that are included in the *Business Content*, are available for analyzing document flows. This includes:

- Number of sent documents (by service, document class, sender, recipient, date),

- number of received documents (by service, document class, sender, recipient, date),

- trend analyses of the sent/received documents for each business relationship in a period and

- trend analyses of the sent/received documents by document class in a period.

The following figure shows a sample trend analysis of the documents sent through an EM in a certain time interval.

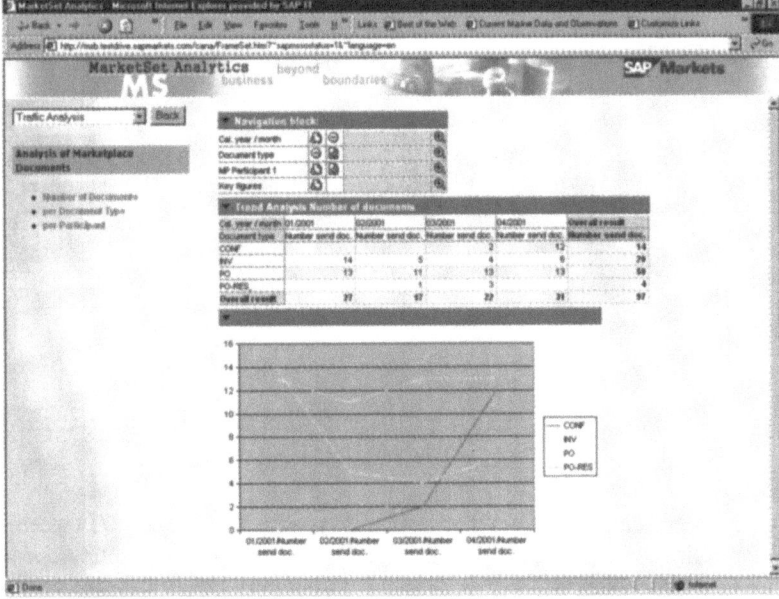

Figure 6.23: Trend analysis of sent documents by participant and month

The participants in an EM can use MarketSet Analytics, on the other hand, for the analysis of operative and strategic processes, for example from the areas e-procurement, e-selling and dynamic pricing. Various predefined information models are available due to a Business Content geared towards the application components used within a marketplace (see chapter 4).

Different front ends, for example an especially set up BI Cockpit (see chapter 4), can be used to call up a query. It is additionally possible to view queries using the front end of the source application, such as EBP.

Below follow some sample analyses from the area e-procurement that are triggered and viewed using EBP. SAP supports the analysis of expenses, suppliers, contracts and orders in the area of Internet-supported procurement.

Purchase orders, received goods and services, order confirmations, or invoices can be analyzed by cost centers within an expense analysis.

A further standard analysis supports marketplace participants with the selection of suppliers.

Central influence parameters are historical price and quantity variances as well as deliveries not received on time. Contract Management ties in with this and allows further analyses with regard to the renewal or extension of contracts with different business partners.

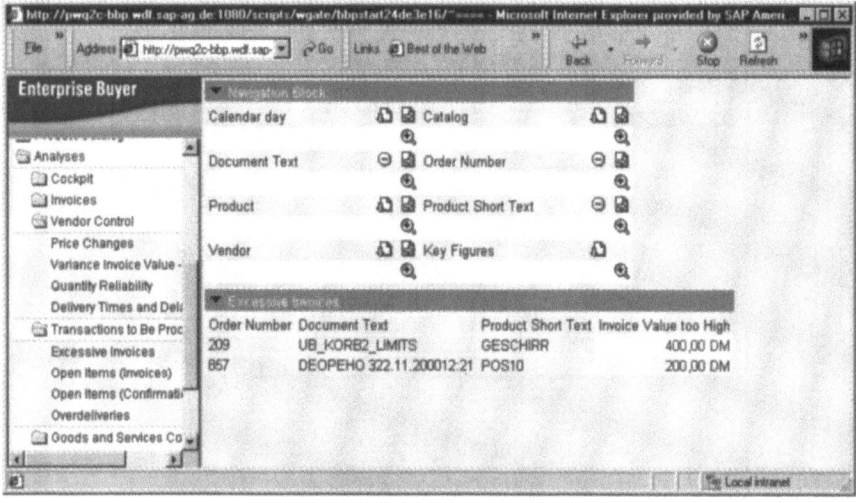

Figure 6.24: Order analysis

The analysis of purchase orders that can be initiated both from an R/3 system and an EBP application component, is the central instrument for controlling operative procurement processes. MarketSet Analytics therefore supports different views, for example the analysis of purchase orders, confirmations, product and cost center accounting, outstanding orders and invoices, late deliveries, lead times as well as price and quantity variances. Figure 6.24 shows the analysis of an order at document level.

6.3 Electronic Marketplaces based on mySAP Exchanges: An Overview

Finally, the following table lists EM, which are operated on the basis of SAP technologies and systems.

Table 6.2: Electronic marketplaces based on SAP technologies and systems

Name of the marketplace	Type Line of industry	Traded goods	Used SAP applications	Operator
Jet2Web Bizmarket http://www.bizmarket.at	horizontal neutral	Office equipment, electronic goods, industrial services and means of transport	mySAP.com marketplace	
CorProcure http://www.corprocure.com.au	horizontal neutral	Office equipment, electricity, MRO	Hosted BuySide Supply Order Auction Services Requisite Bugseye	14 of the 100 largest companies of Australia, including for example Australia Post
Emaro http://www.emaro.de	Horizontal neutral	Office equipment, Telecommunications, IT and industry supplies	MS Procurement	SAP
Enporion http://www.enporion.com	vertical Energy	Gas, electricity	MOE 4.1 (MSB and MSP) MS Procurement MS Order Management Content Engine	Allegheny Energy Inc., ALLETTE's, Ameren Corporation, CMS Energy Corporation, Key Span, PPL Corp., UGI Corporation
HUBWOO http://www.hubwoo.com	horizontal neutral	MRO	MS Procurement	
Quadrem http://www.quadrem.com	vertical Mining	Minerals, metals	MS Procurement Supply Order BW 2.0B	21 of the worldwide leading mining companies, such as Alcan Ltd., Newmont Mining Corp., Rio Tinto
SupplyOn http://www.supplyon.com	vertical	System parts, modules and others	Dynamic Pricing Engine	Bosch, Continental, INA, ZF Friedrichshafen, SAP, Siemens
ec4ec (e-commerce for engineered components http://www.ec4ec.de	vertical Mechanical and plant engineering and construction	non-standardized, coordination-intense components and services,	LCC (EBP/DAB)	(Joint Venture Partner): Babcock Borsig AG, mg technologies ag, VA Technologie AG, SAP AG, Deutsche Bank AG

As the above list of the various EM based on SAP technologies reveals, mainly solutions for supporting procurement processes, in particular MarketSet Procurement, are so far being used, while supply chain management solutions are missing altogether.

Chapter 7 Case Studies from the Automotive Industry

This chapter describes the use of mySAP solutions for the support of supply chain management with the help of five case studies from the automotive industry. The automotive industry has for a long time been molded by an intense cooperation between producers and vendors as well as logistics services providers. Examples for that are already mentioned concepts such as JIT production and vendor-managed inventory. In addition, cooperation between the various suppliers exists when they join forces to form a development partnership in order to play the role of a large system provider. Also manufacturers cooperate, for example, when Porsche buys gear boxes from DaimlerChrysler or vehicles are developed collectively.

In the automotive industry, IT support of business processes has progressed relatively far. However, on a cross-company level one can still observe that this applies in particular to the manufacturers as well as large suppliers while in small and mid-sized companies a lot of these processes are still being carried out manually. Thus only two to three percent of the customers of Goodyear transmit their purchase orders using EDI, for example. These customers are basically the large automotive companies. On the other hand, smaller customers such as supermarkets and service stations, order the tires using a call center or via fax.

The case studies presented below are used to give an impression of the possible use scenarios of SAP solutions in supply chains. The analysis will be carried out from different perspectives: first, the cooperation between DaimlerChrysler and Schenker AG for managing a supply chain for the overseas production of the A-Class and C-Class models. The electronic document exchange using EDI is the focus here. The use of mySAP Supply Chain Management solutions, in particular APO, is described within the framework of the case studies for the suppliers Bosch and Goodyear as well as the manufacturer Porsche. Finally, the status quo as well as potentials of electronic marketplaces will be highlighted using SupplyOn.

7.1   Schenker Case Study: Management of a Supply Chain for Automobile Manufacturing Overseas

Schenker AG is a leading international provider of integrated logistics and shipping services. The company, located in Essen, Germany and part of Stinnes Corporation, has approximately 29,000 employees at almost 1,000 locations. Land transport, air, and sea freight as well as global supply chain management, which will be examined in more detail within this case study, belong to the service range of Schenker AG. Schenker uses the supply chain management to provide potential customers with various system services that consist of components that can be combined in a flexible manner. A focal point of these services is the development and provision of complex IT solutions.

7.1.1   Management of a Supply Chain for Automobile Manufacturing Overseas – Status Quo

7.1.1.1   Overview of the Case Study

This case study is concerned with the management of a supply chain for the production of the A-Class and C-Class model by Mercedes-Benz in Brazil. The factory in Juiz de Fora ensures the supply to the South American markets. Schenker AG undertakes a large part of the organization, structuring, and monitoring of the information and goods flows accompanying the supply chain that ranges from Europe to South America. Figure 7.1 provides a simplified representation of this process.

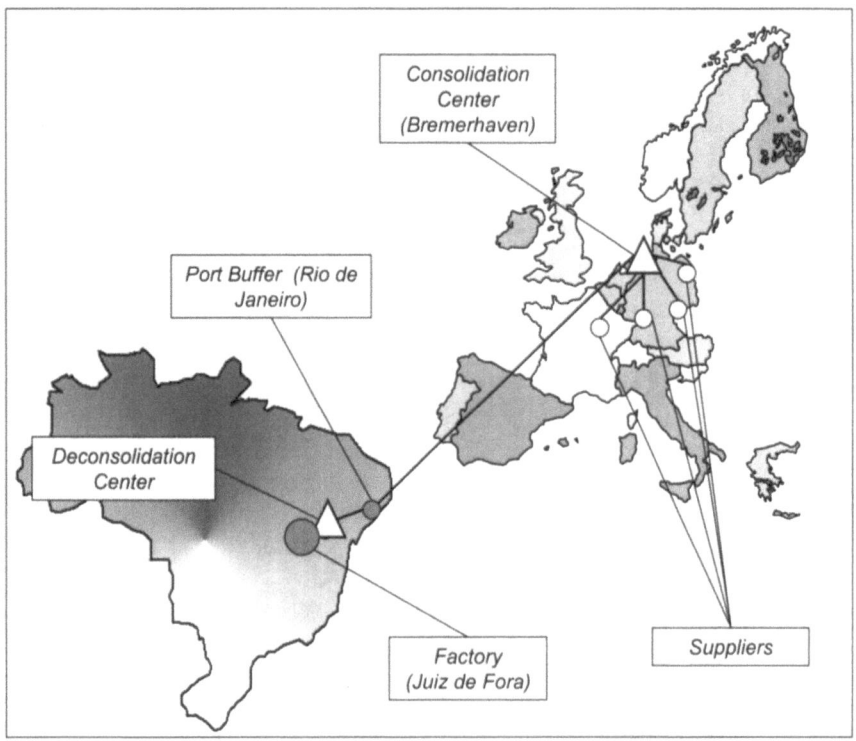

Figure 7.1: Geographical overview of the complete supply chain

Some material requirements for the production in Brazil are the triggering event for activities in the supply chain. Suppliers initially deliver this material to a Consolidation Center (CC) in Bremerhaven (Germany). This CC is a concentration point for goods and information to which specific parts are supplied for the overseas transport to Brazil. They are then packed, placed in containers, and shipped to South America. In exceptional cases, aircrafts are used for the transport. When the parts arrive in Brazil, they are delivered to the Deconsolidation Center (DC). This can be considered as being the opposite pole to the CC in Bremerhaven. The DC has the function of a dissolution point in which the delivered containers are received and unpacked, and customs duties are paid for materials and parts. From there, they are supplied to the factory just-in-time. The DC has the task to provide the consolidated material in the immediate vicinity of the *"point of use"* for the assembly or the production of the customer. Schenker operates the CC in Bremerhaven and the DC in Juiz de Fora.

The following section describes both the physical and informational logistics-related infrastructures as well as the activities and processes within and between the participating companies in the supply chain. The description is based on the four areas distinguished in Figure 7.2.

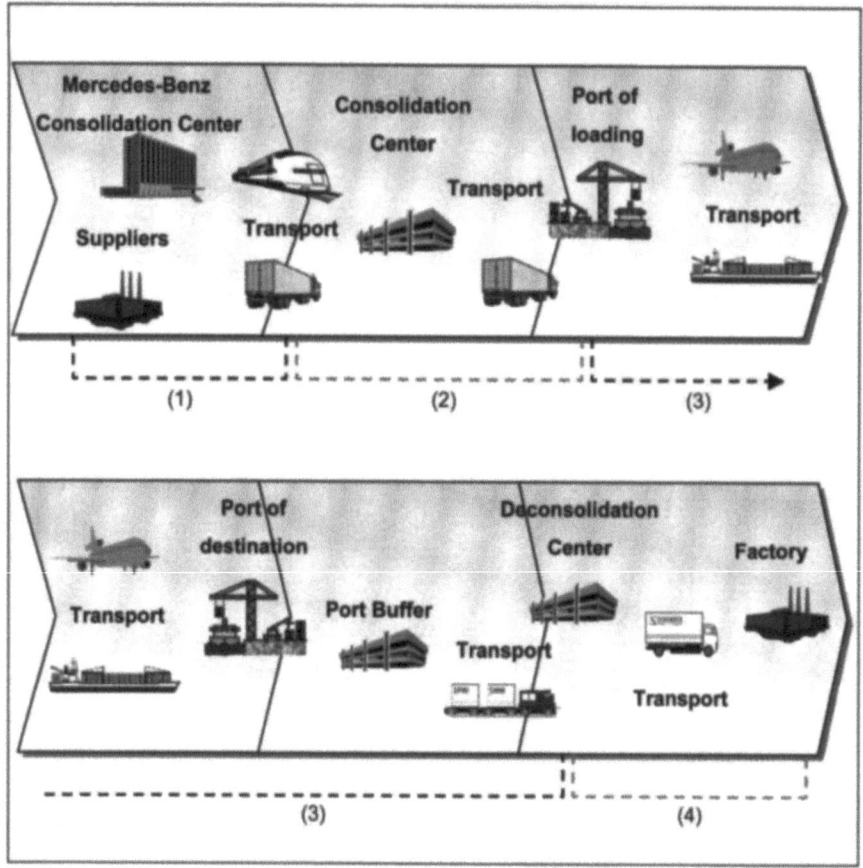

Figure 7.2: Material flow from Europe to South America

Whereas the first considered area covers orders to the supplier through to the receipt of the goods in the CC, area two contains all necessary activities and services through to the loading of the parts for the overseas transport at the port of loading. These two subareas represent the European part of the supply chain.

The physical loading in the port starts area three, and covers all required processes until the parts arrive at the DC in Brazil. Area four follows with the delivery to the factory for the A-Class and C-Class in Brazil. These last two subareas describe the South-American view of the supply chain.

7.1.1.2   *Management of the Processes to Supply the Consolidation Center in Bremerhaven*

The starting point for all activities accompanying the considered supply chain is the Mercedes-Benz (MB) factory in Brazil, which passes its requirements for the production to a Mercedes-Benz Consolidation Center (MBCC) located in the town

Böblingen near Stuttgart (Germany). The first task of this MBCC is to collect, monitor, and further process all the data required for the process along the supply chain. The information originating from Brazil contains the delivery schedule data needed for the production of the A-Class and C-Class and forms the basis for all following activities and processes. The requirements are based on the rough-cut planning that covers a period of six months. These requirements are later ascertained by means of a detailed schedule.

Forecast delivery schedule data is sent as EDI message in VDA.4905 format, converted with an MBCC interface, and processed using the SD module of the R/3 system. A purchase requisition including delivery dates and delivery quantities is automatically created from a sales order. This forms the request for the purchasing department to provide the necessary materials, parts, and services in the specified quantity and at a specific date.

In the further processing, purchase requisitions are automatically converted to purchase orders and produce a scheduling agreement, or also delivery schedule, for the suppliers. These delivery schedules created from R/3 form the basis for the data records that primarily originate from Brazil and that are transmitted to all suppliers in the same format (VDA.4905). As mentioned previously, this occurs six months prior to the actual production in Brazil and provides suppliers with the capability to match their production to the customer's demand.

The transferred data records contain delivery date, article, quantity and often other information needed by the suppliers. Because the MBCC can query the stock levels of the Schenker CC in Bremerhaven, it is possible to match the requirement with the available stock levels. If, for example, there are large stock quantities for a specific product in Bremerhaven, correspondingly smaller subquantities can be requested from the suppliers.

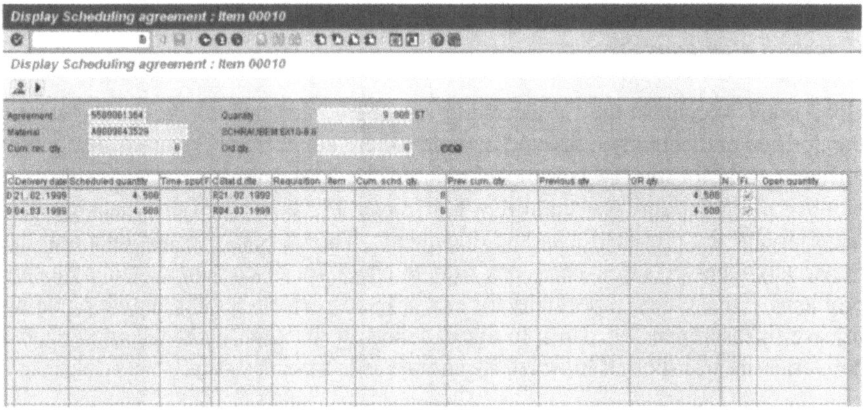

Figure 7.3: Transferred scheduling agreement in the MM module of the CC

The data transferred to the suppliers as scheduling agreement or delivery schedule is also transmitted to the CC in Bremerhaven managed by Schenker. As Figure 7.3 shows, the MM module imports this data and uses them as basis for planning and monitoring processes.

From the data of a scheduling agreement referring to the outline agreement 5500001364, it becomes clear – as Figure 7.3 shows – that 4,500 screws of the material A0009843529 can be expected to arrive on 02/21/1999 and 03/04/1999. Schenker can use this information from the scheduling agreement to check notified and future goods receipts for inconsistencies. The data is generated from the R/3 System of the MBCC by means of modified IDoc messages (see section 3.1), an extension of the DELFOR.01 standard, and imported into the Schenker system by means of a correspondingly modified IDoc interface. These Schenker modifications are necessary, because although the information originating from the MBCC is based on a standard format, it does not fully conform.

The regional freight forwarders used by suppliers and Mercedes-Benz also transfer their data in form of a delivery or shipping notification directly to the R/3 System of the CC. This data is used as a basis for the delivery of parts by the associated regional freight forwarders, which orient themselves on the previously transferred time windows and unloading points. Trucks are used to transport the various goods to the MBCC. In addition to the previously described tasks, the MBCC also acts as supplier. Thus, all components produced by Mercedes-Benz, such as materials from a factory located in Rastatt (Germany), are coordinated by the MBCC and delivered by rail to the CC (which has its own siding).

7.1.1.3 Management of the Processes from the Goods Receipt in the CC Bremerhaven through to the Loading in the Shipping Harbor

Processes after goods receipt

Upon goods receipt in the CC Bremerhaven, there is an immediate comparison of the notified and actually delivered material (there are currently approximately 600 different parts for the A-Class model alone). The goods receipt entry consists of a number of validation procedures, which cover the control of the packing, the material and the provided data and documents. The CC can use this data and the previously received information any time to check for discrepancies and so locate problems. This makes it possible, for example, to perform an alternative planning in case of discrepancies. Thus, to avoid delays in the supply chain, long-delayed deliveries are transported to Brazil by aircraft rather than by ship.

In addition, Schenker AG takes on the supplier evaluation for Mercedes-Benz. The evaluation is oriented on the tasks fulfillment and is stored in the R/3 system. The standard functionality of the MM module is used for this purpose. All vendors can thus be evaluated according to standard criteria; this supports the MBCC purchasing and correspondingly affects the supplier portfolios.

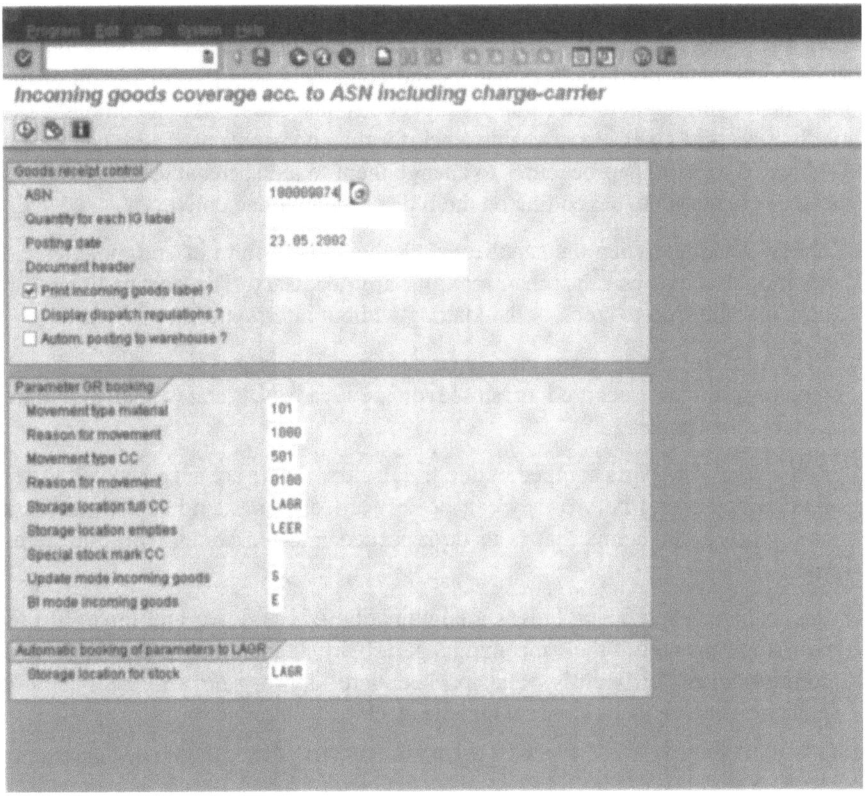

Figure 7.4: Goods receipt posting with regard to an advanced shipping notification in the MM module

Once the data and the physical goods receipts are checked, they are updated through the input template presented in Figure 7.4, with regard to an advanced shipping notification (180009074). This is used to record information about suppliers, freight forwarders, delivered materials, and packing in the R/3 system. The updated data records are automatically transferred by a goods receipt message to the R/3 system of the MBCC, where they are processed in the MM module. The transfer takes place hourly, provided data records to be transferred have accumulated. An IDoc format is used as basis for the data exchange. This format is based on SAP's planned standard format (DESADV.01). However, because this is an extension of the standard format, the data transfer is performed using an interface specially developed by Schenker. The actually delivered and cancelled goods receipts are read using the goods receipt function of the R/3 system of MBCC. Depending on the situation, messages regarding returns to suppliers, scrapping, quantities counted, or stock differences (with reference to the party that caused the discrepancy*)* can be additionally transferred. The performed data transfer causes a redundancy in the two involved Materials Management modules of Schenker and Mercedes-Benz.

Upon the goods receipt in Bremerhaven, further processes that depend on the loading equipment used, such as pallets and containers, and the packaging of the suppliers are initiated in addition to the goods inspection. All incoming parts initially represent a non-dispatchable stock for the goods receipt. These parts must be subjected to various procedures to change them to a dispatchable state. Various processes are possible, depending on the type of the inbound delivery:

1. *Cross Docking*: When the suppliers pack the parts in form of end modules, no additional activities other than marking are necessary. The end modules can pass into the ship-to stock or the loading without interruption.

2. *Reboxing*: Incoming parts are separated from their racks or crates during reboxing and are secured or stored on new racks or crates that are more suitable for handling.

3. *Repacking*: The parts shipped by the freight forwarders are accepted and given special packaging before they can be forwarded. For example, this can be a crate with 5,000 items that is to be repacked into ten crates with 500 items each.

4. *Repacking & Reboxing*: This is a combination of cases two and three. In this two-step process, the incoming parts are separated, relabeled, and commissioned differently, and packed into appropriate lot sizes before transition can be made to the shippable stock.

Goods issue processes

Because Schenker needs not only scheduling agreements but also the appropriate information on concrete delivery dates for the goods receipt, there is a further data transfer from the MBCC to the Schenker system. The data originating from the SD module of the MBCC is transferred in an extended DELFOR.01 format to Schenker's R/3 system by means of a non-standardized IDoc interface. The data is processed through the SD module and it defines from which date or from which cumulative delivered quantity a change status is to be sent to Mercedes-Benz Brazil. An automatic shipment scheduling is performed based on the incoming delivery dates. The ensuring of delivery dates takes the highest priority here.

Figure 7.5 shows a scheduling agreement in the R/3 system of the CC that was sent from the MBCC. This agreement contains planning data that specify when and in which quantity a specific material must arrive in Brazil. Every scheduling agreement is fixed to exactly one material (the material with the number A0005428418 in the example) and can contain different delivery dates (in Figure

7.5 these are 07/01/2001 and 09/10/2002, for example). Additional time restrictions, such as the delivery time to the factory, are not taken into account yet.

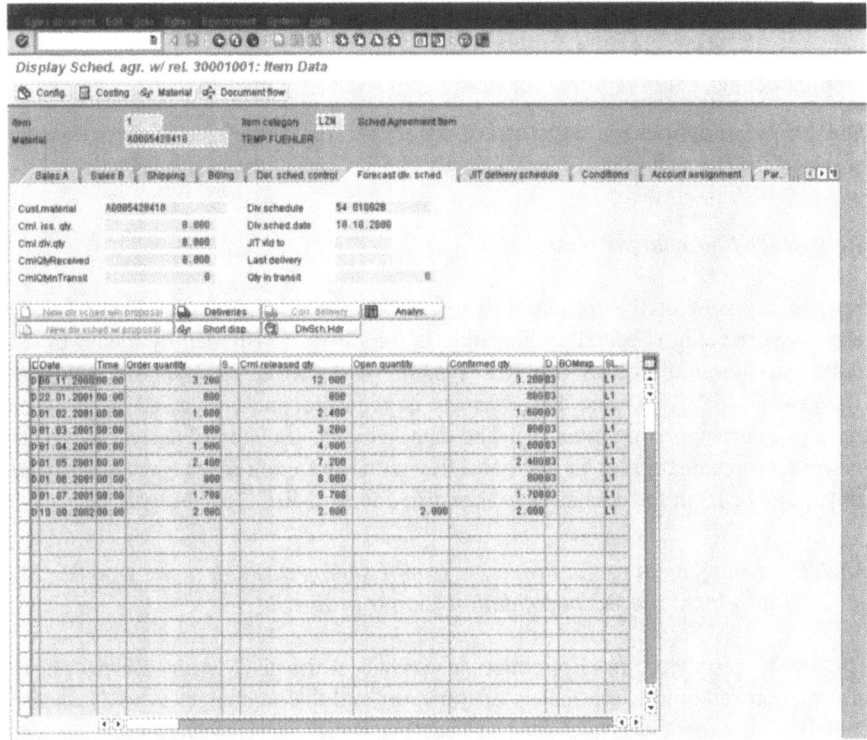

Figure 7.5: Scheduling agreement in the SD module

Once all consolidation activities within the CC have been completed, the containers are transported to the shipping harbor and loaded onto the planned ship. This is represented in the SD system with the posting of the goods issues for the respective delivery. The material issues are deducted from the stocks in the MM module and the status within the R/3 system is updated correspondingly.

The physical loading of the containers onto the overseas means of transport (ship/aircraft) completes the European side of the business transaction and triggers another data transfer. The loading messages, which contain the information on the contents of the containers loaded in Bremerhaven, are forwarded to the MBCC as an advanced shipping notification (ASN). The ASN contains a message regarding the issue of the goods. Provided relevant data has accumulated, it is sent in a frequency of fifteen minutes. In analogy to the previously described modifications, an interface created by Schenker and a data format based on the DESADV.01 standard are used here.

The information on the loaded containers is also forwarded to the DC in Brazil as ASN. In contrast to the previously described data transfer to the MBCC, no modification is needed. The transfer is carried out by using standard interfaces, because the IDoc data format corresponds to the standards (DESADV.01) for shipping notifications. Additional information, for example on damages or supplier details, is not required for further processing by the DC.

The ASN also defines the transition of the processing to the area of responsibility of the DC in Brazil and thus completes all transactions at the European side.

Support for financial processes

For the payment of the freight forwarders, freight data accepted by the freight carriers after being checked by Schenker is forwarded to Bremen by means of the dedicated file interface of the R/3 system. An internal Daimler-Benz format (Inhouse T1499A) is used here, which is received and processed in Bremen through a corresponding interface. The data, which is transferred daily, is used for the invoice verification or to pay liabilities with the freight forwarders and differs in its purpose from the data already forwarded to the MBCC in Stuttgart.

7.1.1.4 *Management of the Processes from Loading through to the Goods Receipt at the Deconsolidation Center in Brazil*

The ASN produced in Bremerhaven provides the DC with all necessary information relating to the means of transport and the containers it holds. It also contains the expected arrival date in the port, which is referred to as *Estimated Time of Arrival* (ETA). Furthermore, it contains a bill of lading for every container (*B/L*). Figure 7.6 makes this clear by listing all notified containers within the R/3 system of the DC.

DC: Advised container/ air freight   A- C L A S S

Ferblegende

Vessel	Container	B/L	RDVI	ETA Port
MSC LEVINA	CARU9048256	MSCUB3733645		13.07.2003
MSC LEVINA	CLHU4044020	MSCUB3733710		13.07.2003
MSC LEVINA	CLHUB046740	MSCUB3733688		13.07.2003
MSC LEVINA	CLHU0103922	MSCUB3733595		13.07.2003
MSC LEVINA	CRXU4504492	MSCUB3733694		13.07.2003
MSC LEVINA	CRXU4715145	MSCUB3733729		13.07.2003
MSC LEVINA	CRXU4871882	MSCUB3733829		13.07.2003
MSC LEVINA	CRXU4948288	MSCUB3733806		13.07.2003
MSC LEVINA	CRXU9250523	MSCUB3733611		13.07.2003
MSC LEVINA	CRXU9370220	MSCUB3733645		13.07.2003
MSC LEVINA	CRXU9464361	MSCUB3733660		13.07.2003
MSC LEVINA	CTIU4032958	MSCUB3733738		13.07.2003
MSC LEVINA	GSTU6354434	MSCUB3733611		13.07.2003
MSC LEVINA	GSTU6748374	MSCUB3733678		13.07.2003
MSC LEVINA	GSTU6746420	MSCUB3733637		13.07.2003
MSC LEVINA	GSTU6746420	MSCUB3733645		13.07.2003
MSC LEVINA	GSTU7449494	MSCUB3733688		13.07.2003
MSC LEVINA	GSTU9904812	MSCUB3733595		13.07.2003
MSC LEVINA	GSTU9074740	MSCUB3733652		13.07.2003
MSC LEVINA	ICSU1079279	MSCUB3733652		13.07.2003
MSC LEVINA	LCRU9685145	MSCUB3733595		13.07.2003
MSC LEVINA	MSCU2870140	MSCUB3733710		13.07.2003
MSC LEVINA	MSCU4045479	MSCUB3733637		13.07.2003
MSC LEVINA	MSCU4066933	MSCUB3733702		13.07.2003
MSC LEVINA	MSCU4070893	MSCUB3733694		13.07.2003
MSC LEVINA	MSCU4089179	MSCUB3733688		13.07.2003
MSC LEVINA	MSCU4100320	MSCUB3733660		13.07.2003
MSC LEVINA	MSCU4122533	MSCUB3733606		13.07.2003
MSC LEVINA	MSCU4122765	MSCUB3733688		13.07.2003
MSC LEVINA	MSCU4127788	MSCUB3733611		13.07.2003
MSC LEVINA	MSCU4144661	MSCUB3733637		13.07.2003
MSC LEVINA	MSCU4153149	MSCUB3733595		13.07.2003
MSC LEVINA	MSCU4179631	MSCUB3733645		13.07.2003
MSC LEVINA	MSCU4181855	MSCUB3733629		13.07.2003
MSC LEVINA	MSCU4199324	MSCUB3733678		13.07.2003
MSC LEVINA	MSCU4210070	MSCUB3733660		13.07.2003
MSC LEVINA	MSCU4297718	MSCUB3733606		13.07.2003
MSC LEVINA	MSCU4314997	MSCUB3733729		13.07.2003
MSC LEVINA	MSCU4334390	MSCUB3733694		13.07.2003
MSC LEVINA	MSCU4612124	MSCUB3733595		13.07.2003
MSC LEVINA	MSCU9053620	MSCUB3733637		13.07.2003
MSC LEVINA	MSCUB251184	MSCUB3733652		13.07.2003

Figure 7.6: Notified containers within the R/3 system of the DC

As the figure shows, the notified containers are on the ship "MSC LEVINA". Provided that the containers are shipped by air, this data is also displayed in the list. This listing allows the DC, which like its European "counterpart" has control over the Brazilian area of the supply chain, to recognize any potential delays and to initiate the appropriate alternative procedures.

Following the overseas transport and the unloading of the containers in the port of destination, the containers are without delay transported by trucks to the customs-free temporary storage facility "Port Buffer" within the port (Rio de Janeiro). In this part of the supply chain, containers are prepared for the forward shipment for the DC. The goods receipt in the Port Buffer initiates the respective update that is forwarded to the DC system as goods receipt message.

This message is transferred as a pure file transfer and is thus imported into the R/3 system of the DC by means of a file interface. It is now that the supplied parts are for the first time maintained as stock in the MM module. The transfer provides the DC with the necessary information on the port of arrival, the ship used, the arrival date, and the number of the incoming containers. It thus provides the capability of monitoring the Brazilian part of the supply chain. The update is performed for the previously received shipping notifications, which allows to control goods receipts and to track any discrepancies.

Following the goods receipt posting in the Port Buffer and the approval for the transport with duty unpaid, all containers are loaded onto trains and sent to the DC. This is located in the immediate vicinity of the factory and, as with the CC, also has its own siding. Compared with transport by truck, the transport by rail has the advantage of more precise arrival times and lower costs.

In case of time-critical situations, the transport is carried out with trucks. This way, a time advantage of approximately sixty percent can be achieved. Once the containers have been loaded, a new file transfer to the Port Buffer (goods issue message) is carried out. The corresponding files contain information, such as the train number, and result in the status being updated in the R/3 system of the DC. This goods issue message has the effect that the containers managed in the storage type Port Buffer transfer to a transit status and remain there until their arrival in the Dry Port or also Container Yard. Figure 7.7 shows an example of this activity in the R/3 system of the DC.

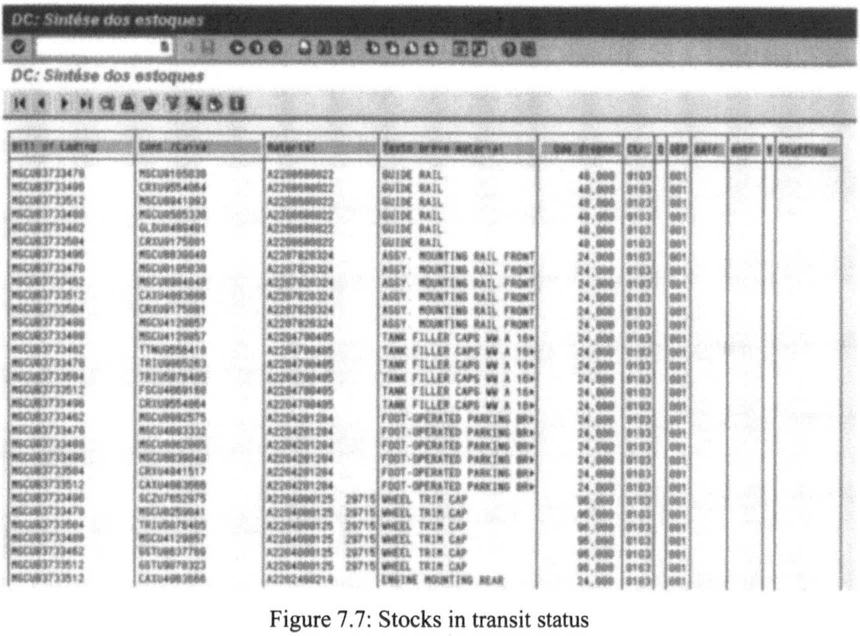

Figure 7.7: Stocks in transit status

This container warehouse is part of the DC (see Figure 7.8) and is located in the immediate vicinity of the actual warehouse, in which the containers are emptied.

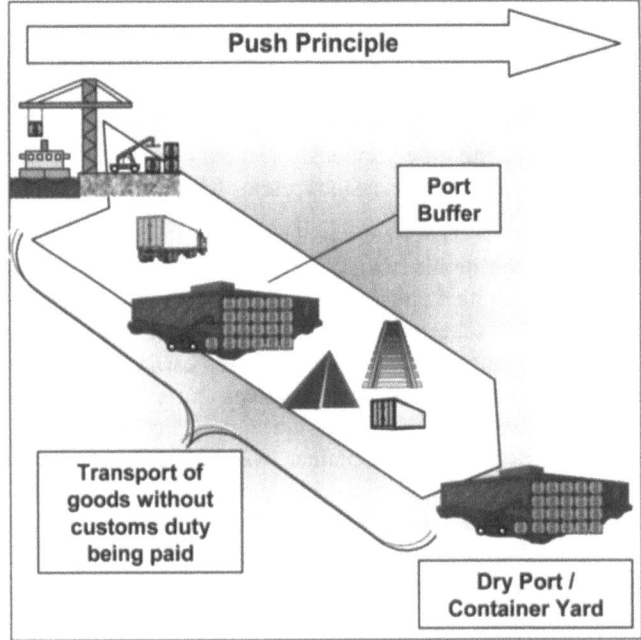

Figure 7.8: The push principle as part of the supply chain

Figure 7.8 illustrates the previously described route of the containers from the acceptance at the port via the temporary storage facility up to the container warehouse. All containers coming from Bremerhaven are recorded and "pressed through" to the container warehouse of the DC by means of the push principle. Up to and including the time of the goods receipt in the container warehouse, the containers or the contained parts are still in a duties unpaid status. To obtain an interest rate advantage, customs duties are paid on the goods just before they are used. The system status is again updated upon goods receipt in the container warehouse. That is, the containers are removed from the transit status, which describes a pending status of the containers between the two warehouse types Port Buffer and Container Yard, and are then entered in the DC container warehouse.

7.1.1.5 Management of the Processes from the Transition of the Containers in the Warehouse through the Delivery to the Factory

The MB Brazil factory now passes additional data to Schenker, that concretizes the general planning previously forwarded to the CC and specifies the parts that are required at the factory within the next 11 days. Thus, containers are no longer involved, but rather a cleared requirement for parts based on the production figures for vehicles becomes the object of consideration. The detailed requirements are transferred to the DC in a standard data format typical for Brazil. The data format used here is an EDI standard that is closely related to the previously discussed VDA format. An external EDI converter transforms the data into the R/3 IDoc format for shipping notifications (DELFOR.01), which is then processed through the sales and distribution processing. A job is used to start an MRP system upon receipt of the scheduling agreement in order to check if the delivery for Mercedes-Benz for a previously defined period can be fulfilled by the stocks of the warehouse, for which customs duties have already been paid.

All represented warehouse types are managed centrally within one system. The MRP system checks the defined stocks and, in case of stock shortage, creates receipt elements that manifest themselves in form of a purchase requisition in the area of the Materials Management system. This means that material from the container warehouse of the DC or from warehouses earlier in the supply chain is required for an on-time delivery of Mercedes-Benz. Note here that upon opening a container, customs duties must be paid for the complete contents or for a complete container delivery. Because the container warehouse is stocked with many containers and different materials in varying quantities, the performed scheduling agreement updates may make it necessary to extract a different container than the one originally planned for a specific period. The availability check is carried out at all warehouse levels on the Brazilian side, that are displayed in the R/3 system with different location numbers for each warehouse type. If the required parts do not exist in the container warehouse, a check is performed as to whether they are available in transit status or in the temporary storage facility at the port. This additional service makes it possible to delay paying customs duties until an optimum time. Because the customs duties for the parts can be associated with some avoidable costs in form of an unnecessary capital lockup, the contents of the containers are analyzed with regard to their further use. Schenker developed a "Container Algorithm" (CA) for this purpose. This algorithm works both value-oriented and volume-oriented. After it has been activated, the algorithm delivers the containers to be extracted from the Dry Port by means of the two target criteria.

The algorithm serves as a decision-supporting instrument since all proposals are made available to the respective decision maker in form of a list. After the decision maker has confirmed a processing alternative, the containers are transferred from the warehouse into the DC warehouse and are removed from the warehouse stock of the container warehouse. After opening the containers in the warehouse, the inventories are again checked and for the first time compared in detail with the notified deliveries of the CC. Customs duty is paid for the parts, which are then separated and some of them are stored as a safety stock. Schenker uses this "minimal stock" to intercept unexpected problems, such as damages to parts or other malfunctions, and thus avoid a potential production standstill.

Figure 7.9 illustrates the areas of the DC and describes the goods flow resulting from the information impulses from Mercedes-Benz. At irregular intervals, the DC receives a JIT (just-in-time) delivery schedule from the IT systems of the production location. Upon arrival of this EDI message that is imported through a file interface, in the extreme case only 90 minutes remain until the delivery to the production location. The detailed schedule is converted into deliveries in the R/3 systems before the goods are delivered by truck to fixed unloading points near the production conveyor belts. The production or assembly can now start. Upon acknowledgement of receipt of goods, that is currently not yet passed electronically to the Schenker's R/3 system, a final posting is made, thus completing the delivery process.

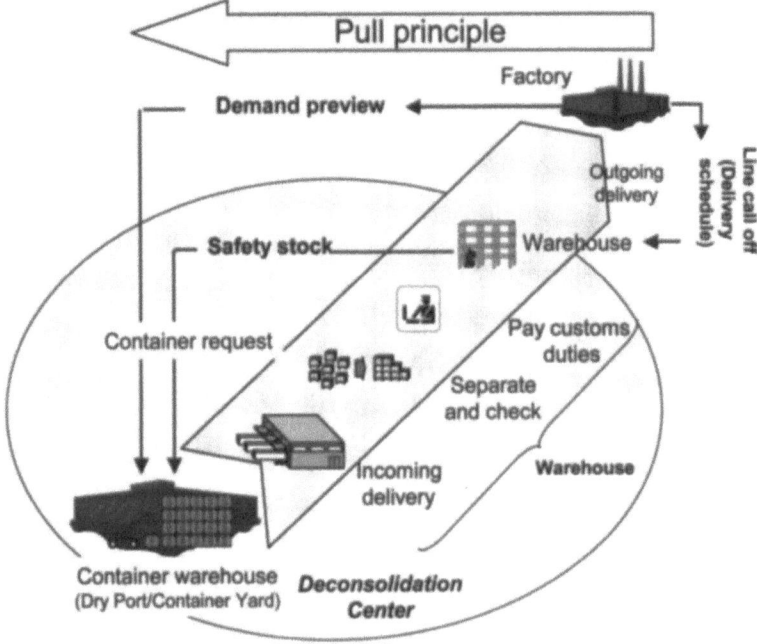

Figure 7.9: Information and goods flows from the container warehouse to the production location

7.1.1.6 Overall Summary of the Logistics-related Information Infrastructure

Figure 7.10 summarizes the information flows alongside the supply chain. The illustration concentrates on the involved institutions, the systems that are based to a large extent on the R/3 system, and the used data exchange formats.

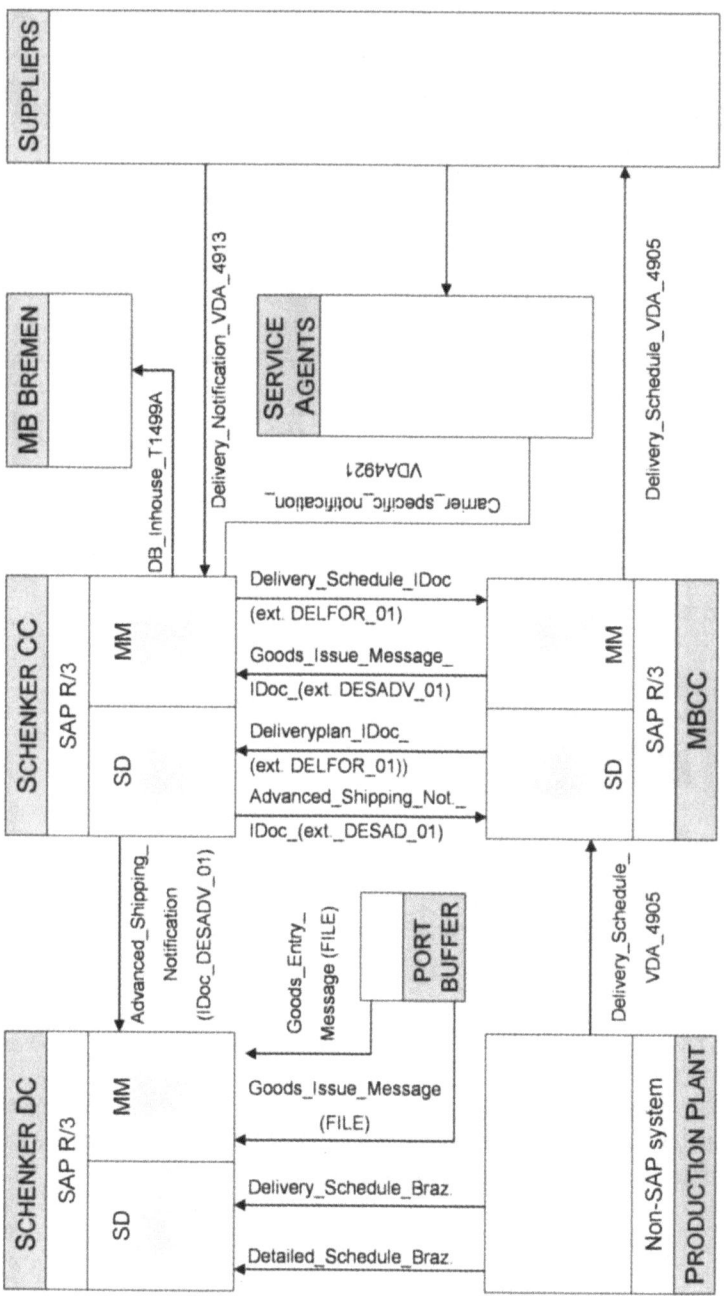

Figure 7.10: Information flows alongside the supply chain

7.1.1.7 Internet-based Reporting (SOURCE)

While in the sections described above solely EDI has been used for the management of the supply chain, this subsection focuses on the Internet-based support of control processes. Schenker has developed an Internet-based tool called SOURCE to allow companies that participate in the processing to have a better insight in the status of the activities. Especially the MRP controller at the production locations is to have a better insight in the time schedule of CC and DC processes. Also, the availability of materials or parts at different stations of the supply chain is to be better monitored with this tool.

In SOURCE, 15 different status points were defined, which reflect the system status (e.g., different IM/WM postings) in the transaction systems that can be queried via the Internet. The technical basis of the SOURCE concept is an Internet Transaction Server in addition to the R/3 system, in which the queryable data is made available in user-created structures (database tables). This is the interface between the ERP systems and the Internet. The logon to the system is carried out via a Web browser and passes a two-step authentication process for reasons of security. The user must first enter a general password and then a special system password. Different information can be queried after the registration, for example:

- All stocks in one or several status points,

- selected materials in one or several status points,

- notified containers (DC),

- carried out goods receipts, or

- freight lists of a container (see Figure 7.11).

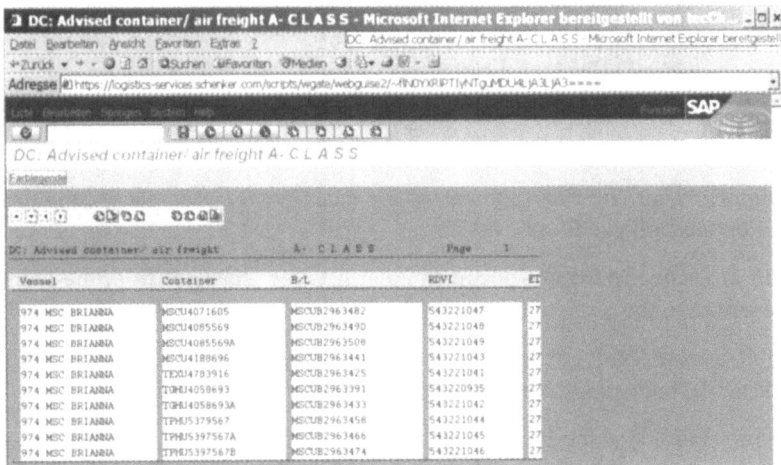

Figure 7.11: Internet-based query of notified containers

The individual queries can be additionally particularized, for instance by entering time intervals or points in time. As the following figure shows, the ASN already described in section 7.1.1.4, for example, can be queried. As with the query via the SAP GUI (see Figure 7.6) carrier, container number, B/L and ETA are displayed. Furthermore, an RDVI number (*Registro de Volumes Importados*), required for the MRP controller at the production location (an index for the entry of the import volume) is integrated. An RDVI number is generated for each B/L.

The MRP controllers can additionally view the complete freight lists of a container to compare these with their planning data. As Figure 7.12 shows, a freight list includes a list of all materials and their quantities.

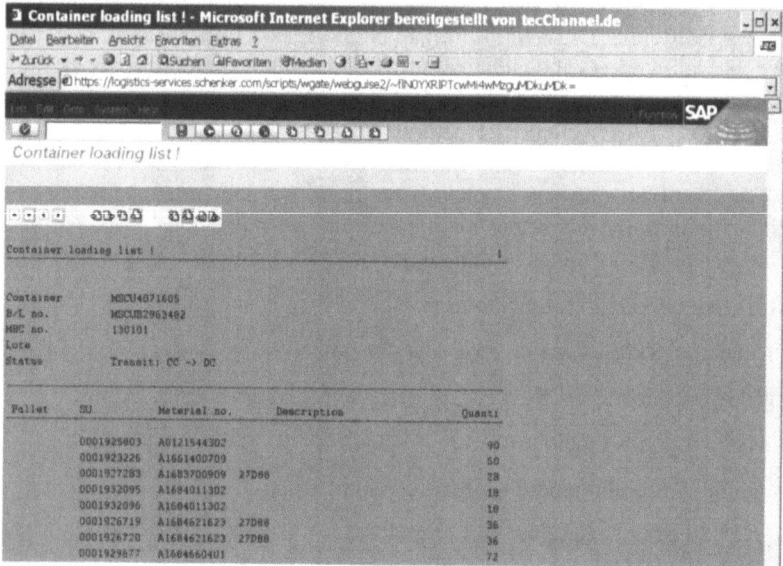

Figure 7.12: Internet-based query of freight lists of a container

The data can also be queried by entering key numbers. As Figure 7.13 shows, this can involve:

- *Shipping Unit Number* (number of the package, for example a container, a pallet or a cardboard box),

- *Bill of Lading* (transport document, that lists the shipment from the point of departure to the place of destination),

- *Lote number* (Portuguese name for lot. It is assigned in the Container Yard for each B/L, following the arrival and the put-away of the containers),

- *DI number* (DI is the Portuguese abbreviation for *Declaração de Importação* (import declaration). The document includes all information required for the payment of goods customs duty),

- *RDVI* (Portuguese abbreviation for *Registro de Volumes Importados* and involves the entry of the import volume per Bill of Lading) and

- *MBC number* (a number range assigned by the MBCC per annum and per containers or air cargo. This number is unique within a year and can be assigned again in the following year).

Figure 7.13 concludes by showing the result of a query regarding a B/L number. The respective RDVI and MBC number as well as the VSE number are displayed. In this case, LOTE and MBC number were not yet assigned.

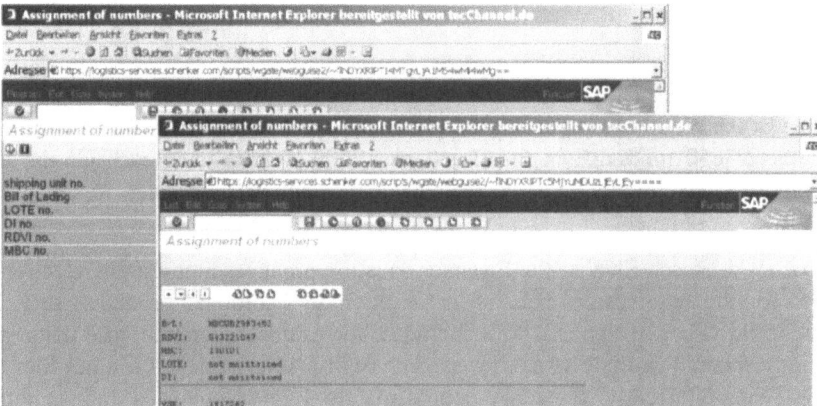

Figure 7.13: Query regarding B/L number

7.1.2   Evaluation and Outlook

According to Schenker AG, no noteworthy problems occurred in the more than three years of operation of the two R/3 systems (Release 4.0) which physically run on a Unix system in Mühlheim an der Ruhr (Germany). The management of the Mercedes C-Class, the assembly of which was taken over by the production location Juiz de Fora only later, could be included in the existing system infrastructure without any problems. At the beginning of the processing, however, the standard R/3 system (Release 4.0 at the time) could not completely meet the requirements of Schenker. Functions for managing handling units as well as required standard processes and reporting structures, for example, did not exist yet and therefore had to be initially developed by Schenker. The current R/3 version indeed provides a usable Handling Unit Management, the made modifications however argue against a release upgrade. The acquired goods associated with a migration due to new standard functions would currently not justify the costs.

Contrary to the two transaction systems, Schenker criticizes the error rate of the Internet Transaction Server. This server is to be replaced in the near future by the Web Application Server sketched in chapter 2.

The SOURCE system, however, brought about a significant reduction of the effort for processing inquiries that were previously handled by telephone. In the future, an event management is to be additionally introduced which automatically displays missed planned deadlines in form of alert messages. For this purpose, further application components of the mySAP Supply Chain Management solution are to be used.

7.2   Case Study for the APO Implementation at Bosch Eisenach GmbH

The Robert Bosch Fahrzeugelektrik Eisenach GmbH (Bosch EhW) is a company of the Bosch group that realized consolidated sales of almost 35 billion € and a net income of 650 million € in the fiscal year 2002. Within the Bosch Group, the automotive technology division produced 23.3 billion € in sales in the same period, approximately 67 percent of the total business volume.

Since 1995, Bosch EhW at the Eisenach location produces high-quality electronic parts for the automotive industry in addition to traditional products, such as windshield wiper equipment. This includes, for example, ceramic base materials (mainly ceramic circuit boards), rev meters, high-pressure sensors and hot film air flow filters. Currently, there are approximately 1.740 employees and, in total, Bosch EhW realized sales of 457 million € with some 5,000 different products in the fiscal year 2002. Bosch EhW is represented in the most important markets in Europe and overseas (the export share amount to over 60 percent for some products) and takes on a leading position in the automotive component supply market. 80 percent of the sales are produced in Europe, 60 percent of which in Germany. Bosch EhW supplies almost all well-known original equipment manufacturers.

The plant ground provides extensive options for continuously extending the production location in Eisenach in the next years. The three main production areas are "Hot Film Air Flow Sensor", "High Pressure Sensor Technology" and "Revolution Probe". In the first area, approximately 800,000 pieces, in the second 500,000 pieces and in the third 2.5 million pieces are produced each month.

Bosch EhW intends to eliminate the information barriers between the individual functional areas (Sales and Distribution, Production, and Purchasing) and the planning levels and wants to ensure an integrated view of the supply chain at all levels of the company. This goal is to be attained with APO (see chapter 5). That way, the currently used systems, mainly proprietary developments, are to be replaced by standard software from SAP AG (R/3 system and APO).

7.2.1   The Challenge

The automobile division at Bosch EhW obtains the largest part of the sales and is the focus of the APO and SAP implementation.

Bosch EhW stores the orders of the customers from the automotive industry in the system as scheduling agreements. The requirements are transferred by means of EDI in form of forecast delivery schedules (FRC) and JIT (just-in-time) delivery schedules. 80 percent of the customers communicate with Bosch EhW by means of EDI (particularly in VDA format in Germany, ODETTE format in Europe). 15 percent of the sales orders reach the regional branches of Bosch by fax; they are entered manually and transmitted to Bosch EhW as an EDI message.

Some customers transfer forecast delivery schedules for a period of up to six months as forecast and transmit delivery-relevant JIT delivery schedules for a period of one to two months; other ones send only forecast delivery schedules for a period of up to 12 months. For various production areas, forecasts for the planning are also used for the production of finished products and assemblies.

First, the sales orders are in this case "roughly" planned by the area Materials Management and in the next step are scheduled "in detail" (in-house production planning) by the area PPE (Production Planning and Execution). The material requirements planning is carried out in the system once a week; order proposals are created every two weeks.

Starting from the date requested by customer, a backward scheduling always occurs. If there are no capacities in production, the planner must intervene, for example by reducing lot sizes, changing dates or by rescheduling to other production lines.

The – timely – material staging for the production is carried out by an external service provider (ESP). The delivery schedules to this service provider are transferred electronically, in the case of which a corresponding lead time must be adhered to. The inbound delivery and put-away depend on the products and occur every two to four hours. Bosch EhW has approximately 370 vendors, 75 percent of which are connected by means of EDI (mainly in VDA format). The largest of these vendors should actively participate in the SupplyOn marketplace (see section 7.5), the smaller ones should be integrated by means of WebEDI.

In the future, selected planning processes at the Eisenach location are to be restructured and APO is to be used to help tap potential benefit. The emphasis here is on the modules PP/DS (Production Planning and Detailed Scheduling) and ATP (Available to Promise), the introduction of which is planned together with the R/3 system. Furthermore, a considerable potential benefit was identified by an implementation of the module DP. The currently existing solution of the demand planning and forecasting and particularly the production forecast based on Microsoft Excel as well as selected areas of the operating level calculation and the sales controlling are henceforth to be represented in an integrated solution based on APO and R/3.

The implementation project is planned to last a total of ten months and has a total budget of 500.000 €. The objectives are:

- Increase of customer satisfaction from 92 percent to 95 percent: This is measured with the system LIWAKS (German abbreviation for delivery fulfillment, retail and control system) that takes into account all variances from the delivery date and quantity requested by the customer.

- Reduction of the WIP and safety stocks by 30 percent: Currently, Bosch EhW stores finished products ten days, the raw materials needed for the finished products 15 days in advance. On the other hand, components of assemblies, such as the ceramic substrates that represent approximately one sixth of the finished product value, are only stored as WIP stock five calendar days in advance.

- Reduction of the costs of an incorrect planning by ten percent: These include, for instance, costs for special trips due to incorrect personal material requirements planning. However, only one shipping error per annum was listed in the last three years on average so that Bosch EhW assesses it to be very difficult to further reduce the costs in this area.

- Reduction of the lead times and the capital lockup costs.

Below follows an introduction of the implementation concept for the areas Demand and Production Planning. Then, section 7.2.3 describes the conceptual design for the Collaborative Management of Delivery Schedules.

7.2.2   Planned Implementation of APO at Bosch EhW

First, only the functions of APO are to be implemented at Bosch EhW, that are necessary to support demand, production, and procurement planning at all company levels and to represent the material flow in an integrated model.

Therefore, the following components or modules were chosen from the range of functionalities and services of APO:

- Demand Planning (DP): This module is to be implemented with almost the complete range of functionality. Only the promotion planning and the Internet-based collaborative planning are not introduced (see also section 5.2).

- Production Planning and Detailed Scheduling (PP/DS): emphasis in this planning area is the optimization using a setup matrix and partly also the block and campaign planning. The characteristics-based planning, on the other hand, is not implemented.

The SNP functionality is only used as an interface between the R/3 system and PP/DS of APO, while the cross-plant availability checks are currently not yet provided (as those of the ATP). Special APO performance features, as those of the CMDS (Collaborative Management of Delivery Schedules), a joint development project of Bosch and SAP, are to be integrated upon completion of the project (see sections 5.6 and 7.2.3). The ND function, on the other hand, is not to be used in the future either. The same applies to the Transportation Planning TP/VS, since Bosch EhW has completely outsourced the company-external logistics to the company Paul Günther Industrielogistik GmbH. This logistics service provider takes on both the material staging and the delivery ex works.

7.2.2.1 Demand Planning

The demand planning environment at Bosch EhW is basically characterized by:

- Long-term sales planning (up to ten years),
- medium-term annual planning with an 80-percent planning accuracy as well as
- mainly production-driven (monthly) planning view in the short-term horizon.

So far, Microsoft Excel is the only system-oriented tool to provide support by representing selected planning processes in different worksheets that are not integrated with regards to functionality and data processing.

The currently rolling monthly planning based on Microsoft Excel will be represented in the DP module of APO in the future (see Figure 7.14). In this case, the following performance features of the demand planning are implemented in APO:

- Creation of demand forecasts using statistical methods,
- collection and synchronization of the planned figures from different planning areas,
- consolidation of the planning results from the individual areas,
- comparison of the demand and production options,
- continuous and automatic monitoring of the planning processes, and
- setup of a reporting using the Business Explorer.

The following figure shows how the individual planning levels and steps should be represented within the framework of the DP and how they should be integrated into the adjacent R/3 system:

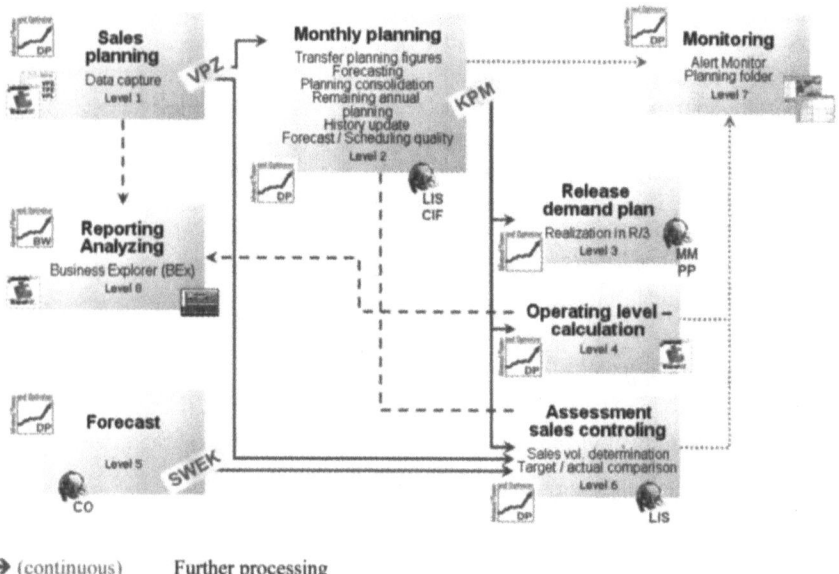

→ (continuous)   Further processing
→ (dashed)   Evaluation
→ (dotted)   Monitoring

Figure 7.14: Rolling monthly planning with APO DP

The functions and application of these planning activities will now be explained:

- *Sales planning* (level 1): it is the priority task of the planning area sales planning to collect and synchronize planned figures that are provided from different positions and business areas based on Microsoft Excel and to represent them in a standard form in APO DP.

  The planning model assumes that the forecast as such is carried out in a non-SAP system and not in the APO DP of Bosch EhW, which is why the transfer of the necessary planned figures to APO must be ensured.

  Accordingly, all necessary storage and reporting functions are supported in this planning area thus enabling the users to completely store, evaluate and further process the synchronized and current, planned figures in APO.

- *Monthly planning* (level 2): The accessibility of the strategic-tactical level (based on Microsoft Excel) with the operative detailed planning level (in PP/DS) is ensured by the monthly planning (see Figure 7.15).

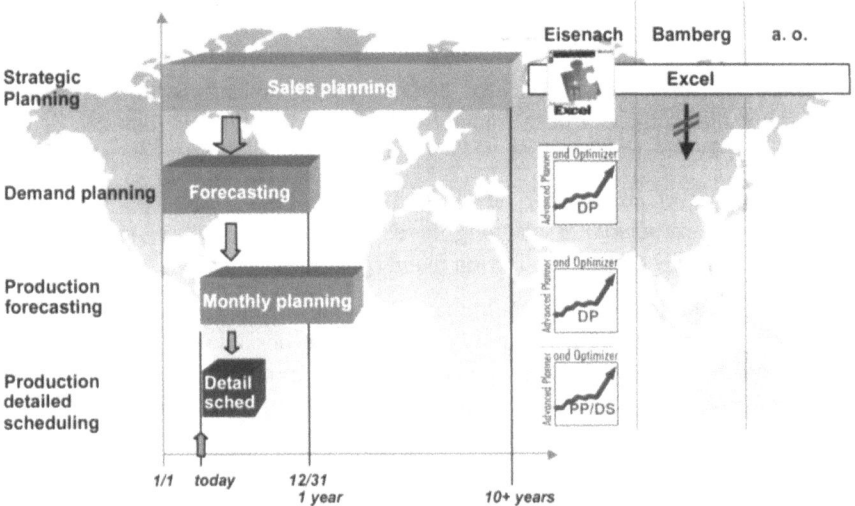

Figure 7.15: Planned planning sequence at Bosch EhW

The monthly planning is the most important planning activity from the view of the production forecast at Bosch EhW. Here the following main functions are supported:

o Rolling monthly planning (quantity planning),

o remaining annual planning (also quantity-based),

o regular update of the production and budget planning (by means of the CIF interface to the R/3 LIS module),

o support for the valuation of the scheduling quality,

o plausibility check of the forecast by using causal analysis,

o restriction-based plan consolidation considering forecast, orders on hand, and warehouse stock as well as the available capacity,

o simulation and valuation of different planning scenarios,

o automatic continuous monitoring of the planning processes, and

o history update and administration for 12 months.

• *Release demand plan* (level 3): The integration of the APO components among one another and into the execution system R/3 allows consolidated demand plans and versions to be transmitted online to the R/3 system and to be tested there at a higher detail level against current production constraints (available resources and stocks) regarding their feasibility.

This means that production-relevant materials planning and planning of products and assemblies, in particular those of secondary or tertiary parts, is carried out after the consolidated demand plan, respectively the continuous monthly planning, has been transferred to the MM and PP modules of the executive R/3 system.

- *Operating level calculation* (level 4): it is the task of the operating level calculation or personnel planning to estimate the workforce requirements starting from the current production planning figures.

The planned figures from preliminary planning areas (such as the monthly planning) are updated regularly (monthly if possible). The scheduling functions themselves are to be understood as approximation procedure; that is, the purpose is not to provide an exact calculation procedure but a rough calculation for the workforce requirements to be expected.

- *Forecast* (level 5): At Bosch EhW the operative goals are mainly defined related to quantity. In parallel, the results of this quantity planning are to be represented and checked regarding their value.

In this case, a sales point of view, in terms of turnover, is to be applied; a product or product line-related profit margin planning within the forecast of product costs is though not planned.

With the determination of the sales, different price structures during the year, customer-specific prices, and discounts as well as different price lists are yet not to be represented (for example for "internal" customers/areas and "external" end customers).

The purpose of this planning area is to provide the costing-based basic data (in this case: the sales prices) for the controlling tasks in the planning area "assessment sales controlling".

The main functions in this planning area are:

- o Transfer of the cost accounting statistics from R/3 (actual data from the CO module),

- o forecast and fixing of these statistics for the next fiscal year, and

- o transfer of the planned statistics into the planning area "assessment sales controlling".

The data volume to be expected is manageable and the data is to be made available from the R/3 system only once a year, which is why at Bosch EhW a download from the R/3 system will probably be realized by means of SAP Query and the replication of the data sources into APO by means of generic extractors.

- *Assessment and sales controlling* (level 6): the operative target/actual comparison is to be automated by means of this planning area. The plan is to identify variances by continuously comparing achieved results with the annual and monthly planning, including the data from the executive R/3 system (LIS module), and to quantify them regarding quantity as well as value. Furthermore, the effects of these plan variances on the planned target are to be projected by means of a remaining annual planning.

The following main functions are supported in this planning area:

o Integration of demand and budget planning (based on the sales planning),

o regular update of the budget planning through monthly planning already consolidated and checked against constraints,

o continuous target/actual comparison with variance analyses as well as a

o remaining annual planning (in the sense of a forecast calculation) as an additive result of the so far achieved results (actual data) and of current plans up to the end of the current fiscal year (planned data).

The (annual) budget planning is carried out once a year based on the sales planning of the business areas. A regular update is always carried out on the basis of the continuous monthly planning.

* *Monitoring* (level 7): This is a cross-application process monitoring and is basically controlled through the alert monitor or the alert browser in the interactive planning folder. For each planner of Bosch EhW, a separate alert profile is provided in this case. The Supply Chain Cockpit and also the Web Reporting as a possible monitoring instrument are currently not provided here.

* *Reporting / Analyzing* (level 8): Reporting is consistently implemented through the APO-internal BW and BEx (see also chapter 4). Here, employees are provided with the option to create their function-specific reports in Excel or to adapt predefined reports to current requirements.

The formatting of planned and actual data should be carried out in the APO-internal BW with the OLAP processor, if required also in the background as a batch process in order to read the data from the OLAP cache of the BW.

7.2.2.2 Production Planning

Prior to the introduction of the R/3 system and APO, the production of assemblies at Bosch EhW was carried out in a repetitive manufacturing for anonymous orders. Finished products were generally produced in an order-specific repetitive manufacturing. Orders for the production of assemblies and finished products were partially created personally and thus had to be scheduled in coordination with the shop floor control regarding the available capacities in the plant.

The assemblies and finished products were produced in larger series in order to avoid the partially very time-consuming setup activities on the production lines as much as possible, which can include the exchange of up to 40 toolkits within a production line. This aspect became important at project startup when it came out that the production range and detail would increase significantly in the near future (currently there are approximately 5,300 materials procured externally as well as 1,200 assemblies and 2,400 finished products).

A production planning run in APO should now enable Bosch EhW to carry out a simultaneous material and capacity planning for in-house production, external procurement, and stock transfer in a producing plant. The result of a production planning run should lead to a more rapid, mostly automated generation of executable production plans.

For critical products, all low-level codes are to be immediately newly planned with every change that is relevant for the plan. Critical products at Bosch EhW are:

- Hybrids (High Pressure Sensor Technology and Hot Film Air Flow Sensor),

- pressure absorber (High Pressure Sensor Technology) and

- modules (Hot Film Air Flow Sensor).

This planning option is especially interesting when the multi-level availability check is used, because an availability date can be immediately determined when a sales order is created. The disadvantage of this planning variant is the resource consumption; it is therefore only applied for the products that involve the largest production complexity and capital lockup. Changes relevant for planning that trigger this online planning are made at least once a day.

On the other hand, the automatic planning should be used in the planning run for less critical products. In this case, every change relevant for planning generates a planning file entry for the product that is then planned again with the next planning run. A run controls when and how often a product is to be planned, and can be executed when the system load is less (e.g., at night).

Further, it is to be possible at Bosch EhW to perform an interactive planning for specific products. The planner can trigger this planning from the product view and the planning boards.

The infinite scheduling strategy is used (backwards) in this case (see also section 5.5), with which, starting from the date requested by customers, a backward scheduling is carried out and the activities are scheduled on the resources without consideration of the capacity utilization. This strategy is the obvious choice in cases where there are only very few bottleneck resources in the production. If the scheduling results in a capacity overload, this is displayed by means of exception messages (alerts); the planner can then manually reschedule in the planning board.

At Bosch EhW, the production planning variant "optimization through setup matrix" is implemented within the R/3 and APO project.

In this case, the setup matrix for every possible setup operation at a work center contains the setup time and the setup costs that are necessary to change the resource from one setup status to another setup status. A setup matrix can be used to represent sequence-dependent setup times and costs with reference to the products to be manufactured on a resource.

The creation and maintenance of setup groups as well as the maintenance of the setup transitions in APO are required for this purpose. The system uses the setup matrix to determine the duration of setup activities as well as the setup time and setup costs-dependent sequence of operations on specific resources during scheduling and optimization.

The automatic scheduling in the best possible setup time allows to schedule individual operations or a group of operations in already existing occupancies on the work center in the graphical and tabular planning board, so that the overall setup time of the occupancy increases the least.

With automatic scheduling, an optimal scheduling position on the target work center is searched for, one by one for every operation. The operations are scheduled one after the other in the sequence previously defined in a strategy profile. With the determination of the optimal position of an operation, it is taken into account whether the newly generated setup transitions are allowed.

At Bosch EhW, setup keys, groups, and matrices are not to be transferred from the R/3 system to APO. Furthermore, for reasons of performance it is recommended to define as little setup matrices as possible and a small number of setup transitions.

The APO system provides extensive optimization functions. It is thus possible to define corresponding costs for every setup transition in a setup matrix. Then, scheduled operations on a resource, that are not in an optimal position with respect to the setup costs, can be changed to an optimized scheduling sequence with the help of an optimization function by heavily weighting the setup costs.

The optimization function in APO can be executed through the product planning table as well as the detailed scheduling sheet (see Figure 7.17 and Figure 7.18). In the initial screen of these planning boards, the corresponding products and resources must be selected, for which an optimization run is to be carried out. For this purpose, there are different profiles (planning board profile, strategy profile, and optimization profile) that can be preset user-specifically. Results of optimization runs can be saved in simulation versions and compared with one another. Then the planner can copy the optimal solution to the active planning.

Furthermore, the following scheduling strategies are to be used to a lesser extent:

- *Block planning*: block planning is a forecast or preassignment of production capacities for certain products with the objective to achieve a more efficient utilization of the capacities. This can involve classified products, that is, such products that have certain attributes in addition to the part number, that clearly identify it. Non-classified products, however, can also be used for block planning.

In different industries, such as the metal or paper industry, the operations are scheduled on the different production lines not only due to their date sequence or remaining capacity. It is in fact necessary to summarize products with same attributes in a preliminary planning, since processing these articles requires the same setup status of the installation and setup can thus be reduced to a minimum.

Blocks do not exist in the R/3 system. From the R/3 system, the work centers are only transferred to APO; there, they are referred to as resources in the master data. At Bosch EhW, the block planning is thus to be maintained in the APO system for the respective resource. For this purpose, a corresponding time interval is defined in weeks, days or also hours in APO for the block planning. Only certain products can be produced on the resource within this time interval. The automatic scheduling of planned orders for all products that can be produced on a resource (e.g., production line), considers the time intervals of the block planning, that is, products, the characteristics of which are provided for another block, are also scheduled correspondingly. The defined blocks are displayed as a graphic in APO on the resources and also in the different planning tools, such as the product planning table or the detailed scheduling sheet (see Figure 7.17 and Figure 7.18).

- *Campaign planning*: campaign planning is a summary of planned and process orders with the objective to manufacture a certain quantity of a product over a certain period on a production line without interrupting the sequence. The campaign planning includes the scheduling of campaigns, their assignment to resources and the availability check of the resources.

In the APO implementation of Bosch EhW, a production campaign is to be created, whose function is called from the menu or from detailed scheduling sheet (see Figure 7.17). All orders that are scheduled on a resource are displayed and can be copied to a campaign. Both new and already existing orders are copied to the campaign. APO is to automatically transfer the data of the production campaign to the R/3 system for execution and settlement.

7.2.3   The Process of the Collaborative Management of Delivery Schedules at Bosch

Following the estimated completion of the implementation project in the first quarter of 2003, the integration between the R/3 system and APO as well as the CMDS enhancement are to be carried out. Below follows an explanation as to how the interaction of APO and R/3 system will look like using the sales order process as an example (see also section 5.6).

The activities that will occur during the processing of collaborative scheduling agreements can be subdivided as follows:

- *Receipt of the outline agreement*: a sales order is generally entered through the sales system EVA. From there, it is transferred to the R/3 system through IDocs and stored there as a scheduling agreement in the SD module.

  The original scheduling agreement is transferred to APO by means of the CIF interface and saved there as forecast/planning delivery schedule. Then the outline agreement is split into monthly or weekly quantities in APO according to the settings determined in the sales scheduling agreement control profile. The due delivery schedules result from that.

- *Feasibility and admissibility check*: Every due delivery schedule passes the admissibility and feasibility check:

  The admissibility check compares the last processed due delivery schedule with the newly received one. The variances are checked against the tolerance values set in the control profile. A variance up or down within the defined tolerances results in the status "admissibility ok". If the tolerance limits are exceeded, the status "admissibility not ok" will be assigned. The feasibility check is not run in the case of "admissibility not ok".

  The feasibility check determines whether the new due delivery schedule with the currently valid period splits (plant scheduling) can be realized without violating defined constraints, such as minimum days' supplies. The difference between admissibility and feasibility check therefore is that the first checks the incoming delivery schedule with regard to quantity or schedule variances, while the feasibility check tests for stocks and days' supplies.

- *Transfer of confirmed due delivery schedules to the R/3 system*: If the admissibility and the feasibility check have not generated any conflicts or alerts, the due delivery schedules are transferred back to the R/3 system as confirmed due delivery schedules. If the customer later confirms these delivery schedules, APO generates operative delivery schedules from them (see Figure 7.16).

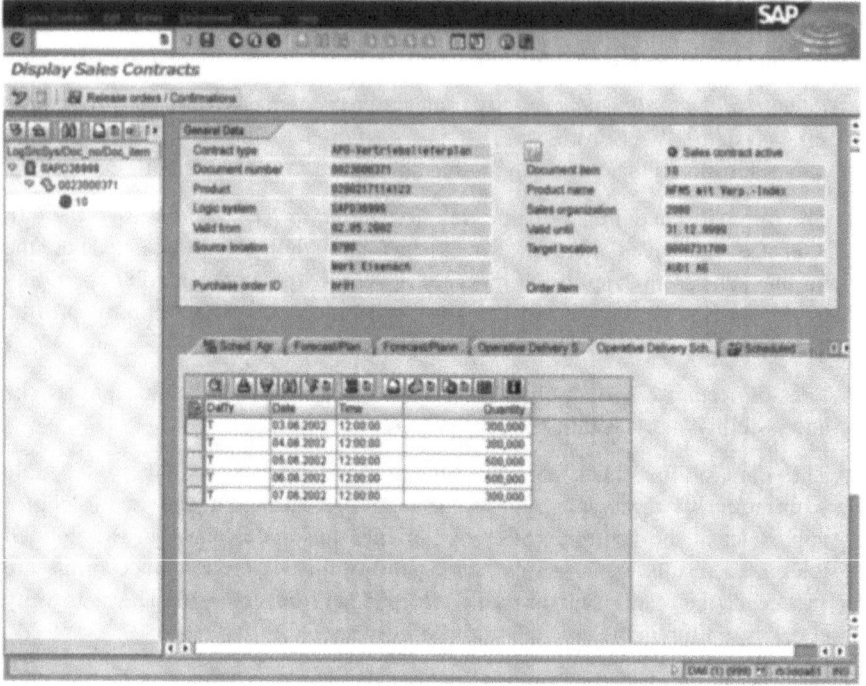

Figure 7.16: Operative delivery schedules in APO

- *Planning the production*: Production planning is now carried out in APO for the confirmed due delivery schedules. At Bosch EhW, the planning is only carried out for packaging activities since the production planning is already carried out in advance.

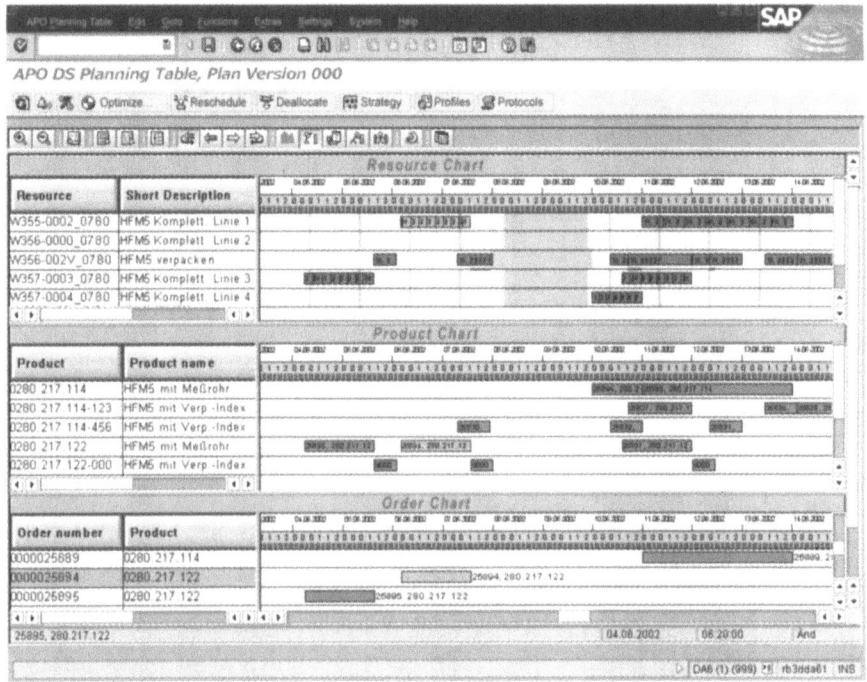

Figure 7.17: Planning the packaging activities of JIT delivery schedules

Figure 7.17 shows how product 0280.217.122, for example, is packed upon completion. Planning the packaging activity (see under product number 0280.217.122-000) is only carried out if the admissibility and feasibility check were successful.

- *Receipt of the JIT delivery schedules*: If the customer confirms the framework order through JIT delivery schedules, it is compared with the previously received due delivery schedules (see Figure 7.18). An admissibility check is again carried out, in order to detect large variances compared to the former framework orders (also called planned (PL) orders). In case of passed admissibility and feasibility check, the JIT delivery schedules (also called sales scheduling agreement (SSA) releases) are turned into operative delivery schedules that can be executed and sent in the R/3 system.

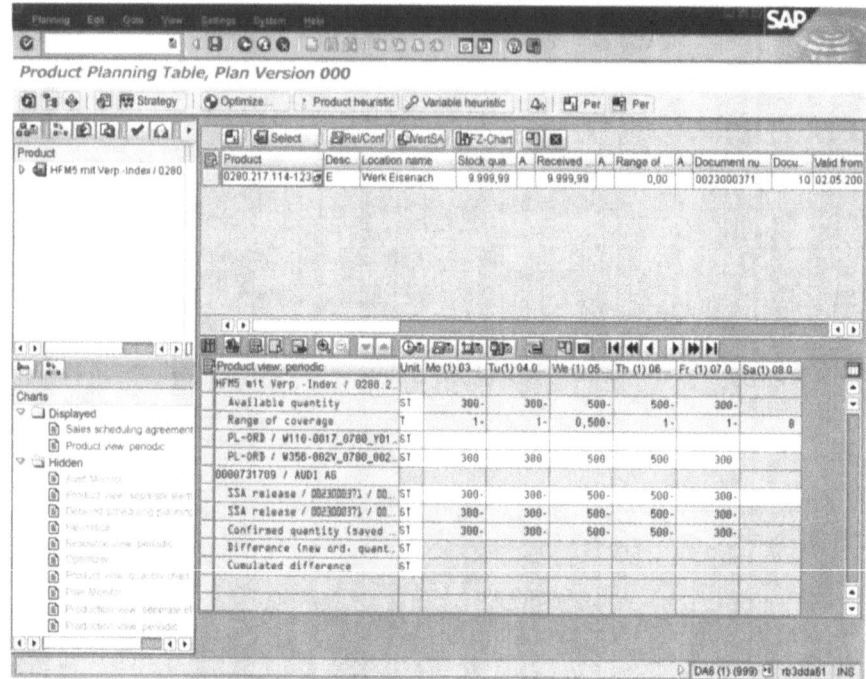

Figure 7.18: Comparison between planned orders and scheduling agreement releases in APO

Figure 7.18 shows the planning board for product 0280.217.114-123. The lower table shows how the confirmed due delivery schedule from Figure 7.16 (SSA release) exactly matches the previously received framework order (PL-ORD).

This Collaborative Management of Delivery Schedules can also be integrated with the R/3 and APO system at the recipient's site. The details on this are described in section 5.6.

7.3   Case Study Goodyear: Use of mySAP Supply Chain Management

The Goodyear Tire & Rubber Company with 95,000 employees worldwide and a daily production of more than 500,000 tires is one of the largest tire and rubber manufacturers in the world. The company possesses six rubber plantations and operates 84 factories in 26 countries (see Figure 7.19). Development centers exist in the United States, Japan and Luxembourg.

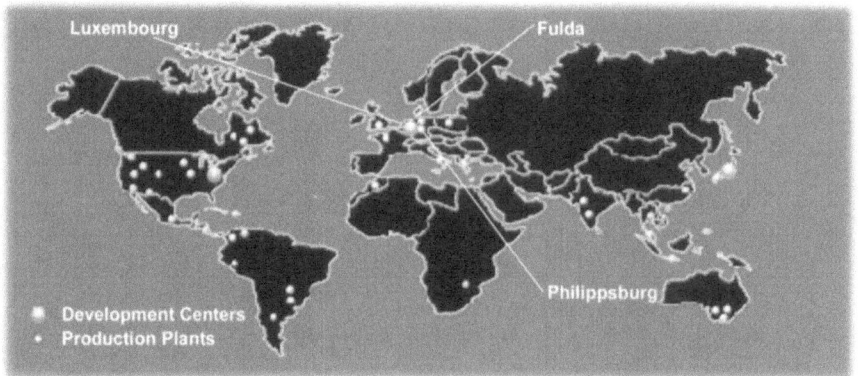

Figure 7.19: Global positioning of production plants and development centers

The company operates with the brands Goodyear, Fulda, Kelly, Lee, Delta, Voyager, Debica and Sava, and is represented in 42 countries, in which the Goodyear products are distributed through over 25,000 sales branches. In Europe, the corporate group operates under the name Goodyear Dunlop Tires Europe B.V. since the alliance with the tire manufacturer Dunlop: In Germany alone, more than 60,000 points of delivery are supplied with products from the corporate group. In addition to the large automobile manufacturers, franchise holders and service companies, the customers comprise both large and small companies such as service stations.

In addition to two central R/3 systems at the Luxembourg and Kelsterbach locations (near Frankfurt), Goodyear Dunlop Tires Europe uses a distributed IT architecture consisting of different components of the mySAP Supply Chain Management solution to plan and control logistics processes. This is an APO system, a Logistics Execution System (LES) and a BW system. These components are operated in Philippsburg, where both the production plant and central warehouse are located.

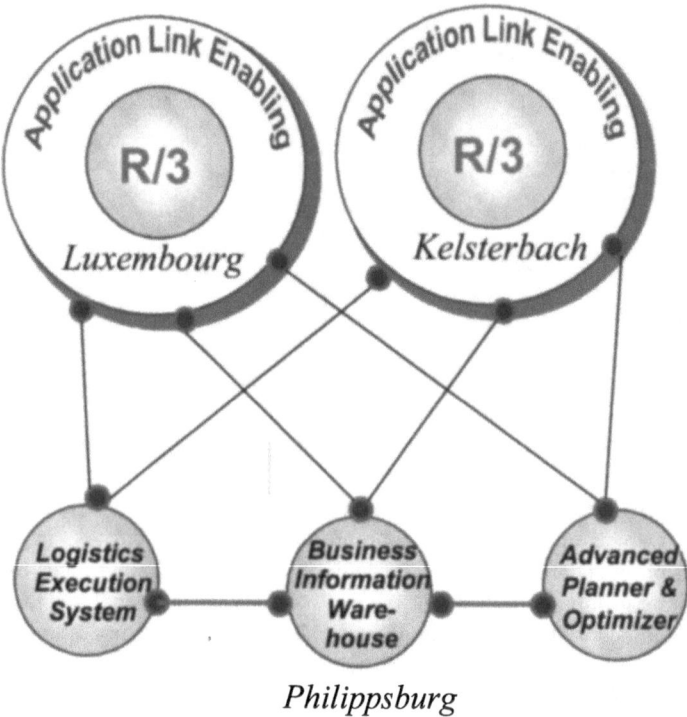

Figure 7.20: Goodyear IT architecture

The properties of the individual application components and their relationships are described below.

7.3.1   APO

7.3.1.1   Task

Goodyear has various locations all over the world that produce specific types of tires and that are supported by independent SAP application components. The individual production locations do not offer the entire Goodyear or Dunlop product range, which makes a mutual product transfer based on a collaborative planning necessary and therefore an interaction between the different SAP applications for the supply of the sales markets. Figure 7.21 shows the global value distribution of the Goodyear systems.

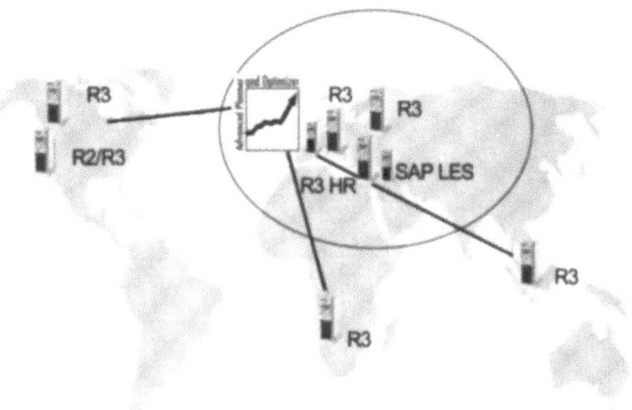

Figure 7.21: Targeted radius of action of APO

With APO, Goodyear targets a global sharing of the ERP systems. So far two central European systems, in which the order receipts of Goodyear (Luxembourg) and Dunlop (Frankfurt) are managed, are connected in Europe. This results in a larger transparency since the data records can be used for collaborative planning in both ERP systems in the areas demand, stocks, production, and distribution of goods. In the long run, this aims to reduce the stock and transport costs by 20-30 percent, increase the processing speed by 25 percent, and improve the product availability and delivery by more than 95 percent.

Alternative options regarding supply or distribution of goods are available for supplying different locations as Figure 7.22 shows with regard to a subarea of the European Goodyear distribution structure. With an assortment of currently 8,000 articles (approximately 4,500 of which are Goodyear products) it must be additionally considered that the product type (A, B or C article), the utilization, and the priority have effects on the specification of the optimal transfer planning. Simultaneous planning that is necessary for a cross-country optimization of logistics processing requires a common approach to different orders across all instances of the involved systems. For the transportation management, this involves the determination of the optimum route, the selection of the transport equipment, and the transport type as well as the determination of the required loading sequences from a general perspective. It should be possible, for example, to develop an optimal, dynamic delivery strategy between locations from a group view, considering various factors such as costs and time.

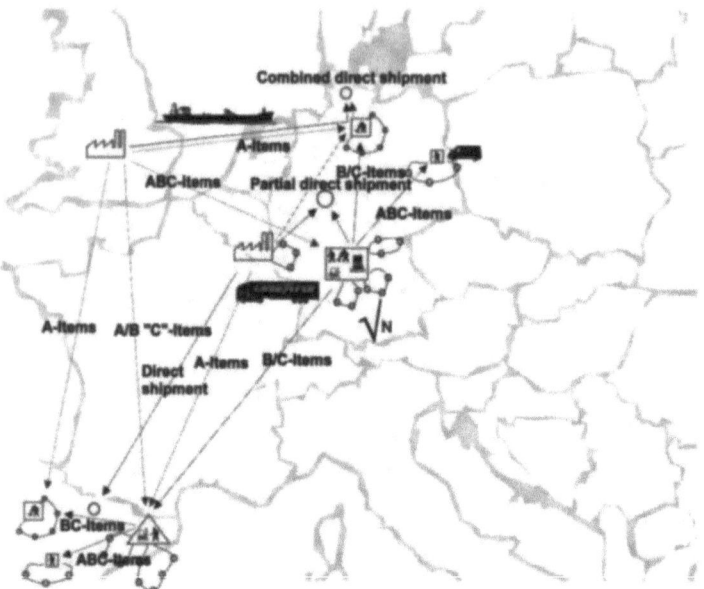

Figure 7.22: Strategies of the delivery between different locations in Europe

7.3.1.2   Using APO

This section describes the use of APO components and their functions for the previously presented task. In a first phase, starting in 1998, Goodyear implemented basic functions for Demand Planning, Supply Network Planning and Deployment, Production Planning, and Available to Promise. The SCC displayed in Figure 7.23 shows an overview of all locations integrated within the model and their relationships.

Here, the two central European systems were connected with the APO system by means of Application Link Enabling (ALE) and CIF technology. ALE designates an SAP-specific technology for the integration of loosely-coupled, independent applications with physically separated R/3 systems. This is a medium for the asynchronous coupling of distributed systems without a shared database. The communication within the ALE technology is performed by means of messages and is established between two applications with Remote Function Calls (RFC). An advantage of ALE is that also different R/3 systems of different releases are able to communicate with one another. This was important in the case of Goodyear since they used different releases for a long time. Currently, release 4.6c is being used in all over Europe.

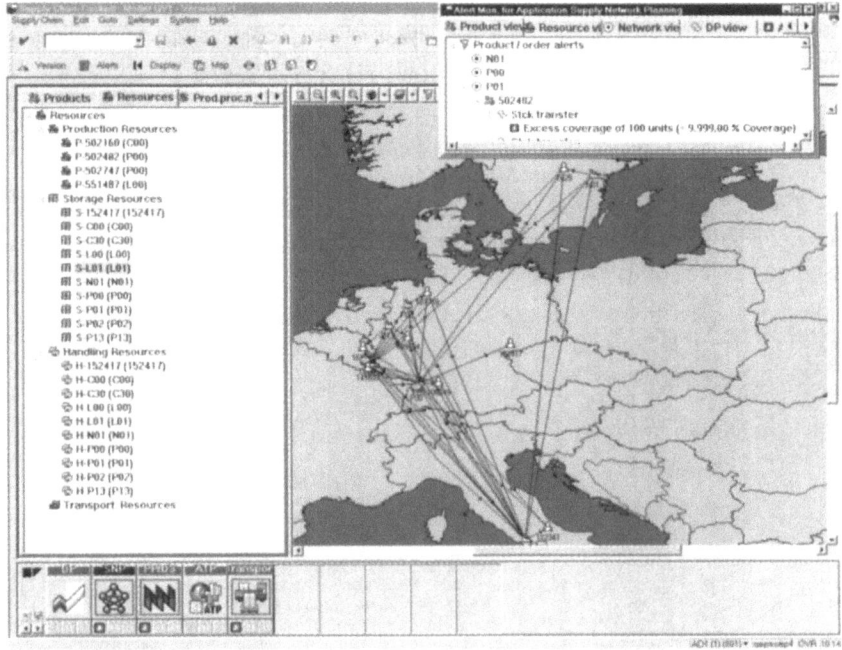

Figure 7.23: Supply Chain Cockpit (Goodyear)

Each individual central system manages a specific number of distribution centers, plants, delivery and consignment warehouses that have been modeled by means of the Supply Chain Engineer. The model contains a number of restrictions. These are

- Production constraints (e.g., the capacity of a production plant),

- transport constraints (transport capacities on different lanes), and

- warehouse constraints (warehouse capacity, number of doors, processable volume, equipment).

The following section introduces the used APO planning modules.

7.3.1.3 Demand Planning

The Demand Planning module includes order data and information from the MM module in the company planning and evaluates them. The sales forecasts are created with the help of seasonal trend models, multi-linear regression and exponential smoothing, whereby factors such as a sudden beginning of winter, registration figures of cars and trucks as well as test results of the ADAC (German automobile club) and their effects on the demand for special products are automatically included in the forecast. The user can freely configure the planning horizon as well as the volume of the used history-oriented data.

7.3.1.4 Supply Network Planning and Deployment

The forecast data is passed to the Supply Network Planning and Deployment module. The forecast of the product demand is broken down using heuristics and assigned to the various locations.

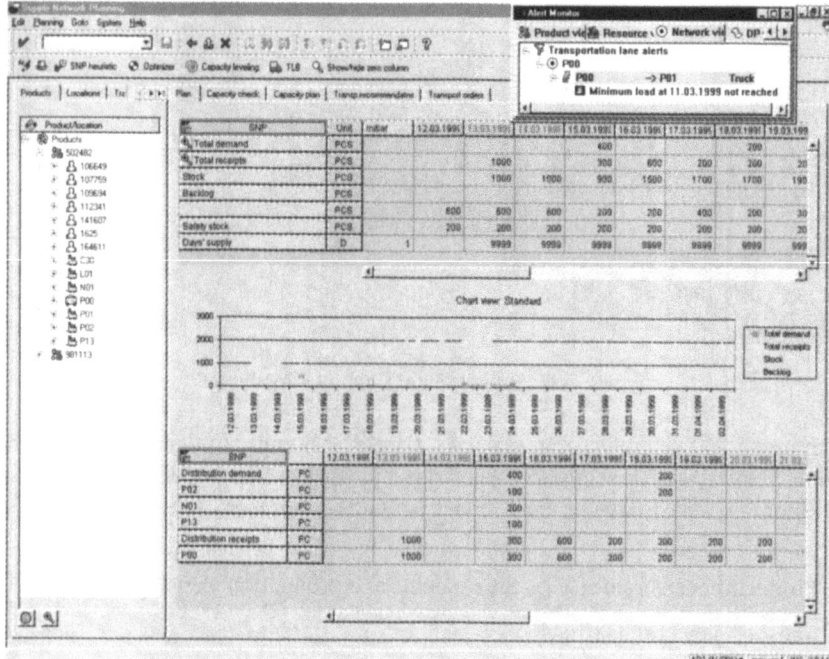

Figure 7.24: Supply Network Planning

As Figure 7.24 shows, the user receives a summary of all available inventory, safety stock, potential supply bottlenecks and distribution information. Supply bottlenecks can be avoided by using production and procurement plans that are forwarded to the respective factories. From a plant viewpoint, a production plan is the request to produce a certain quantity of one or more products for a certain date and time. If raw materials are also required here, the corresponding suppliers that can also be a Goodyear plant, are informed.

The planning results are so far only sporadically passed on to the Transport Load Builder that in this case carries out a cross-system transportation planning and determines how and in which form the deliveries are to be carried out between the individual locations of the corporate group.

7.3.1.5 Available to Promise

By connecting the two central systems, Goodyear can submit availability queries not only on country-specific systems but in future also at a global level (provided that further continental systems are integrated). An ATP cost rate has been defined as restriction, which, when exceeded, causes the rejection of a delivery. In future, the ATP functionality should be extended to production and transport orders.

7.3.1.6 Supply Chain Reporting

In addition, Goodyear developed a special reporting concept, by means of which data can be used for analyses directly from the APO *live*Cache. This allows to include logistics data in analyses already during their processing in APO on different levels of granularity. More details on this will follow within the description of the BW in section 7.3.3.

7.3.1.7 SAP APO – An Evaluation

The project for implementing APO started in November 1998. In June 1999, production started for some selected products. Only then, it was released for the entire range of products. Difficulties occurred mainly with the complex integration work, through to the mutual exchange of information between APO and the participating R/3 systems.

A second implementation phase, starting midyear 2002, was delayed due to the merge with Dunlop. The objective here is to implement further APO functionalities, such as the so far neglected Detailed Scheduling and aspects of the Strategic Planning. The latter, for example, should enable the analysis of alternative location decisions and their effects on costs and time. In addition, Goodyear strives for implementing a vendor-managed inventory with approximately 600 business partners.

The first results from using APO suggest significant cost savings in the entire European network. Extrapolated to the implementation of the complete product range, savings of 25-30 percent in the stock area (stock costs) and 20-30 percent in the area of transport costs can be expected. The standard ATP scenarios so far implemented for the two European central systems lead to a significant reduction of the response times, both for external customers and also for corporation-internal queries.

7.3.2   Support for Logistics Processes Using the SAP Logistics Execution System

7.3.2.1   Starting Point and Task

Goodyear has three central facilities in Germany that required an instrument to improve the processing in the warehouse and transport areas. This includes:

- a delivery warehouse in Duisburg with a storage area of 15,000 square meters,

- a factory warehouse in Fulda (production location including warehouses with a product range consisting of A, B and C articles) with a space of 13,000 square meters as well as

- the location in Philippsburg (Germany) that produces goods and also serves as distribution center for A, B and C products manufactured worldwide. The warehouse area of the location amounts to 70,000 square meters. Tires produced in Asia, for example, are distributed to other locations of the Goodyear Group or to customers via Philippsburg.

The management of these locations was initially realized within a central R/3 system in Luxembourg. However, this resulted in the following problems:

- The high data arrival rate meant that the realization within the R/3 architecture was possible only to a limited extent, because, depending on the utilization, the response times of the central system as result of the data storage on a database could be very long.

- Updates to the central system, for example because of release changes, affect the availability of the systems at both locations.

- The functionality for the support of decentralized warehouse and transport processes provided with the R/3 system (Release 4.5) did not suffice for an efficient support of these business processes at the locations.

With this background, a SAP pilot project with the implementation of a decentralized system physically located in Philippsburg was started in February 1997. The objective was to keep the central order management in Luxembourg and provide lasting support for the warehouse and transport processes at the two locations through new functionality. As Figure 7.25 shows, the R/3 applications were connected using ALE.

The LES manages the Fulda and Philippsburg locations since September 1997. In this case, the logistics processing in Philippsburg was supported by the forklift guiding system Mobile Operating Business (MOB) from the company Witron, which will be discussed in our Porsche case study (see section 7.4). The MOB system was, however, replaced in the course of a release upgrade (4.6.c) and by different proprietary developments that according to Goodyear lead to advantages compared to the previous solution.

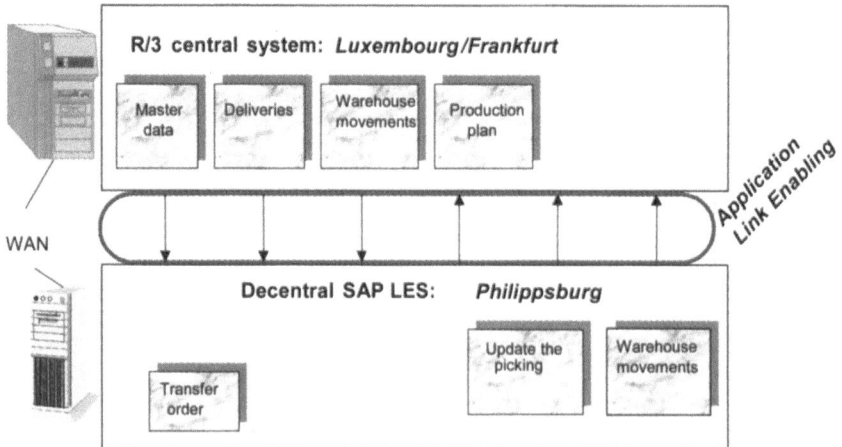

Figure 7.25: Goodyear Dunlop Tires Europe B.V System architecture

LES supports the warehouse management, transport, and distribution functions within the R/3 system in Luxembourg (now also those of the Dunlop systems in Frankfurt). From the view of the two locations, this peripheral system with physical headquarters in Philippsburg has two very important advantages: First, it is available 24 hours per day and seven days a week and secondly, it runs independently from administration, utilization, and technical problems of the central system.

The following section discusses the transportation management and picking, two central processes in logistics, and their support provided by the LES.

7.3.2.2 Transportation Management with LES

Orders are managed with the central ERP systems in Luxembourg and Frankfurt. In general, a distinction is made between incoming orders from large customers and from day-to-day business. The major customer business involves, for example, orders from large automobile manufactures. The orders are linked to outline agreements and are characterized by a large volume. JIT deliveries are characteristic for this type of business. A delivery schedule is automatically imported into the central system in Luxembourg by means of EDI and is ascertained by a detailed schedule up to four hours prior to the production of the original equipment manufacturer. Figure 7.26 shows the interaction of the central system (in this case Luxembourg) and LES.

Depending on time restrictions and distances, the resulting delivery can be made either from one of the two locations or from a consignment warehouse. Confirmations and shipping notifications, which are currently still handled by the central system, are in future to be replaced by the LES.

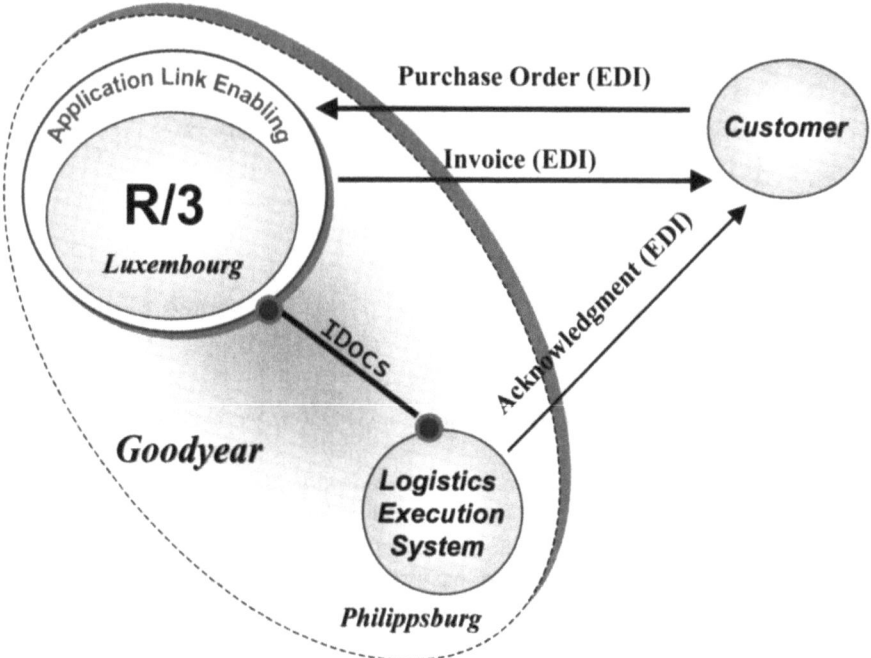

Figure 7.26: Information exchange with the major customer business

For the day-to-day business, small companies often order the required products at the telephone call center in Cologne. These are in most of the cases smaller order quantities. The information is entered there into the central system without further delay. This is necessary because Goodyear provides a 24-hour service from incoming order to delivery for this type of business. The order volume currently lies between 10,000 and 30,000 orders per day for Europe.

Regardless of the type of the incoming order, deliveries are generated from the orders (exactly one delivery is generated from one order). As the following Figure 7.27 shows, the tire business is characterized by seasonal fluctuations. The outlier in November can be explained with the changes in weather and the associated switch of the user from summer to winter tires.

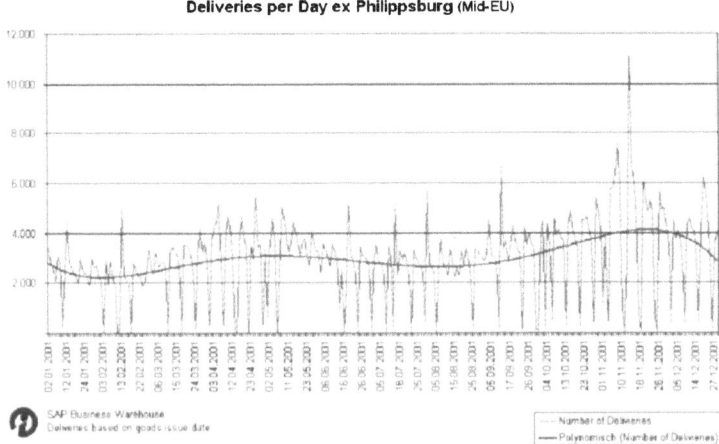

Figure 7.27: Deliveries outgoing from Philippsburg

A preselection, from which location (Fulda or Philippsburg) the customer is to receive the delivery, has already been decided in the central system upon receipt of the orders. Since the physical services, such as picking, are managed by the LES in these locations, the LES receives a copy of the delivery. The transfer is carried out almost in real-time based on the previously discussed ALE technology.

The description of the delivery in the system contains the goods recipient, the ordered articles and the number of units, the total weight, the goods issue date, and all information needed for further processing (see Figure 7.28).

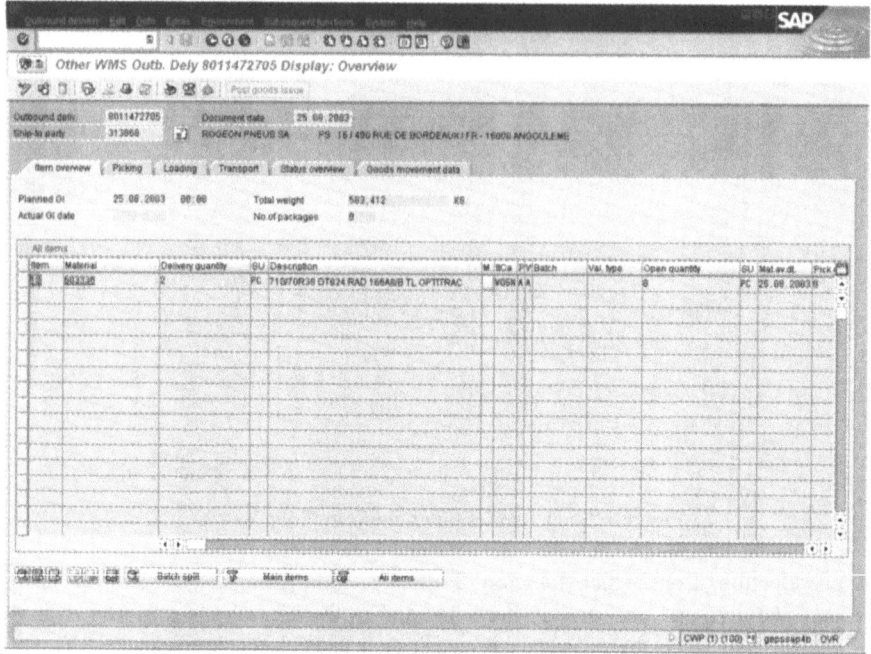

Figure 7.28: Description of the delivery in the decentralized system

Whereas the large volume and thus full capacity use of the transport medium for orders from major customers result in a direct delivery ex works, the supply of smaller customers usually takes place as a multilevel transportation chain. The individual purchase orders are distributed to smaller delivery sites through various service agents, from where they are then delivered to the customers. The transportation chain thus consists of a main leg (up to the delivery warehouse) that is then followed by a fine-tuned distribution (to the customer). The partner companies are responsible for the coordination of the fine-tuned distribution. To ensure the 24-hour service, fixed doors or loading ramps and time windows are assigned to the freight forwarders involved in the processing and thus the loading and inbound delivery times are synchronized so that the distribution warehouses and thus the customers can be supplied on time.

The 24-hour service offered by Goodyear requires a comprehensive transportation planning for deliveries by trucks. For this purpose, transfer orders, which are called shipments in the SAP terminology and contain all the information needed for the transportation processing, are created.

The transportation planning is made via a transport monitor especially developed by Goodyear, that provides the user with extensive options for grouping deliveries (e.g., for one truck).

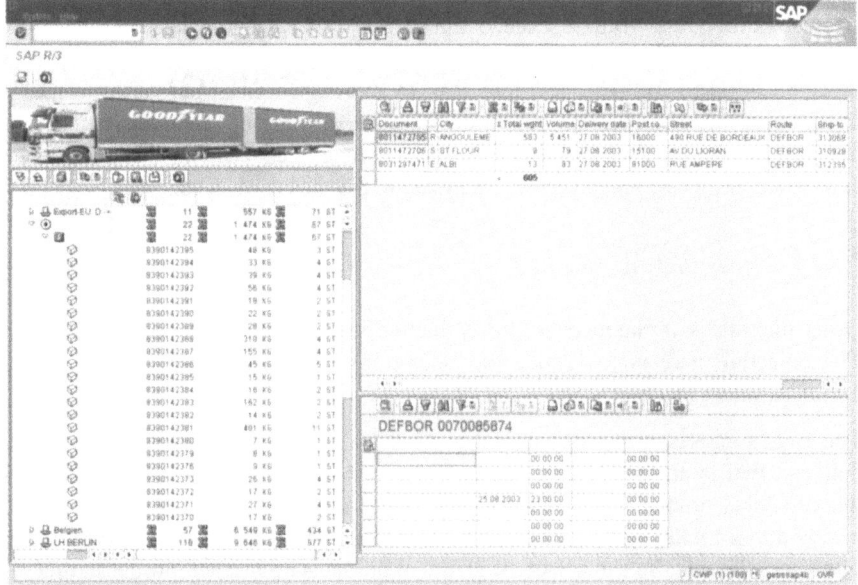

Figure 7.29: Transport monitor

The following information shown in Figure 7.29 is available:

- The transportation route,

- the freight forwarder,

- the total of the deliveries grouped together to a transfer order as well as

- the total weight of the deliveries grouped together to a transfer order or the tires contained within.

Furthermore, the loading times and the start of the transport as well as the end can be queried via the transport monitor.

The grouping of the deliveries is supported by different, individual Goodyear strategies. This includes:

- Automatic strategy determination,

- grouping by country, postal code and street,

- grouping by routes, and

- grouping by transportation zones.

The system automatically predetermines the shipment route, freight forwarder, and loading gate. However, these are only suggestions determined based on rule-based criteria, which the user can change at any time. Information on the loading times is needed for controlling the subsequent picking of the deliveries. Transport start and end are used for a later analysis of the transports.

Should the delivery volume exceed the capacity of a vehicle, the deliveries are automatically distributed among other vehicles. A "greedy algorithm" as well as the application of further algorithms lead to an assignment of deliveries to means of transport that is essentially based on a simple sort order. The algorithm starts a new run as soon as the capacity of the first vehicle is exhausted. This assignment ends when all deliveries have been assigned to the means of transport.

7.3.2.3   Order Picking with LES

Order picking is initiated once the collective shipments have been put together. The objective here is to reduce the operations within the warehouse and thus minimize the associated work.

The LES supports a two-step picking. This picking is not restricted to a single delivery, that is not oriented to customers and individual deliveries, and provides the capability to pick products from different deliveries in a single step. This means that a picker sees just the tires to be picked and not the associated order. Thus, for example, he can select all identical products of a transfer order in one.

Goodyear developed a special monitor (picking monitor) for this as well. The LES provides a suggestion that makes an assignment in "picking waves". Goodyear refers to this as a grouping run. This specifies which tires are to be picked when and by whom. The different articles of a delivery can therefore be assigned to absolutely different waves.

The assignment or division of the deliveries and their parts is carried out based on rules. The rule set contains, for example, information on the warehouse personnel and available operating facilities, such as forklift truck. Depending on the size, the volume and the storage bin, it is taken into account which devices are required for the picking. A distinction can be made here, for example, between picking in bulk storage and picking in a shelf warehouse. Different devices are needed for the processing depending on the storage location. Because the personnel also have different qualifications, not all products can be "picked" by any employee.

Once the individual products have been assigned to different picking waves, this data is directly passed on to the workers within the warehouse by means of data radio frequency technology. The system shows them the priorities of the shipments and also which storage locations contain the respective tires. It also determines the shortest path through the warehouse.

If the times determined for a picking process are exceeded, a corresponding alert message is displayed in the picking monitor. The withdrawn tires are automatically confirmed directly in the forklift truck. The labeling of the tires is performed in the same sequence, in which the transfer orders were picked, and is initiated directly by the forklift truck driver's activities.

A delivery-related goods issue posting is made after loading has been completed. Each individual delivery is passed to the central system as an IDoc (see section 3.1) and an EDI transfer to the customer or the distribution center is initiated. Thereby, date confirmations and invoices are exchanged. In future, the confirmations will be made directly from the decentralized system.

7.3.2.4 SAP LES – An Evaluation

From Goodyear's point of view, the implementation of a stand-alone LES produced the following results:

- The effort for the system administration was reduced to 20 minutes per month and satisfied the expectations placed on the LES.

- The personnel costs for the maintenance of the system could be significantly reduced in comparison to the old system.

- According to Goodyear, no hardware and software error occurred even after more than three years of operation.

- The average response times, which (depending on utilization) were extremely long due to the data administration by the central system, could be reduced to a third by switching to the LES.

- The personnel and warehouse planning has been facilitated.

- The commissioning of the LES has resulted in an improvement in productivity. Specifically, 30 percent more deliveries could be handled with the same number of personnel.

- The times for the assembly and picking of the deliveries are less than two hours and have been reduced by approximately 60 percent.

- The handling effort for the loading and unloading of a means of transport was affected only to a small extent and lies below ten minutes. The error-proneness has been reduced and thus the quality of the in-house processes improved.

7.3.3   Use of the SAP Business Information Warehouse at Goodyear

To manage and process the comprehensive information of the two systems previously discussed, the system architecture in Philippsburg was extended by SAP BW in 1999. This application runs on a Windows NT server with two processors and a random access memory of 2 gigabyte. The BW has the following main uses:

- remove mass data from the operative systems, such as the created deliveries and transport orders,

- provide data to perform analyses and reports, and

- provide a historical data basis for APO planning runs.

Due to the high data volume in the area of logistics execution, the performance of the transaction systems already deteriorated by approximately 50 percent after two years. Because the mass data must not have any affect on the day-to-day activities, a transfer to the BW has been carried out. This elimination of data from the transaction systems has restored the original performance. In addition, the administered information can now be viewed in the BW at any time and included in a later company planning.

In addition to the performance improvement, the BW is primarily used to perform comprehensive analyses and reports. Figure 7.30 shows the various InfoCubes Goodyear defined for this purpose. This includes Material Requirements Planning, Inventory Management, Demand Planning, Purchasing and Quality Management, for instance (see left side of screen). Within the BW, the individual InfoCubes are represented by a technical statement, for example 0FIAA.

So far, Goodyear primarily uses sales order data and deliveries for analyses. The transfer from the two central systems is carried out automatically by means of the corresponding information models of the Business Content (see section 4.2).

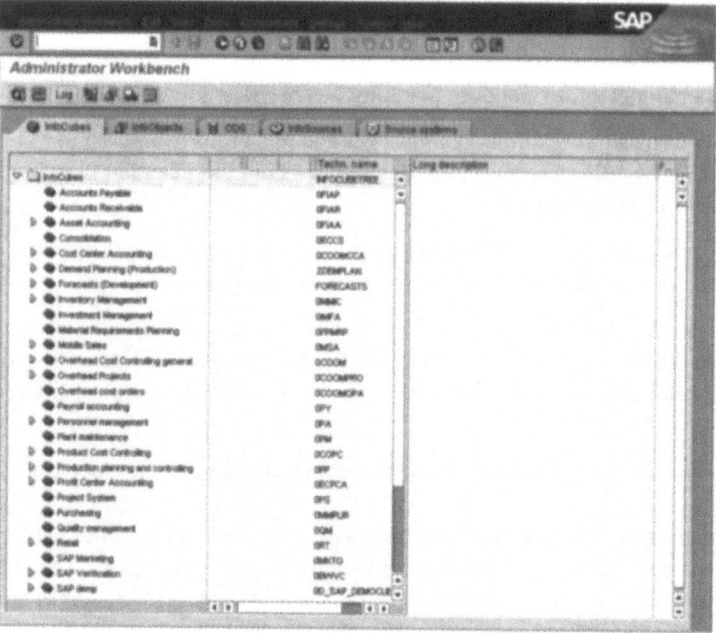

Figure 7.30: InfoCubes

The resulting data or information form the basis for a supply chain-related activity-based costing. The main objective is to generate process-oriented and thus cross-application information on costs. This information can be used strategically to improve the product/customer cost planning as well as operatively to identify and quantify optimization potentials. To be able to quickly and purposefully influence the costs, the cost management in the distribution area not only needs information on which costs originate from where in the company but also

- the services performed there,

- the required resources,

- possible cause-effect relations between costs and services as well as

- relations between activities and product costs.

With regard to the valuation of the cost-to-serve, Goodyear configured various analyses and reports, such as delivery costs per month and location, and various detailed analyses, for example distribution costs at a location on a certain day.

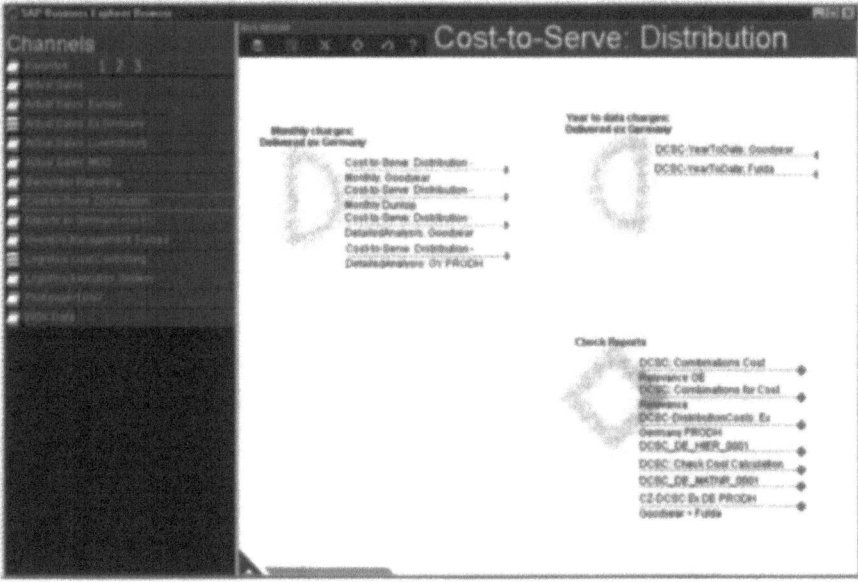

Figure 7.31: Cost-to-serve analyses

The individual queries are started via the Business Explorer. As already described in section 4.2.6, data from the APO *live*Cache can also be called via the BW front end.

After a query is called, the data is displayed in MS Excel. Here, the user has the option to expand aggregated data in order to access a higher detail level, for example the document level. The following figure shows the example of a detailed analysis in the area of the distribution for a special tire. The spreadsheet (see Figure 7.32) contains information on tire deliveries, differentiated by country (e.g., Belgium, France, Germany), by sales organizations (see left side of the

screen) and by tire type. The deliveries of the different articles are added for every
country and displayed in form of a total.

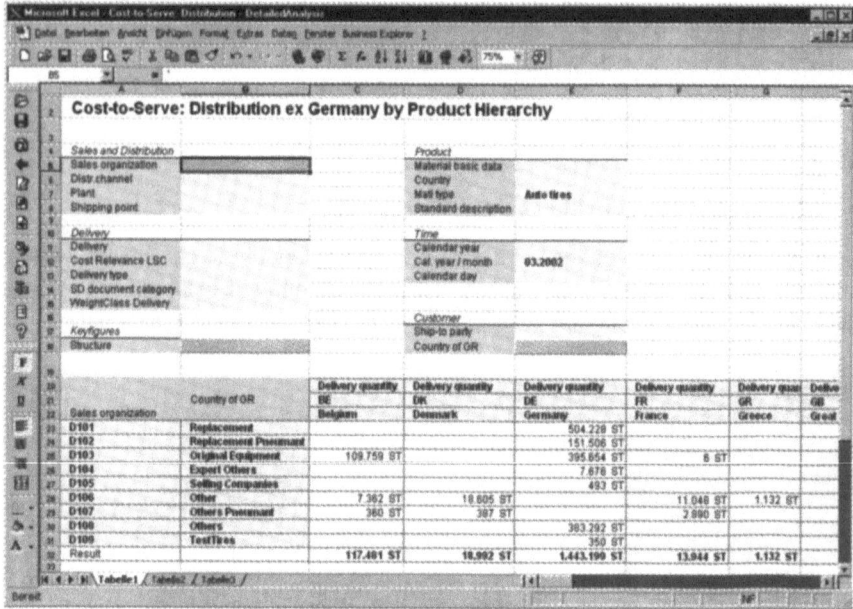

Figure 7.32: Analysis of deliveries by countries

According to Goodyear, the cost-oriented supply chain analysis has been
influencing the entire European corporate group strategy for over two years now.
It helped to identify, analyze, and to a large extent eliminate weak points.

In the future, the data maintained within the LES is to be used for analyzing the
utilization of the vehicle capacities, the workload, the arrangement of the products
within the corporate group warehouses, and for checking the effectiveness of the
picking.

The BW is a useful addition to the previous system infrastructure, since APO data
can be stored in the BW. These are order and delivery data as well as forecasts
from the Demand Planning module. If all data records were permanently held in
APO, this would result in an unsatisfactory system performance and thus real-time
information could no longer be provided.

7.4   Case Study for Spare Parts Logistics at Porsche

Porsche AG is a comparatively small, globally operating original equipment
manufacturer that was founded in Germany and supplies the premium sports car

sector with the two model series Porsche Boxster and Porsche 911. The cross-country vehicle Porsche Cayenne joins in as third model series, which denotes the entry into the market segment of Sport Utility Vehicles (SUV).

The company has some 7,916 employees and realized sales amounting to 4.86 billion € in the fiscal year 2001/02, when they sold 54,234 cars. Porsche AG sells their vehicles in a total of 78 countries, whereby the North American markets, USA and Canada, are the most important with sales amounting to 41 percent of the total sales. The domestic market, Germany, makes up 32 percent and the European market 21 percent of the total sales. The remaining 6 percent is sold in the other geographical markets, mainly in Asia. The central production location of the company is in Zuffenhausen (Germany), while the central warehouse, from which all dealers and importers all over the world are supplied with 80 percent of the spare parts, is located in Ludwigsburg (Germany). 20 percent of the spare parts are distributed directly from the production warehouse in Zuffenhausen. The main development site is in Weissach (Germany) where also the Porsche AG racing division is located. Finally, the cross-country vehicle Cayenne is manufactured in Leipzig (Germany).

The real-time supply of Porsche customers with spare parts is to be ensured in addition to the sales of new vehicles. Within a global logistics strategy defined in 1999, Porsche decided to introduce SAP software for the support of the spare parts logistics in order to improve this process. First, the strategic background leading to this decision is explained below. Then, the process of the implementing and applying SAP software in the parts logistics will be described.

7.4.1 Strategic Background

In 1999, Porsche phrased a global logistics strategy, by means of which, among other things, the supply of the dealers of the nine subsidiaries is to be improved. The following figure provides key figures from these companies.

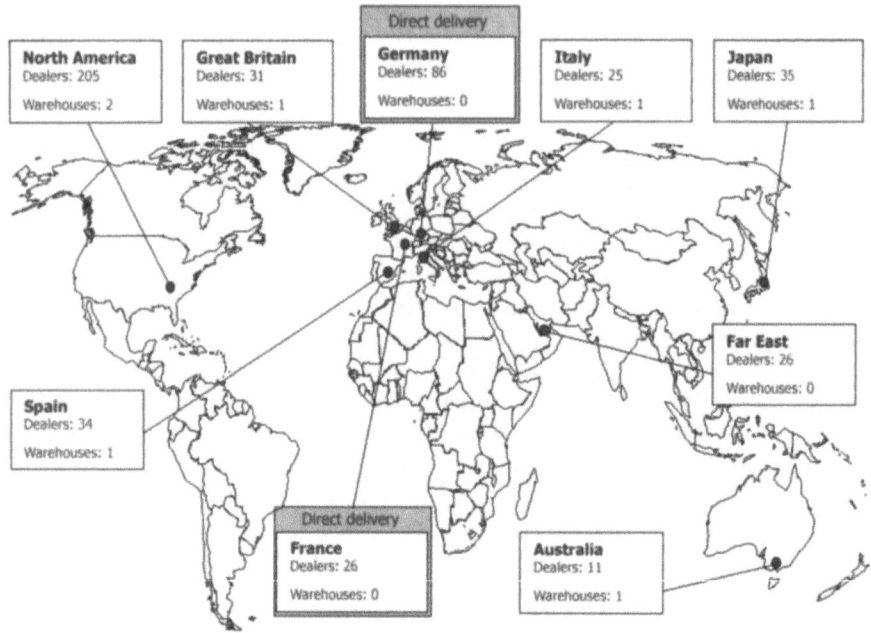

Figure 7.33: Global Porsche dealer network

This strategy pursues two main goals: until 2003, a value-based reduction of 15 million € of the worldwide warehouse stocks kept in readiness together with a reduction of the safety stocks by 20 percent. The other goal is to improve the service level by six percent. Prior to the implementation of this strategy, the supply chain was as follows:

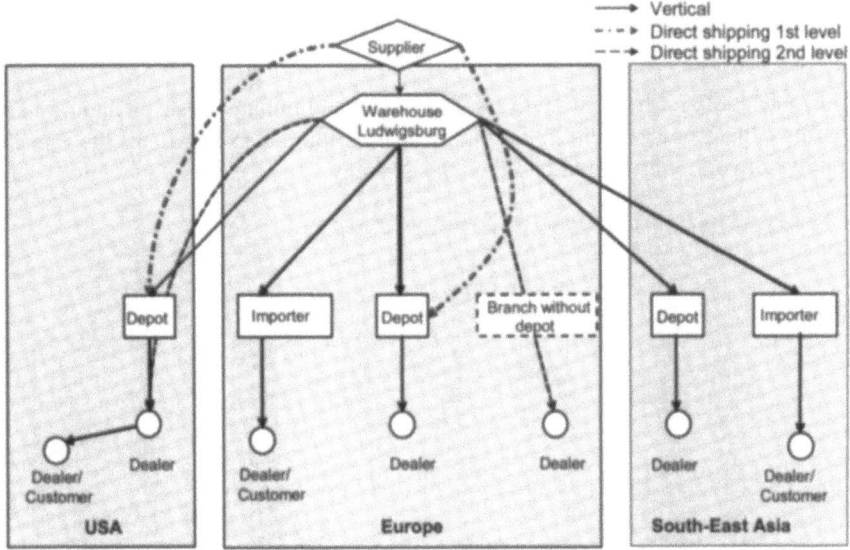

Figure 7.34: Spare parts supply chain of Porsche prior to the restructuring

The central warehouse in Ludwigsburg (PAG Ludwigsburg) was supplied with the respective spare parts through approx. 1,200 vendors. From this central warehouse again, 16 worldwide distributed depots were supplied, that in turn supplied the approximately 500 Porsche dealers. Only in exceptional cases, also both a direct supply of the depots through the vendors and of the dealers through the central warehouse was possible.

Therefore, each member of the supply chain was generally in direct relationship only with the immediately preceding or subsequent level: The demand was calculated and a corresponding purchase order was posted. The importers and dealers used different software systems to support these ordering and delivery processes, which lead to incompatibilities and complicated the global collaboration.

The missing software integration was one of the causes for the lack of transparency within the supply chain, due to which it was not possible, for example, to determine where a certain part was located at a certain time. It was also not possible to react to changes within less than three to five days so that, for example, the adjustment of the stocks to special sales deals was delayed and therefore could partially not occur in time. In total, the delivery times were very long, which even resulted in some business transactions not materializing.

Reliable forecasts of the demands were also not possible: On average, variances of approximately ten percent of the forecasted quantities occurred, since these forecasts were mainly based on the experience or the intuition of the MRP controller. Each member of the chain kept high safety stocks in readiness to compensate for the risk resulting from the low-speed response times as well as the minor planning accuracy.

The new global partial strategy is expected to eliminate these difficulties and optimize the processes within the supply chain. Figure 7.35 represents the Porsche supply network restructured based on this strategy.

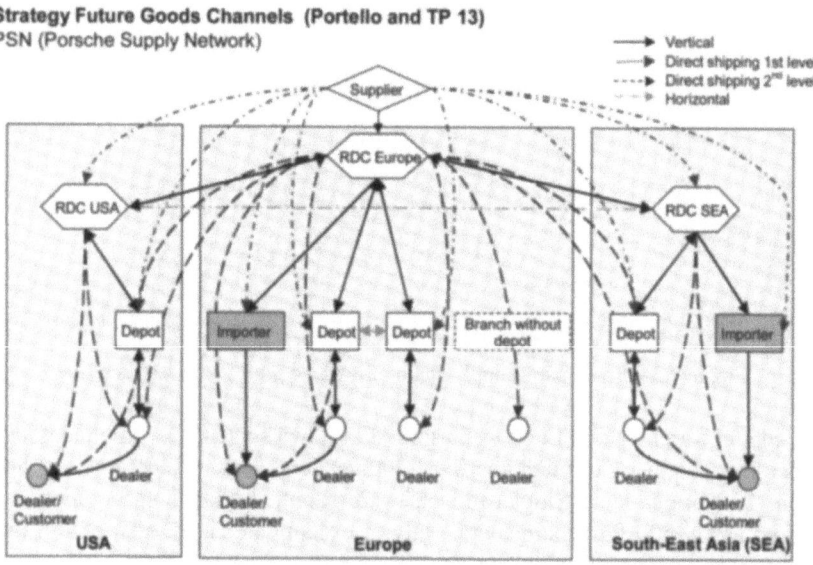

Figure 7.35: Spare parts supply chain of Porsche after the restructuring

The new strategy, on the one hand, plans to set up new regional distribution centers (RDC) in the most important markets (USA and Asia) in addition to Europe. Furthermore, the number of direct deliveries to the regional RDCs and the depots in these regions through the suppliers is to be increased. The number of dealers to be directly served through the RDCs, on the other hand, is also to be increased. Also the exchange at one level (e.g., between depots) is to be enabled. The RDC Europe in Ludwigsburg will still be supplied with spare parts by the vendors. There, approximately 56,000 articles are stored; between 8,000 and 9,000 shipments are sent all over the world every day. The majority of these deliveries goes to the two other RDCs North America and Southeast Asia. These three RDCs supply the depots, which in turn supply the individual dealers. The local depots are to ensure a high service level within a region. The most important objectives of the new global logistics strategy are:

- One software system for all importers,
- interface to the dealer management systems,
- high level of transparency of the entire supply chain,

- forecasts and purchase orders based on the customer demand,

- automatically generated proposals for the replenishment for importers,

- automatic replenishment of the dealers' stocks,

- global leveling of the stocks,

- global spare parts locator in case of emergencies,

- reduction of the safety stocks by 20 percent,

- minimization of the total transport and stockholding costs through optimized delivery frequency and quantity,

- increased flexibility due to earlier notification about changes, and

- tracking and tracing.

7.4.2 Project Structure and Process

The realization of the global logistics strategy of Porsche was carried out in two subprojects with a total volume of approximately 20 million €. The first one, "PorTello" (German acronym for Porsche Spare Parts Logistics), concentrates on the optimization and restructuring of the spare parts business in the German market. The second subproject Polaris (Porsche parts logistics and replenishment international system) includes the plan to introduce the system implemented in Germany within PorTello at a global level. This means that in a first step the importers and in a second step also all dealers are to be connected worldwide.

The realization of the second subproject has been completed in the area North America and is to be extended to the other markets step-by-step.

Porsche made the decision to support the global logistics processes mainly using products from SAP AG. A reason for this decision was that the R/3 system was already being used when the first subproject (PorTello) was started, and thus little compatibility problems were to be expected.

PorTello ran from October 1999 through August 2001 and called for an average of 50 employees for this period, whereby the project team consisted of a third each of external consultants, employees from the user departments and employees from the local IT departments.

Extensive decisions were made already before PorTello started. This includes, on the one hand, the selection of APO (version 3.0) for the support of the supply chain management. APO 3.0 was marketed only after PorTello had already started; Porsche was one of the first pilot customers for implementing and using it. Porsche, however, accepted the risk associated with this because this version covered the defined requirements better than the previous ones. An example for this is the function of the Supply Chain Cockpit that is to be used as the basic reporting system for the global logistics. It was furthermore decided to use the Transport Management System (TMS) of the company Witron that takes on the entire warehouse control and thus adds to the functionality of the SAP WM (Warehouse Management) module.

In a third step, it was decided to upgrade from R/3 4.0 to version 4.6.

The project PorTello was processed in eight phases:

The first phase of PorTello included the recording of the actual processes in order to define the target processes on this basis in the second phase. These processes, however, could only be realized to a certain extent due to the constraints resulting from the use of SAP systems, from which Porsche concluded that the focus of IT or reorganization projects should not necessarily be on a detailed description of the new processes but rather on the definition of targeted goals.

The third phase focused on whether the project ET2000 from Volkswagen AG should be copied by Porsche in modified form. The decision was made that this would not be useful and so a second "Blueprint" was created in the second half of 2000, which transferred the target processes into implementation plans.

The fourth phase of the project – the implementation – claimed the second half of the year 2000. Here, on the one hand, the system was customized. This was necessary due to the fact that Porsche has special software requirements because of its relatively small size and its particular market. On the other hand, Porsche developed various additional programs and add-ons to make further functionalities available. The modeling of substitution chains, for example, is supported by individual software. A substitution chain is given if, in case of a return call, a part is not replaced by an individual spare part but by several spare parts. A new headlight, for example, is not built in as a whole but each part, the bulb, the reflector and so on, are built in separately. Due to the *live*Cache technology it is very time consuming to extend APO to include such situations. This can only be solved by additional programs.

An add-on for processing the exchange open item account was developed, for example. The exchange open item account controls the value-based adjustment of the stocks from dealers when they transfer high-quality parts of a car for reprocessing or when they build in reprocessed parts instead of new spare parts.

Furthermore, interfaces were developed during the execution phase to link the SAP systems with other software systems in the company. Finally, module tests were also carried out in this phase.

The last three project phases fell into the year 2001. Within the fifth phase, all development objects were refed to the Porsche system SAP R/3 4.6. The sixth phase included all preparatory measures for the production startup of PorTello on August 1st, 2001. This includes, for example, various integration and productive tests, extensive training (in total 1,700 person days) and the overprovisioning of the importers and the dealers. This overprovisioning is to ensure that no stock-outs occur even in case of difficulties when starting the new system. During the tests it was partially not possible to carry out mass tests, in which all processes run through as in reality.

The project was completed by the support phase, in which for the last four months of 2001 measures for the stabilization and optimization of the system were taken and the users were specifically supported.

Now that the project structure and its process have been introduced, the actual realization of the processes will be described, which run within the spare parts logistics based on the SAP systems.

7.4.3 SAP-based Processes in the Spare Parts Logistics at Porsche

Within the processes for the spare parts delivery at Porsche, service providers, freight forwarders, and vendors are connected to the system by means of EDI (mostly based on the standards ODETTE, VDA and EDIFACT), telephone, fax and e-mail. The process and the interaction and functionality of the components that are used in the spare parts logistics at Porsche are described now. The processes can be divided into three segments "inbound", "warehouse" and "outbound" (see Figure 7.36).

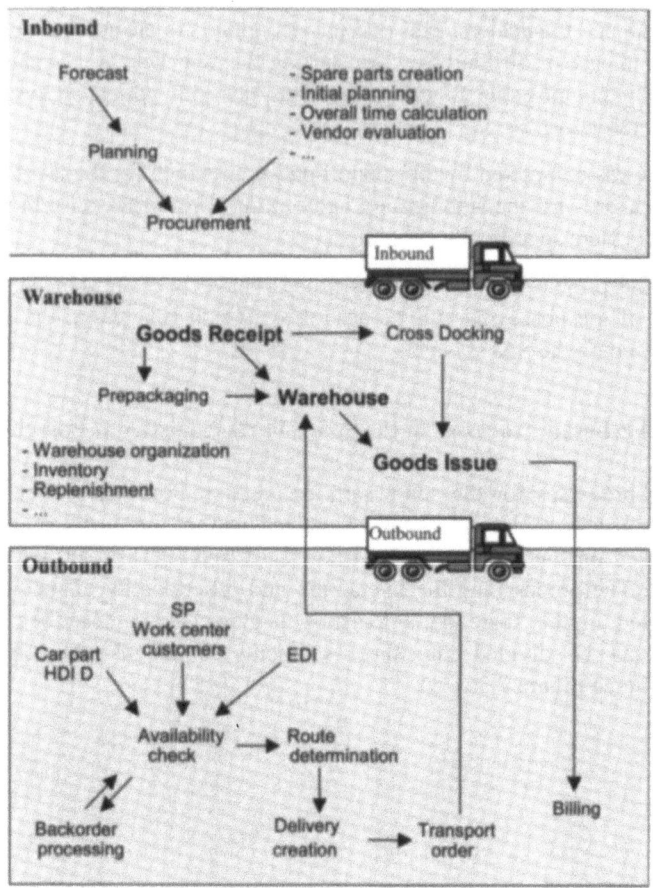

Figure 7.36: Segments of the processes of the SAP-based spare parts logistics

Within the inbound process, the question is how the right quantity of the right goods arrives at the right warehouse at the correct time. APO is used to ensure this: APO is capable of exchanging the master and transaction data required for the planning with the R/3 system at runtime by means of a CIF interface. An example for exchanged information is data from locations that is first entered in the MM module of the R/3 system and is then extended in APO by information relevant for planning, such as geographical data. In APO, there are 180,000 material numbers stored, of which 90,000 parts can be ordered. From these again 50,000 parts are storable and are therefore planned completely in APO. The enhanced master data in APO serves as a basis for generating forecasts on future demands of the importers and dealers; these are created by means of the APO component Demand Planning. The DP module in this case draws on the history of a part, planned sales deals as well as human corrections and uses different forecasting models for this (see section 5.2). If a new part is involved, which consequently does not have an own history yet, the planner can either use the history of a similar part to determine the demand or use the histories of other various single parts to derive the demand for the new part. The determination of these additive demands is again carried out by means of a Porsche-specific add-on that passes the determined history on to APO.

The forecasts are in turn the basis for the material requirements planning with the APO SNP module as well as for the Production Planning and Detailed Scheduling. The planning results are purchase requisitions to vendors that are transferred to the R/3 system. There, the scheduling agreement schedule lines are converted; the dealer and importer, however, can still correct these using an SAP GUI. Furthermore, planners can modify the delivery quantities and dates. Figure 7.37 shows the input template for changing transfer orders. These are generated in the SD module of the R/3 system.

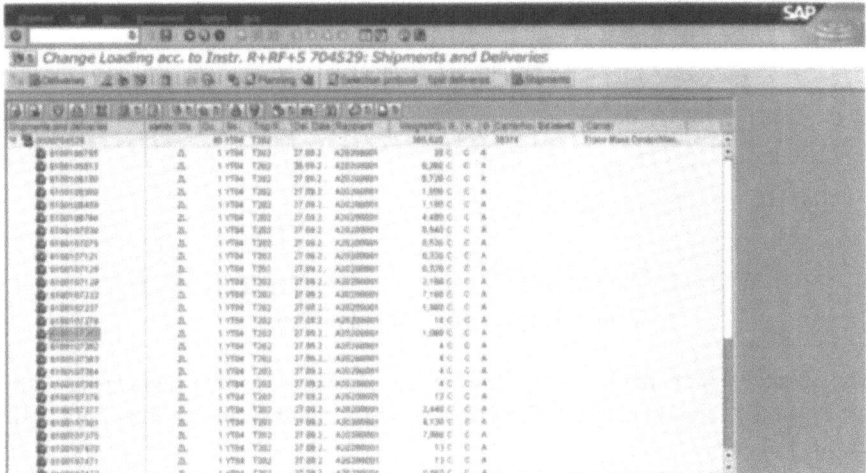

Figure 7.37: Changing an SD transfer order

The transfer order displayed in Figure 7.37 consists of many partial deliveries (for instance, packages with parts), all of which are to be delivered to a single dealer (A20200001).

The described interaction between APO and the R/3 system as well as the tasks that are taken on by APO with the partial logistics are summarized in Figure 7.38.

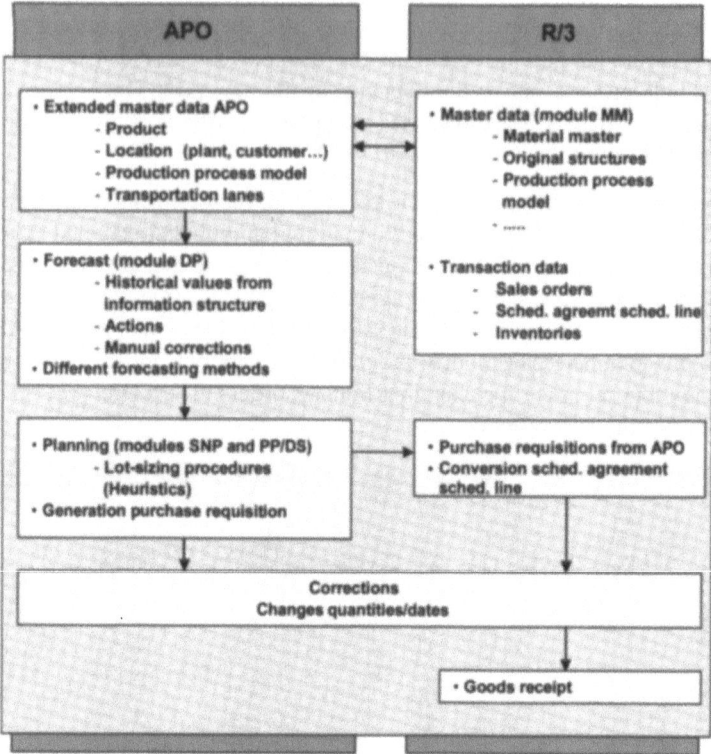

Figure 7.38: Interaction between APO and R/3

The quantities procured by or delivered to the central warehouse Ludwigsburg are based on the sales forecasts that were created for the dealers and importers with the help of APO.

The procured spare parts are now placed in storage in Ludwigsburg; hereby, the warehousing is supported by the WM module as well as by the TMS system of the company Witron. The value-based and quantitative stock for a certain part is in this case always recorded in the WM module that was modified and extended by add-ons. An adjustment was made, for example, so that returns can be taken into account upon goods receipt. A further add-on was created for the packaging processes.

Examples for tasks taken on by TMS are the route optimization and the control of the vehicles via radio. In addition, TMS enables the prioritization of the orders, that is, it can be weighed which part should be delivered and which can still be postponed.

Figure 7.39 shows the operations in the warehouse from the goods receipt up to the goods issue and also what is processed within the R/3 system or where the TMS is used.

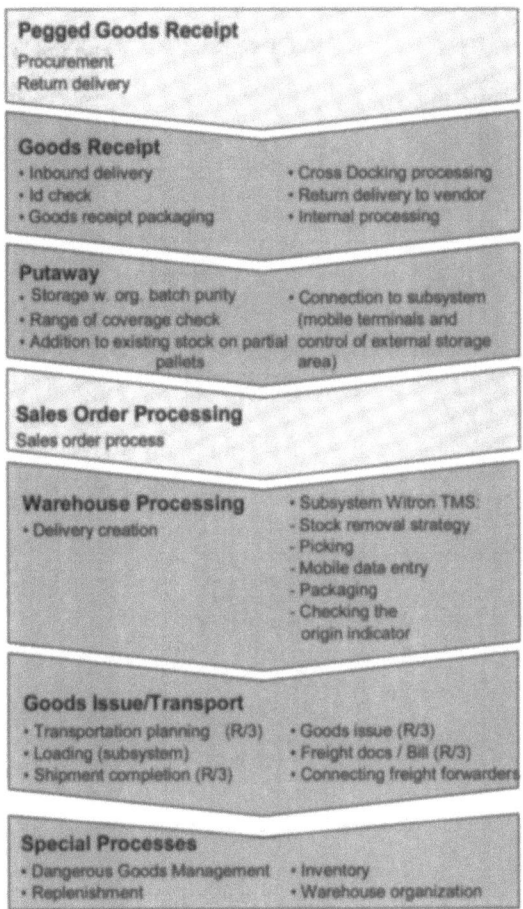

Figure 7.39: The warehousing process

The delivery of the spare parts represents the transition between the process sections warehouses and outbound. In this case, 70 percent of the delivered parts are sent from the central warehouse in Ludwigsburg and 30 percent from the production warehouse in Zuffenhausen. The process section "outbound" is triggered by the orders, that is, purchase orders of the importers and dealers. Figure 7.40 shows how the sales order processing is structured.

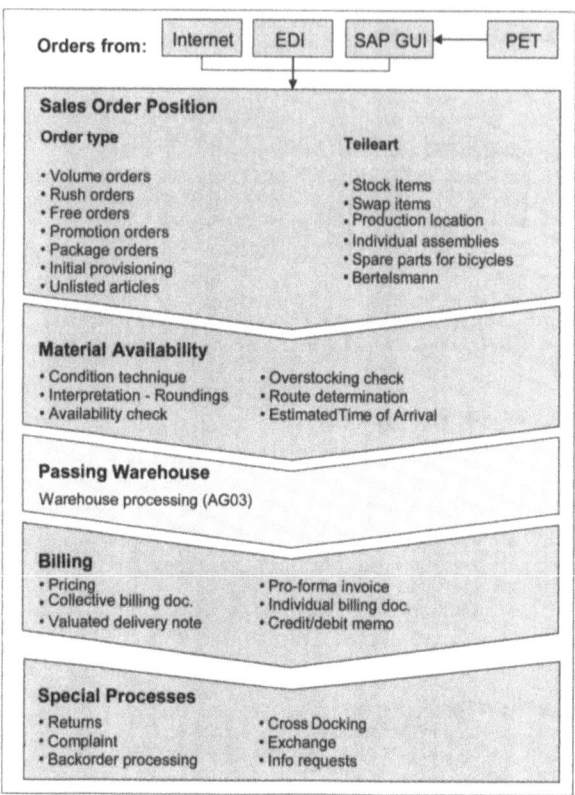

Figure 7.40: The sales order processing process

Within the subproject PorTello, 90 German dealers and 20 worldwide distributed importers were equipped with SAP GUIs. By means of an ISDN link, they can transfer, for example, purchase orders or complaints to the APO system (see Figure 7.41). This link first goes to VW in Wolfsburg (Germany) and from there over a leased line to the Porsche SAP systems. This cooperation for the common use of a communication infrastructure is inasmuch self-evident as most Porsche dealers are at the same time VW dealers.

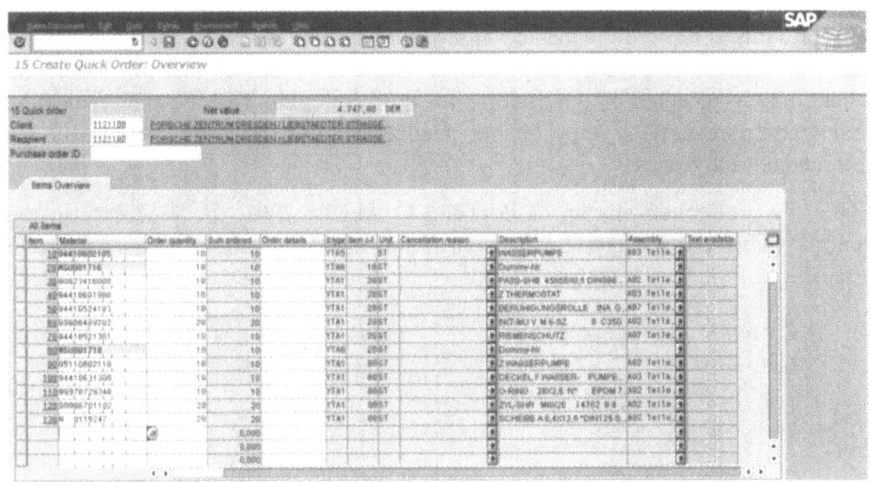

Figure 7.41: Incoming orders of a dealer by means of the SAP GUI

Currently, the large importers only use the SAP GUI to process their complaints but not the purchase orders. Importers with AS400 can place purchase orders using P files (Porsche files, a proprietary EDI format) or EDIFACT, whereby EDIFACT is used rarely. Small markets can place the purchase orders using the Internet in connection with digital X.509 certificates. Furthermore, the dealers and importers can access Porsche Electronic Parts Catalog (PET) from the company Lexcom, which contains the detailed information, including CAD data, on all available parts. The PET catalog has an interface to the MM module of the R/3 system. The parts are entered through the FSI system (German abbreviation for vehicle spare part system) and the Lexcom PTK editing system (see Figure 7.42).

The dealers can select the required spare part from the PET and place an availability query to the dealer management system to first check whether they have it in stock themselves. If this is not the case, a collective purchase order is triggered and the estimated time of arrival is calculated. For this, Porsche – for stability reasons – uses an individual solution and not the APO Available-to-Promise (ATP) functionality. The generated transfer order (Figure 7.37) is directed to the warehouse, where the purchase order is processed. With the goods issue, the billing process is triggered and within this process the dealer is informed of the early delivery in form of a valuated delivery note. The applicable customs regulations are maintained in the customs system (see Figure 7.42).

In addition to this purchase order triggered by the dealer, there is still the automatic stockpiling. The basis is that every change in stock of a certain dealer is reported through the dealer management system at Porsche. This is used for the calculation of which new spare parts this dealer will need soon. This is finally the base for his automatic stockpiling. The thus required calculations are still not performed with the APO system but with the spare parts system (see Figure 7.42).

In future this is to be implemented in the APO system in North America and will then be "rolled out" step by step to other markets. To ensure that this automatic stockpiling is accepted by the dealers, it is most important that they can return the delivered spare parts if they do not need them after all. The spare parts are returned once a year.

Since the production startup of PorTello in August 2001, the processes in the central spare parts store Ludwigsburg are based on the following system architecture:

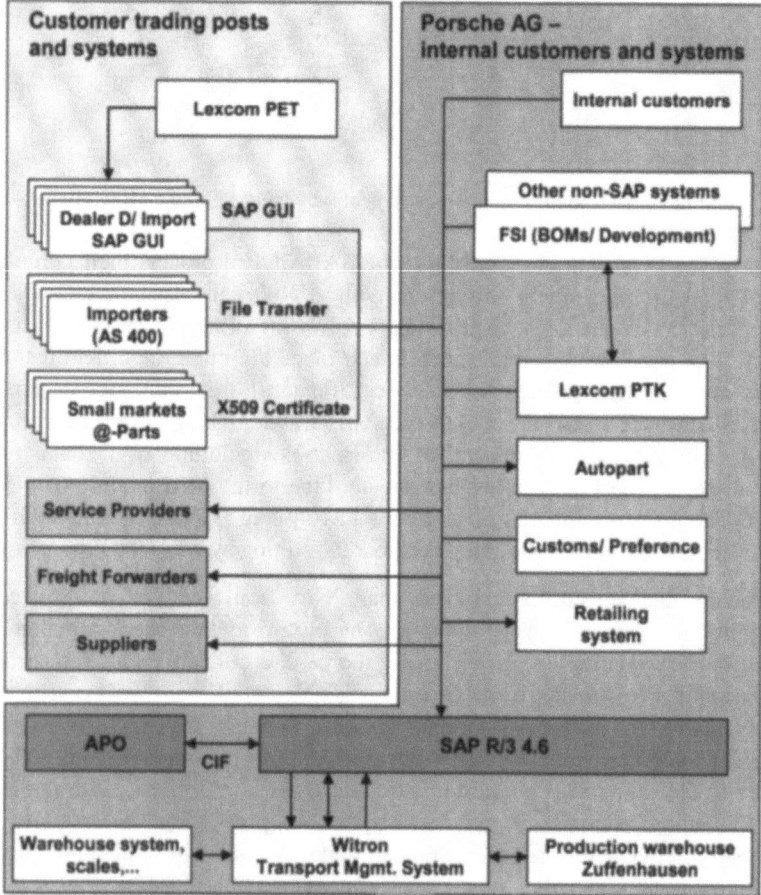

Figure 7.42: The system architecture of the spare parts logistics at Porsche

7.4.4   Evaluation of the SAP-based Spare Parts Logistics at Porsche

The transport costs could be reduced already a few months after completing the first subproject (PorTello). On the other hand, changes to the cost situation in the storage area can currently hardly be reported. Within the second subproject (Polaris), however, Porsche anticipates a significant improvement of the storage cost situation.

The delivery service level has not improved due to the new strategy. The reason for this is that the delivery is only a problem in cases where the part in question is not available, that is, in case of incorrect planning or unexpected mass purchase orders. In both cases, forecasting through the APO system cannot help either.

Demand Planning with APO has turned out to be partially problematic at Porsche. This can be attributed to the special features of this company, in particular the small size compared to other original equipment manufacturers, such as VW. Problems occur, for example, if an unexpectedly large purchase order "buys" up the entire warehouse stock. Due to the low transaction volume it is not easy for Porsche to compensate for such extreme variations. In contrast, at large companies, unexpected mass purchase orders do not preponderate due to the high total volume.

The order lead times were considered optimal already before the SAP systems were implemented and could be maintained after APO was implemented. The interaction with the *live*Cache proved to be problematic, which at the beginning was not persistently stable and due to its design did not allow to link add-ons directly to the APO system. Therefore, all enhancements developed by Porsche are integrated in the R/3 system.

7.5 EM in the Automotive Industry – Case Study SupplyOn

The SupplyOn AG with headquarters in Hallbergmoos near Munich (Germany) offer a platform with the same denominator as electronic marketplace (EM) that supports the trading of goods and services between suppliers of different value-added levels in the automotive industry (http://www.supplyon.com). The company was founded in the summer of 2000 by the automotive component suppliers Bosch, Continental, INA and ZF Friedrichshafen. Since 2002, also Siemens VDO belongs to the shareholders. In the meantime, approximately 700 companies (status of June 2002) from over 30 countries are registered on SupplyOn as participants. The range of services of the marketplace includes integrated solutions for the business-related functional areas purchasing, sales and distribution, logistics, and product development.

First, we describe the reasons that gave rise to the foundation of SupplyOn. Then the characteristics of the marketplace, for example target groups and revenue model as well as the functions and services used by SupplyOn for the support of inter-organizational business processes, will be examined. The chapter concludes with an evaluation and an outlook.

7.5.1   Creation of SupplyOn (Operator Collaboration)

SupplyOn emerged from individual e-business initiatives of the four mentioned suppliers. The main goal was particularly to efficiently operate inter-organizational processes. The focus of Bosch, for example, was on the setup of electronic catalogs, WebEDI (see chapter 3) and Internet-based purchasing (e-purchasing) (see section 6.2.2.1) of direct goods and services. ZF Friedrichshafen also dealt with electronic supplier information systems and directories (*business directory*) and additionally with requests for quotation (RFQ) (see section 6.2.2.3). In addition to auctions and e-purchasing of direct goods, INA was also interested in indirect goods or their procurement. Continental already gained experiences with setting up e-business solutions with the tire-specific marketplace RubberNetwork (see http://www.rubbernetwork.com) and now concentrates on auctions as well as procurement of indirect goods.

Based on these experiences, it was recognized that the individual initiatives were very similar or partly congruent, and that by bundling the resources, especially know-how, the implementation and operating costs for the individual companies could be reduced. Adventitiously, many suppliers of upstream value-added levels (tier 2 through tier n) supply several association partners simultaneously, thus providing extensive options for standardizing processes and IT infrastructures. In this case, a tier-2 company on average supplies five tier-1 companies in this market.

These considerations resulted in the establishment of the SupplyOn AG. Here the members of the operator association are in almost all conceivable business relationships. From the viewpoint of electronic parts, such as ABS systems, Bosch and Continental are competitors, for example. While INA is a supplier for all other companies, Bosch and ZF collaborate in the area of electronic components in order to use synergies.

Furthermore, SAP became a partner in the newly established corporation. The reasons for this mainly had to do with the integration of inhouse systems with SupplyOn and the utilization of network effects. SAP solutions are popular in the automotive industry, particularly in large companies that include the operators (Fricke et al. 2002); they are used by all consortial partners. SAP sees an advantage in participating in SupplyOn in the acquisition of know-how about automobile-specific processes and problems, that in turn can be used in other SAP applications, for instance in form of "Best Practices". In return, SAP provides the necessary technologies and applications for operating the EM.

7.5.2   Marketplace Characteristics

SupplyOn is an open, internationally oriented EM for the automotive industry that supports the trading of direct goods and services. Suppliers of the automotive industry and related lines of industry, in particular make-to-stock manufacturers, are addressed. Unlike purchasing platforms, used by manufacturers only to request goods (such as BMW Exchange), in principle also other companies can act as suppliers and enquirer on SupplyOn. Prerequisite is a contract that authorizes the participants as sellers or purchasers. According to the operator association, SupplyOn is understood as an addition to the purchasing platforms of the original equipment manufacturers that particularly aim at linking tier-1 vendors.

Collaborations with other marketplaces are nevertheless possible. SupplyOn and Volkswagen, for example, agreed on an intense collaboration regarding their marketplace activities. The goal is to harmonize the information exchange in the automotive industry and to contribute to the standardization of Internet-based systems and processes within the line of industry. Suppliers should one day be able to access SupplyOn as well as Volkswagen-specific inquiries (RFQs) through a standard user interface. Another advantage is that companies must be registered only on one of the two platforms, which reduces the administrative efforts both for the operator and the participant. Similar agreements with other OEM initiatives are also aspired.

SupplyOn becomes collaborative due to the applied revenue model: to make one-time transactions via the EM less attractive and to establish the platform on a long-term basis, the participants pay fixed amounts. The fixed costs of participation as seller on the EM depend on the sales revenue of the company as well as the number of the registered users. A standard supplier with ten users and a sales revenue of up to € 5 million pays € 220 per month. The following table gives an overview of the SupplyOn price model for sellers.

Table 7.1 SupplyOn price model (Seller)

Sales	User	Charge per month
> € 5 million.	10	€ 220.-
€ 5 -10 million.	10	€ 440.-
> € 10 million.	10	€ 660.-

The participants receive different basic services that are used through a special Web cockpit (SupplyOn Supplier Cockpit). So far, no standardized price model exists for the purchaser side. The costs for this depend on various factors, for instance whether the company already acts as a seller. Variable, transaction-specific costs are so far not included in the revenue model.

To take the requirements of further marketplace participants (in addition to the operators) into account better, these can influence the structure of the EM, for example processes and process structures, in form of work groups. Companies that actively contribute to the structure of the EM are referred to as associated members.

7.5.3   Inter-organizational Processes with SupplyOn: Support of Various Forms of Requests for Quotation

The core business of SupplyOn is the support of the procurement of goods and services (E-Sourcing) as well as the operative settlement of logistics processes within supply chain management. In addition to direct goods requiring subscription, indirect goods can also be traded on the EM. For this purpose, a special catalog management system operated by an external service provider was integrated into the EM.

The emphasis within the procurement activities is in the support of various forms of requests for quotation that SupplyOn refers to as opportunities. Supply chain management functionalities are also provided. These are mainly operative processes, such as the exchange of business documents via WebEDI. The documents can be, for instance, delivery schedules, delivery and transport data, credit notes, stock movements or shipping notifications.

So far, the marketplace does not use any SAP applications in the supply chain management area. SupplyOn together with the software provider Atos Origin, another technology partner, jointly developed the available services. Functions for the support of the collaborative development of products are currently being implemented.

Below, the focus is on the requests for quotation on SupplyOn. In this case, these requests for quotation are supported through the application component Dynamic Pricing Engine (see section 6.2.2.3). SupplyOn distinguishes three different forms of requests for quotation that will be explained in more detail below:

1.   Request for Quotation (RFQ),
2.   Live Bidding as well as
3.   Online Bidding.

7.5.3.1   *Request for Quotation*

RFQ is a form of request for quotation that is targeted at medium to long-term items. In this case, no end is defined at the beginning of these requests for quotation. In general, RFQs are used for production-linked goods, thus subject to subscription. Examples are electronic parts, gearwheels and gearboxes. On SupplyOn, the following possible configurations for RFQs are available:

*   *Rules* that define the submission of quotations through vendors,

*   *Header data*, thus basic information, such as terms of delivery/payment and material pricing groups that apply to the entire opportunity,

*   *Vendors* that are narrowed down, for example, by means of distribution lists,

- *Items,* in which products to be traded are described in more detail as well as

- *Attachments*, that is files, such as purchasing conditions, subscriptions, that are attached to an opportunity to specify this in more detail.

You create a request for quotation by defining the rules for submitting quotations. Examples are:

- *Calculating the level in evaluations*: Various quotations are transferred to a ranking order. The level of a bid is determined based on a special field (SupplyOn calls it "price per price unit") that the vendor must fill in when submitting the quotation. Only purchasers or initiators of a request for quotation can change the ranking order of the bids.

- *Defining start and end time of the opportunity:* Here the times are defined for the submission deadline or the end of the request for quotation.

- *Quotations per item (Broken Lot):* The suppliers must enter the prices per quotation item when submitting bids.

- *Fixed quotation per item & RFQ quantity:* When submitting a quotation, suppliers cannot change the quantity per item the purchaser specified. If this rule is activated, no subset quotations are possible.

Once rules have been defined, header data has to be defined in a next step. Examples are:

- *Specification of a distribution list*: In this case, previously selected suppliers are asked for a quotation, that is, only invited suppliers can participate in the request for quotation. A distribution list consists of one or several vendor lists as well as the selection, which persons are to be informed by e-mail about the status of the opportunity. If no distribution list is specified, all vendors of the EM can participate in this operation.

- By means of the *material pricing group*, the purchaser determines which form his vendors have to fill in for a request for quotation and whether in addition to the "standard quotation fields" (e.g., price per price unit, additional costs, non-recurring costs, quotation valid until) comments as well as further fields are required. Additional information can depend on the selected material pricing group and can be used for a more exact query of the cost items of an item, for example.

A vendor list includes all vendors and their employees that are to participate in requests for quotations. Vendor lists are used to group suppliers together to material pricing groups or areas and to then use these lists again in the respective opportunities. A purchaser can summarize, for example, possible suppliers of turning workpiece in Europe in a vendor list and can then access this list in case of inquiries for turning workpieces.

Item data is defined to characterize the individual items of the request for quotation more precisely. This includes:

- RFQ quantity,

- unit of measure,

- product number, material pricing group (internal) and product name as well as

- delivery date/time or demand period, currency and price unit.

All saved individual items of the request for quotation appear in a corresponding list. Figure 7.43 shows an item list with the different products to be procured.

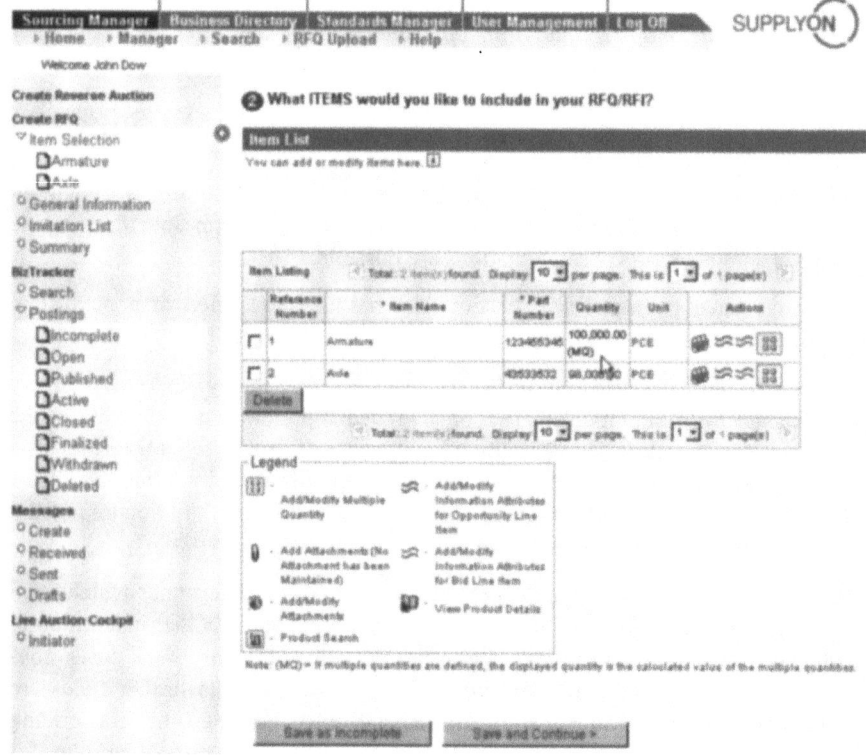

Figure 7.43: Item list

File attachments allow to define extensive product specifications, technical drawings and alike for business partners. Just as with the attachment functionality of the purchaser, vendors can also add attachments to their quotations.

The myBizTracker can be used to view the data of an operation (e.g., an RFQ). Purchasers are provided with the following options:

- Publishing/activating opportunities and viewing their status information,

- changing/converting/copying opportunities, and

- viewing and analyzing quotations of the vendors.

An opportunity can be in different statuses regardless of the process. The status of an opportunity changes if the purchaser triggers this (action) or sets rules that cause this change automatically. As long as an opportunity has the status "active", suppliers can transmit quotations and change already existing quotations. The submission of a new quotation of the same supplier replaces existing entries. A final comparison of bids is thus not possible until the opportunity reaches the status "closed" or "completed".

By using the myBiz-Tracker (see section 6.2.2.3), the initiator of the quotation can view quotations both while and after an opportunity is being/has been processed. Figure 7.44 shows a simple example:

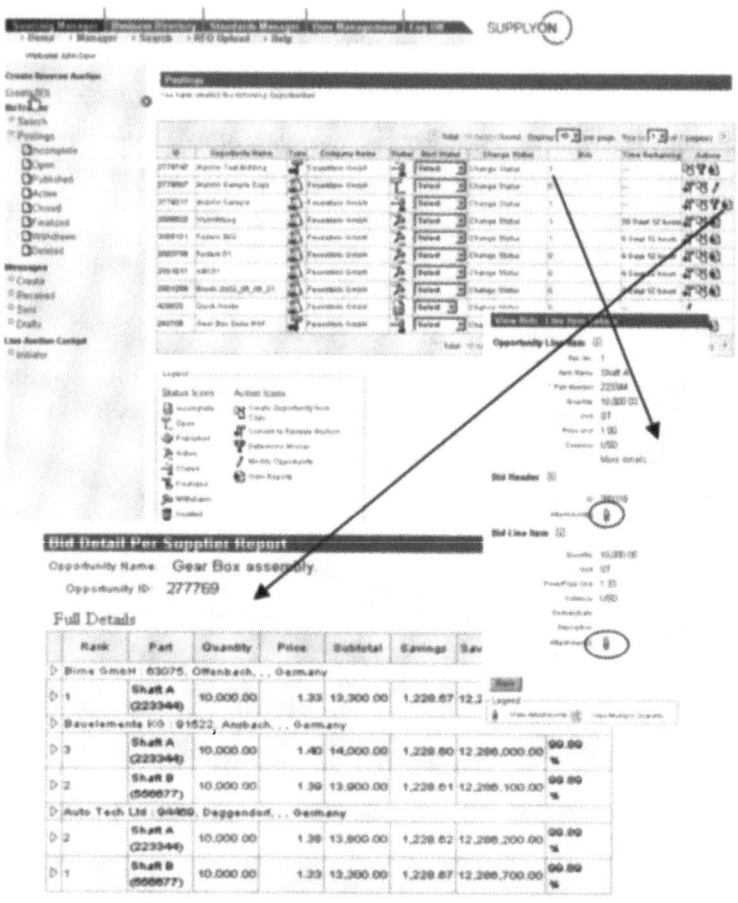

Figure 7.44: myBiz-Tracker

Within the myBiz-Tracker, the type of the opportunity of a company and their status information is displayed. In "Postings" (top part of the screen), the reference "View Reports" (Actions) displays all submitted quotations of the suppliers for each item in a new screen (bottom part of the screen). The details of the quotation (price fields, comments etc.) can be called by means of the reference "Bids" in the top part of the screen.

The formatting and analysis of quotations is supported through different reports. Figure 7.45 for example shows an evaluation of bids.

Figure 7.45: Standard evaluation of bids

7.5.3.2 Online Bidding

A further form of quotation provided by SupplyOn is Online Bidding. Unlike RFQs, the bidders can view the currently best bid without knowing who submitted it. A tier-1 company, for example, places his request for automotive components into the system; vendors anonymously can view the respectively best bid and improve their own bid. The duration of an Online Bidding is defaulted and generally takes a few days. Online Bidding, such as an RFQ, that precedes the Online Bidding, is used for the procurement of goods requiring subscription, for example punching, drawn and bent parts.

An Online Bidding is initiated by first defining opportunity and response rules. Examples are:

- *Overall bid* (a quotation for all items together).

- *Specification of start time and duration of the opportunity:* the duration of an opportunity can also be determined (max. 23:55 hours) instead of an end time.

- *Automatic extension of the opportunity:* The bidding can be extended by automatically setting this rule. The specifications "period without activity", "extension period", and "number of possible extensions".

   Example:
   If no quotation was submitted within the last ten minutes (this is the period without activity), the opportunity is automatically closed. If on the other hand a quotation is submitted within the last ten minutes, the bidding is extended by 15 minutes (extension period). This can be repeated a maximum of four times. Then the system automatically completes the opportunity. Human interventions for changing the parameters Extension and Closing are possible for the initiator at any time during the auction.

- *Underbidding of the company bid/best bid:* This defines whether a new quotation must appear below the previous own quotation (company bid) or below the best quotation of all participants.

- *Price improvement:* New quotations must fall below the current quotation by at least the entered step. The step variants unrestricted (this does not define a predefined step), absolute (absolute size), and relative (in percent) are possible.

After defining the rules, the header data is fixed analogous to RFQs, distribution lists are inserted and the item lists are created.

The header data is extended by bidding-specific fields according to the rule selection and the item data additionally contains a start price and a reduction step. Online Bidding actually allows to select a classification, but the supplier is provided only with default fields for submitting a quotation (no specific cost items of the selected material pricing group can therefore be displayed).

The purchaser can see the received bids for each item, whereby the following additional fields are displayed in comparison with an RFQ (see Figure 7.46):

- Bid of the supplier,
- best bid,
- ranking of the supplier (only with selected rule) as well as
- salesperson name.

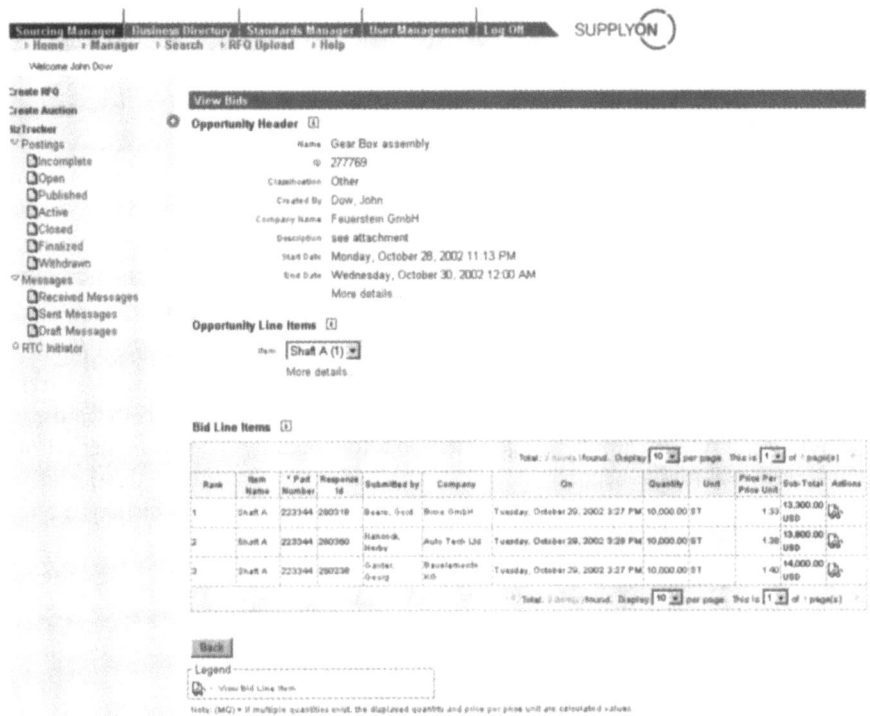

Figure 7.46: Quotation overview

As with the application of an RFQ, reports (evaluations) are also possible. Already existing RFQs can be converted to an Online Bidding.

7.5.3.3 Live Bidding

Live Bidding is a third form or request for quotation SupplyOn provides, that is preceded by an RFQ, as with the Online Bidding. The Live Bidding variant allows selected suppliers to submit quotations in a limited time period (generally one to two hours). A chat window additionally allows purchasers and sellers to communicate directly. Status lines and symbols automatically inform about changes made to opportunities. Live Bidding is also used for production-linked goods. The process resembles that of the Online Bidding, whereby additional functionalities are available to the involved participants:

- A special Live-Bidding Monitor is used for controlling this.

- New quotations are immediately displayed both as graphic and by means of text functions.

- Extended graphical evaluations of the quotations are possible.

- The connection status of the providers is displayed.

- Substitute bids (Proxy Bidding) can be submitted (only in cases where the vendor has technical problems).

Rules, header data and item data are defined as with the Online Bidding.

The Live Bidding application consists of two areas: the Live-Bidding Monitor (view of the initiator/purchaser) and the Live-Bidding Response (view of the bidders). They both are called through the myBizTracker. With Live Bidding, exactly one user (seller) per company can participate.

The Live-Bidding Monitor publishes all active opportunities (1) (see the following figure). By clicking on one of these opportunities, the purchaser fills the monitor with the operation data and thus sees the individual items (2) as well as the current status. In case of active opportunities the "remaining time" (3) runs backwards. In addition to an automatic control, it is possible to manually extend the period (4) (click on hour-minute-second specification to enter the extension time) and to complete the transaction early. A completed operation is no longer displayed after closing and reopening the monitor.

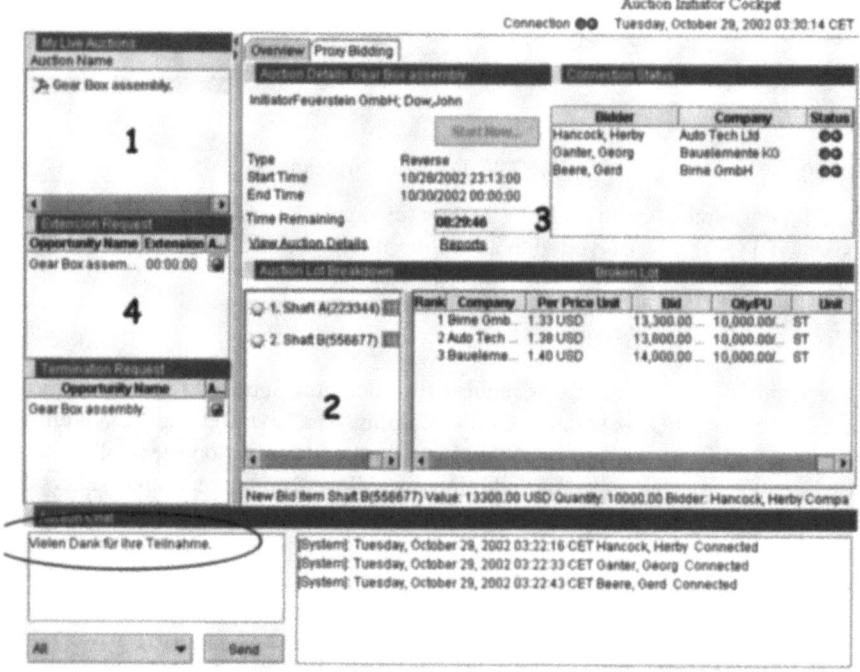

Figure 7.47: Live-Bidding Monitor (Purchaser)

The purchaser can also recognize which of his vendors have just set up an active connection to the marketplace (status green). Other vendors without active connection are indicated with the status red. When new bids are entered, the purchaser receives a message in the status line. This is additionally indicated by a yellow light bulb next to the item in question. By clicking on this item, the purchaser can view more detailed data regarding the offer on the right-hand side of the screen (see Figure 7.47). He can furthermore call up a graphic evaluation or one of the reports (evaluations analogous to the bid invitation). The "Reports" link in the purchaser monitor refers to the evaluations. When the user clicks on the symbol next to the corresponding item, the respective graphic with the bid processes is displayed (see Figure 7.48).

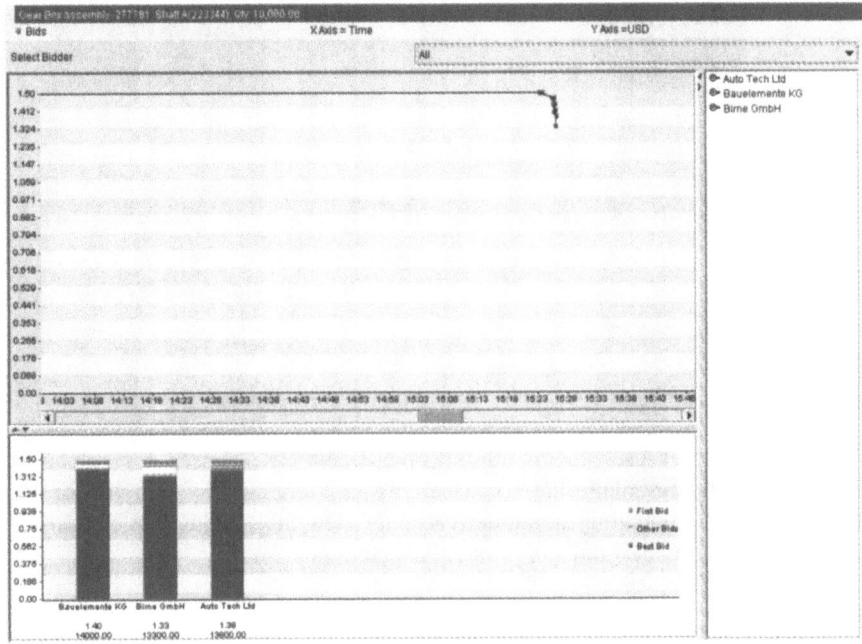

Figure 7.48: Evaluation

It is possible to select all or individual vendors as well as the best bid. In accordance with a chat forum paradigm, the purchaser sends messages to all participants or only to certain ones. Vice versa, the seller can only send messages to the purchaser.

In exceptional cases and only in cases where the vendor encounters technical difficulties (for instance, he cannot access the Internet), the purchaser can submit substitute quotations on behalf of the seller if the vendor in question has closed his monitor (see Figure 7.49). The seller transmits these offers by fax or telephone, for example. The purchaser receives an overview of the current quotation status through the numerous functionalities and can select the contract partners upon completion of the Live Bidding.

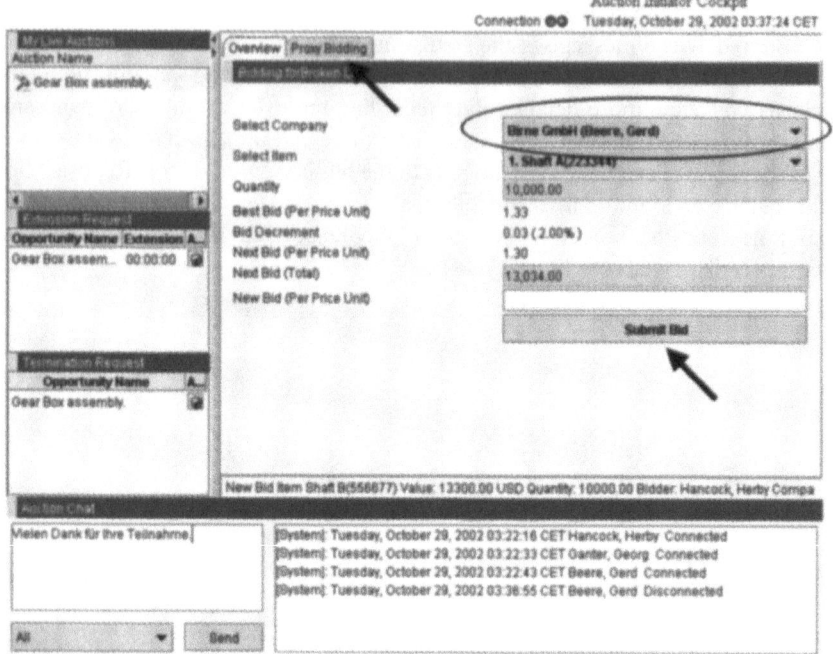

Figure 7.49: Substitute quotation (Proxy Bidding)

The invited vendor uses the monitor "Live-Bidding Response" for responses within Live Bidding. While the purchaser has an overview of which vendor has submitted which quotation, the bidder can only view his submitted quotations as well as the currently best bid and possibly his rank.

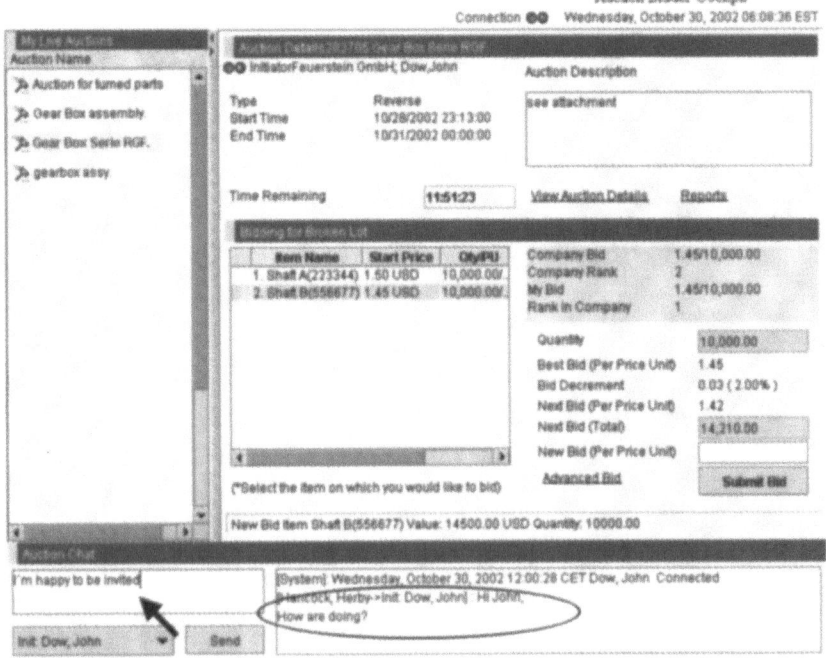

Figure 7.50: Live-Bidding Response

7.5.4   Evaluation and Outlook

60 percent of the participants of SupplyOn are German companies. 21 percent of the participants are located in other European countries and 19 percent in non-European countries (particularly the U.S.). Already 21 of the 30 largest European suppliers belong to the registered SupplyOn participants. Currently, mainly the founder members appear as purchasers of goods and services.

A total of some 3,000 persons are authorized to use the EM. This includes purchasers, sellers and administrators. In the E-Sourcing area, 3,000 marketplace transactions were carried out up to the beginning of June 2002. 90 percent of these are primarily bid invitations or RFQs. Online Bidding and Live Bidding amount to only ten percent. In case of a request for quotation on SupplyOn, on average five other companies are involved in addition to the initiator. This means that within the performed transactions some 15,000 companies were involved in the E-Sourcing processes on the EM. According to SupplyOn, the number of the marketplace transactions continually increases.

In future, the participants on SupplyOn will be able to use the DMS of the MarketSet LCC application already described in chapter 6 within the collaborative product development. Furthermore, SupplyOn plans the usage of further SAP solutions, particularly for the support of SCM processes.

Abbreviations

ABAP	Advanced Business Application Programming
ACP	Auto Catalog Publisher
ALE	Application Link Enabling
ANSI	American National Standards Institute
APIs	Application Programming Interfaces
APO	Advanced Planner & Optimizer
ASN	Advanced Shipping Notification
ATP	Available to Promise
B/L	Bill of Lading
BAPIs	Business Application Programming Interfaces
BASDA	Business and Accounting Software Developers Association
BC	Business Connector
Bex	Business Explorer
BI	Business Intelligence
BW	Business Information Warehouse
CA	Container Algorithm
CAD	Computer Aided Design
CC	Consolidation Center
CIF	Core Interface
CIM	Common Information Model
CMDS	Collaborative Management of Delivery Schedules
CO	Controlling
COM/DCOM	Common Object Model/Distributed Common Object Model
CORBA	Common Object Request Broker Architecture
COSA	Cooperative Simulated Annealing
CPFR	Collaborative Planning, Forecasting and Replenishment
CRM	Customer Relationship Management
cXML	Commerce XML

DC	Deconsolidation Center
DEDIG	Deutsche EDI-Gesellschaft
DI	Declaração de Importação
DIN	Deutsches Institut für Normung e.V.
DMS	Document Management System
DP	Demand Planning
DPE	Dynamic Pricing Engine
DS	Detailed Scheduling
DTD	Document Type Definition
DW	Data Warehouse
EAN	International Article Numbering Association
EANCOM	International Article Numbering Association – Communication
EBP	Enterprise Buyer Professional
ebXML	Electronic Business using Extensible Markup Language
EC	Electronic Commerce
ec4ec	e-commerce for engineered components
EDI	Electronic Data Interchange
EDIFACT	Electronic Data Interchange for Administration, Commerce and Transport
EJB	Enterprise JavaBeans
EM	Electronic Markets
ERP	Enterprise Resource Planning
ETA	Estimated Time of Arrival
FI	Financials
FTP	File Transfer Protocol
FVA	Fertigungsvorbereitung und Ausführung
GA	Genetic Algorithm
HRNP	HyperRelational Protocol
HTML	Hypertext Markup Language
HTTP	Hypertext Transfer Protocol
HTTPS	HyperText Transmission Protocol Secure
ICM	Internet Communication Manager
ID	Identification
IDocs	Intermediate Documents
IGS	Internet Graphic Server
IM	Inventory Management
ISDN	Integrated Services Digital Network
IT	Information Technology
ITS	Internet Transaction Server
J2EE	Java 2 Enterprise Edition
JIT	Just-in-Time
JMS	Java-Message-Services-Standard

KPI	Key Performance Indicators
LAN	Local Area Network
LDAP	Lightweight Directory Access Protocol
LES	Logistics Execution System
LIS	Logistics Information System
LIWAKS	Liefererfüllungs-, Waren- und Kontrollsystem
LLNL	Lawrence Livermore National Laboratory
MAW	Materialwirtschaft
MB	Mercedes-Benz
MBCC	Mercedes-Benz Consolidation Center
MIME	Multipurpose Internet Mail Extensions
MM	Materials Management
MOB	Mobile Operating on Business
MOM	MarketSet Order Management
MOLAP	Multidimensional On-Line Analytical Processing
MRO	Maintenance Repair and Organisation
MRP	Materials Requirement Planning
MSP	MarketSet Procurement
NDM	Network Design & Modelling
OAGIS	Open Applications Group Integration Specification
ODS	Operational Data Store
OEM	Original Equipment Manufacturer
OLAP	Online Analytical Processing
OLE DB	Object Linking and Embedding Database
OLTP	Online Transaction Processing
PCD	Portal Content Directory
PDA	Personal Digital Assistant
PDM	Product Data Management
PET	Porsche Elektronischen Teilekatalog
PIN	Personal Identification Number
PorTello	Porsche Teilelogistik
P-Files	Porsche Files
PP	Production Planning
PPM	Production Process Modell
PSA	Persistant Staging Area
QM	Quality Management
RDC	Regional Distribution Center
RDVI	Registro de Volumes Importados
RFC	Remote Function Call
RFI	Request for Information
RFP	Request for proposal
RFQ	Request for Quotation

ROLAP	Relational On-Line Analytical Processing
SA	Simulated Annealing
SAS	Scandinavian Airlines System
SAP	Systeme, Anwendungen und Produkte
SAPGUI	SAP Graphical User Interface
SC	Supply Chain
SCC	Supply Chain Cockpit
SCE	Supply Chain Engineer
SCOR	Supply Chain Operations Reference
SD	Sales and Distribution
SDMS	Secure Document Management System
SEDAS	Standardregel einheitlicher Datenaustauschsysteme
SM	Service Management
SMTP	Simple Network Mail Protocol
SNP	Supply Network Planning
SOAP	Simple Object Access Protocol
SOURCE	Stock Overview Using Relevant Control Events
SOX	Schema for Object-oriented XML
SSA	Sales Scheduling Agreement
SSL	Secure Socket Layer
SSO	Single-Sign-On
STO	Stock Transfer Order
SUVs	Sport Utility Vehicles
SWIFT	Society for Worldwide Interbank Financial Telecommunication
Taglib	Tag Library
TMS	Transportation Management System
TCP/IP	Transmission Control Protocol/Internet Protocol
TP	Transportation Planning
TPDs	Trading Partner Directories
TRADACOMS	Trading Data Communications Standards
UDDI	Universal Description Discovery and Integration
UNSMS	United Nations Standard Messages
VANs	Value Added Networks
VDA	Verband der Automobilindustrie
VMI	Vendor-Managed Inventory
VS	Vehicle Scheduling
VW	Volkswagen
WAP	Wireless Access Protocol

WebDAV	Web-Based Distributed Authoring and Versioning
WM	Warehouse Management
WML	Wireless Markup Language
WMS	Warehouse Management System
WSDL	Webservice Definition Language
WWW	World Wide Web
xCBL	XML Common Business Library
XML	Extensible Markup Language
XPC	XML Portal Connector
XSLT	Extensible Stylesheet Language for Transformations

References

Anahory, S.; Murray, D. (1997) Data Warehousing in the Real World: A Practical Guide for Building Decision Support Systems. Addison-Wesley, Bonn et al.

Bakos, Y.; Brynjolfsson, E. (1993) Information Technology, Incentives, and the Optimal Number of Suppliers. In: Journal of Management Information Systems, Vol. 10, pp. 37-53.

Baldi, S.; Borgman H. P. (2001) Ownership-Structures of Electronic B2B Marketplaces – Multi-Perspective Analysis. In: Buhl, Huther, A.; Reitwiesner, B. (Eds.) Information Age Economy, Proceedings of the 5th International Conference Wirtschaftsinformatik (WI/IF 2001), Augsburg, Germany, pp. 589-603.

Bellatreche, L.; Karlapalem, K.; Mohania, M. (2001) Some Issues in Design of Data Warehousing Systems. In: Developing Quality Complex Database Systems: Practices, Techniques, and Technologies. Idea Group Publishers, Hershey, PA.

Bichler, M. (2001) The Future of E-Markets: Multi Dimensional Market Mechanisms. Cambridge University Press, New York et al.

Brandenburger, A. M.; Nalebuff, B. J. (1996) Coopetition. Doubleday, New York.

Buxmann, P.; von Ahsen, A.; Martín Díaz, L. (2003) Economic Evaluation of Cooperation in Supply Chains – Models and Results from an Empirical Study. Currently in review.

Chamoni, P.; Gluchowski, P. (2002) Business Information Warehouse. Springer, Berlin et al.

Codd, E. F. (1993) Providing OLAP (On-Line Analytical Processing) to User-Analysts: An IT-Mandate. Unpublished manuscript, E. F. Codd and Associates.

Cooper, M. C.; Lambert, D. M.; Pagh, J. D. (1997) Supply Chain Management: More than a new Name for Logistics. In: The International Journal of Logistics Management, Vol. 8, pp. 1-14.

Dearing, B. (1990) The Strategic Benefits of EDI. In: The Journal of Business, Jan./Feb., pp. 4-6.

Erlenkotter, D. (1990) Ford Whitman Harris and the economic order quantity model. In: Operations Research, 38, pp. 937-946.

Fricke, M.; Hoppen, N. (2002) Electronic Markets in the European Automotive Industry - Results from an Empirical Study. In: Proceedings of the 9th Research Symposium on Emerging Electronic Markets; Rheinfelden/Basel, Switzerland, pp. 53-68.

Fricke, M.; Weitzel, T.; König, W.; Lampe, R. (2002) EDI and Business-to-Business Systems: The Status Quo and the Future of Business Relations in the European Automotive Industry. In: Proceedings of the 6th Pacific Asia Conference on Information Systems (PACIS), Tokio, Japan.

Gartner (01.16.2002, visited: 09.08.2003), SAP's tough, but not invincible, url: http://zdnet.com.com/2100-1107-816190.html

Gebauer, J.; Buxmann, P. (2000) Assessing the Value of Interorganizational Systems to Support Business Transactions. In: International Journal of Electronic Commerce, Vol. 4, No. 4, pp. 61-82.

Handfield, R. B.; Nicols, E. L. (1999) Introduction to Supply Chain Management. Prentice Hall, Englewood Cliffs, NJ.

Harris, F. W. (1913) How many parts to make at once. In: Factory, The Magazine of Management, Vol. 10, pp. 135-136 and p. 152.

Helms, M. M.; Ettkin, L.; Chapmann, S. (2000) Supply chain forecasting. Collaborative forecasting supports supply chain management. In: Business Process Management, Vol. 6, pp. 392-407.

Inmon, W. H. (1996) Building the Data Warehouse, 2nd Edition. John Wiley & Sons, New York et al.

Jakovlievic, P. J. (08.23.2000, visited: 09.08.2003), SAP Remains Solid While Transi-tioning, url: http://www.technologyevaluation.com/Registration/TEC .asp?url=/research/researchhighlights/businessapplications/2000/08/news_anal ysis/na_ba_pj_08_23_00_1.asp&

Kachigan, S. K. (1986) Statistical Analysis: An Interdisciplinary Introduction to Univariate & Multivariate Methods. Radius Press, New York.

Ketterer, N. (2002) Hierarchische Supply-Chain Planung mit SAP APO 3.0 bei einem Serienfertiger. In: Dangelmaier, W.; Emmrich, A.; Kaschula, D. (Eds.) Modelle im E-Business. ALB-HNI-Verlagsschriftenreihe, Paderborn, pp. 241-254.

Knolmayer, G.; Mertens, P.; Zeier, A. (2002) Supply Chain Management Based on SAP Systems – Order Management in Manufacturing Companies. Springer, Berlin et al.

Kotok, A. (08.02.2000, visited: 09.08.2003), Extensible and more. An Updated Survey of XML Business Vocabularies, url: http://webservices.xml.com /pub/a/ws/ 2000/08/02/ebiz/extensible.html

Kurz, A. (1999) Data Warehousing Enabling Technologies, MITP. Bonn, Germany.

Liautaud, B.; Hammond, M. (2000) e-Business Intelligence: Turning Information into Knowledge into Profit. McGraw-Hill, New York.

Lincke, D. (1998) Evaluating Integrated Electronic Commerce Systems. In: Schmid, B.; Selz, D.; Sing, R. (Eds.) EM – Electronic Transactions. EM – Electronic Markets, Vol. 8, pp. 7-11.

Martín Díaz, L.; Buxmann, P. (2003) The Value of Cooperative Planning in Supply Chains: A Simulative Approach. In: Proceedings of the 11th European Conference on Information Systems (ECIS 2003), Naples, Italy.

McDonald, K.; Wilmsmeier, A.; Dixon, D. C.; Inmon, W. H. (2002) Mastering the SAP Business Information Warehouse. John Wiley & Sons, Hoboken, NJ.

Meier, M.; Sinzig, W.; Mertens, P. (2002) Enterprise Management with SAP SEM/Business Analytics. Springer, Berlin.

Oliver, R. K.; Webber, M. D. (1982) Supply-chain management: logistics catches up with strategy. Outlook (reprinted in: Christopher M. (Ed.; 1992) Logistics: The Strategic Issues, pp. 63-75, Chapman & Hall, London).

SAP AG (2001a, visited: 06.03.2002), IT Landscapes: Architecture and Life-cycle Management of Distributed Environments, url: http://www.sap.com/solutions /netweaver/pdf/landscape.pdf

SAP AG (2001b, visited: 09.08.2003), mySAP Technology for Open E-Business Integration – Overview, url: http://www.sap.co.kr/solutions/technology/pdf/ overview.pdf

SAP AG (2001c, visited: 09.08.2003), Portal Infrastructure, url: http://www. sap.co.kr/solutions/technology/pdf/portal.pdf

SAP AG (2001d, visited: 09.08.2003), Security: Secure Business in Open Environments, url: http://www.sap.com/solutions/netweaver/pdf/security_ whitepaper.pdf

SAP AG (2001e, visited: 09.08.2003), Web Application Server: Web ApplicationTechnology and Web Dynpro, url: http://www.sap.co.kr/solutions/ technology/pdf/web.pdf

SAP AG (2002a, visited: 09.08.2003), SAP Web Application Server: Support for Open Standards, url: http://www.sap.com/solutions/netweaver/pdf/tb_1937.pdf

SAP AG (2002b, visited: 09.08.2003), Global Solutions without Boundaries, url: http://www.sap.com/solutions/netweaver/pdf/ GlobalSolution .pdf

SAP AG (2002c, visited: 09.08.2003), Exchange Infrastructure: Process-Centric Collaboration, url: http://www.sap.com/solutions/netweaver/pdf/XI_50052041 .pdf

Scharl, A.; Gebauer, J.; Bauer, C. (2001) Matching Process Requirements with Information Technology to Assess the Efficiency of Web Information Systems. In: Information Technology and Management, Vol. 2, pp. 193-210.

Silver, E.A.; Peterson, R. (1985) Decision systems for inventory management and production planning, 2nd Edition. Wiley, New York et al.

Stanford Technology Group (1995) Designing the Data Warehouse on Relational Databases. Whitepaper, Stanford.

Sun (01.14.2002, visited: 09.08.2003), Messaging Systems and the JavaTM Message Service, url: http://developer.java.sun.com/developer/technicalArti cles/Networking/messaging/

Stanford Technology Group (1995) Designing the Data Warehouse on Relational Databases. Whitepaper, Stanford.

W3C (11.16.1999, visited: 09.08.2003), XML Path Language (XPath) Version 1.0, url: http://www.w3.org/TR/xpath

W3C (05.08.2000, visited: 09.08.2003), Simple Object Access Protocol (SOAP) 1.1, url: http://www.w3.org/TR/SOAP/

W3C (03.15.2001, visited: 09.08.2003), Web Services Description Language (WSDL) 1.1, url: http://www.w3.org/TR/wsdl

Weitzel, T.; Harder, T.; Buxmann, P. (2001) Electronic Business und EDI mit XML. dpunkt, Heidelberg, Germany.

Westarp, F.; Weitzel, T.; Buxmann, P.; König, W. (1999) The Status Quo and the Future of EDI. In: Proceedings of the 7th European Conference on Information Systems (ECIS 1999), Copenhagen , pp. 719-731

Wigand, R. T.; Mertens, P.; Bodendorf, F.; König, W.; Picot, A.; Schumann, M. (2003): Introduction to Business Information Systems. Springer, Heidelberg et al.

Wüstner, E.; Hotzel, T.; Buxmann, P. (2002) Converting Business Documents using XML/XSLT. In: Proceedings of the 4th International Workshop on Advanced Issues of E-Commerce and Web-based Information Systems (WECWIS 2002), Newport Beach, California, pp. 61-68.

Index